Kinkead's Cookbook

KINKEAD'S COOKBOOK

Recipes from Washington D.C.'s Premier Seafood Restaurant

BOB KINKEAD

PHOTOGRAPHY BY TIM TURNER

TEN SPEED PRESS
Berkeley | Toronto

Ten Speed Press
P.O. Box 7123
Berkeley, California 94707
www.tenspeed.com

Distributed in Australia by Simon & Schuster Australia, in Canada by Ten Speed Press Canada, in New Zealand by Southern Publishers Group, in South Africa by Real Books, and in the United Kingdom and Europe by Airlift Book Company.

Cover design by Betsy Stromberg
and Catherine Jacobes

Interior design by Betsy Stromberg

Photography by Tim Turner

Photography assistance by Takamasa Ota

Library of Congress Cataloging-in-Publication Data
Kinkead, Bob, 1952–
  Kinkead's cookbook : recipes from Washington D.C.'s premier seafood restaurant / Bob Kinkead.
    p. cm.
  Includes index.
  ISBN 1-58008-522-9
  1. Cookery (Seafood) 2. Kinkead's (Restaurant) I. Title.
  TX747.K535 2005
  641.6'92—dc22
                          2004007407

First printing, 2004
Printed in Hong Kong

1 2 3 4 5 6 7 8 9 10 — 08 07 06 05 04

Dedication

This book is dedicated to
Marie Brennan Kinkead, my father's mother,
from whom I inherited what cooking talent I possess,
and
George Alfred Turgeon, my mother's father, from whom I inherited
my appreciation of good food and dining well.

My grandmother, Marie Brennan Kinkead, was an exceptional cook who every day of her adult life baked dozens of cookies and rolls, breads, three or four pies or cakes, and dinner for several families. Everything was made from scratch and it all went to feed her own family, neighbors, and folks down on their luck. Hers was not a wealthy family, but she was a genius at making the most of inexpensive fish, cheaper cuts of meat, and leftovers. She was a great user of bacon fat for cooking and lard for baking. It was all incredibly delicious (if not unhealthy) and the Kinkead grandchildren always looked forward to special Sunday suppers with Grandma, Grampa Kink, and all the cousins.

During the depression and the early part of the war, her back door became famous to those out of work. They learned that her generosity, hot food, and justifiably famous apple pie could always be counted on. Grandma Kinkead was a woman with a very generous heart who simply loved to cook.

I would like to say that I learned to cook at my grandmother's apron, especially since my grandmother was one of the greatest natural cooks I ever knew. However, that would be a bold-faced lie. Growing up, I couldn't have cared less about learning to cook or toiling in grandma's kitchen. Fortunately, my father was paying a great deal more attention, so many of Marie Kinkead's creations have lived on.

As good a cook as my paternal grandmother was, my maternal grandfather was a better eater. George Alfred Turgeon was president of a construction company started by his father and run by his three brothers and himself. While Fred liked tools, electronic gadgets, and tinkering, he lived to go to restaurants. In particular, he enjoyed going to check on jobs with his oldest grandson (that's me) and then taking him to a restaurant. He would have loved the career I chose.

Between my two grandparents, I guess I was genetically predestined for a career as a chef. That, and coming from a family of ten children, one learned early on to feed oneself. At the Kinkead dinner table there were two types of diners: the fast and the hungry. Fussy eaters went without.

Contents

Acknowledgments

The people who are most deserving of my gratitude are the cooks, managers, waiters, bussers, food runners, and dishwashers who have made Kinkead's the wonderful restaurant it is.

Over the years there have been many people in the various restaurants where I was chef who allowed me to excel at this craft and who have made me look good. At Kinkead's, my thanks go to Mimi Schneider ("my secret weapon"), Manager George Ronetz, and Wine Director Michael Flynn, who have been with me since the restaurant opened and whose dedication to providing a professional and warm dining environment has resulted in Kinkead's being awarded nearly every accolade in the industry. Thanks also go to my chefs, Jerry Cousson and Todd Schiller, and my pastry chef, Chris Kujala, who kept the restaurant running on an even keel during the writing of this book. I would like to thank Bill Collison, Tom Kahoe, and Jung Wi, who are not only superb waiters but who also make me and the rest of the staff laugh a lot.

Thank you to my partners at Kinkead's and Colvin Run Tavern, Alan Sherman and Pat McGivern, who not only invested in me and our restaurant, but who built it as well.

My sincere gratitude to my good friend Jeff Gaetjen, the chef at Colvin Run Tavern and one of the most gifted cooks it has been my pleasure to work with. His diligence, creativity, and hard work make for one less headache in my busy life.

I am indebted to Mallory Buford, who tested many of the recipes in this book, and to Ris Lacoste, a great friend and collaborator over many years and many restaurants who, with her team, tested the remaining recipes.

Special thanks to Tracy O'Grady, who opened Kinkead's with me and who worked her way from garde manger to chef de cuisine. She eventually became America's representative at the Bocuse d'Or.

I would like to acknowledge Scott Bryan ("the Verm"), Jasper White, Jimmy Burke, Jeff Buben, Ben and Karen Barker—all great chefs and good friends.

My thanks to Louis and Marlene Osteen, wonderful friends over many, many years who have been through the many ups and downs of the restaurant business.

To Chris Schlesinger, my friend and tormentor for several decades and one of the most enjoyable cooks I ever had in my employ, thanks for your friendship and your unique sense of humor.

Others who deserve thanks, whom I have had the pleasure to know or work with: Chick Walsh, David Marconi, Guy Savoy, David Ryan, Pat and Nitzi Rabin, Ruth and Cliff Manchester, Jim Arseneault, Stan Bromley, Phillip Cooke, Mark Furstenberg, and Doug Pellecchia.

Heartfelt thanks go to Bob and Sue Kinkead, my parents, and my nine siblings, good eaters all. Particularly, I want to thank David, with whom I am about to embark on a new endeavor.

My special thanks to Tim Turner, whose easy temperament and brilliant photography made this a much better book than I could have imagined.

Finally, my love and gratitude go to Dianne, my in-house editor and greatest supporter.

Foreword

People constantly ask me, presumably because of my writings and not because of my waistline, "What's the best meal that you've ever had?" Wrong question, because you can't usefully compare a feast eaten in one of France's three-star temples of haute cuisine to a parade of exquisitely crafted dim sum in Hong Kong. What they should ask is, "Where do you most enjoy eating, day in and day out?" If they did, my answer would be perfectly straightforward: Kinkead's in Washington, where I live most of the year.

The place is a mirror of the man: jolly, welcoming, and unpretentious, which is one reason it attracts not only Washington big shots—cabinet members, senators past and present, television correspondents, lobbyists, the occasional Georgetown grande dame—but also little shots, out for a rare night on the town to celebrate a birthday or an anniversary. Another lure is the jazzy piano of Hilton Felton in the bar. A third is the wine list, lovingly assembled by Michael Flynn, the sommelier, which ranges well beyond California, France, and Italy to offer fine bottles from Austria, Spain, and Australia.

But the main reason people go to any restaurant—sensible people, anyway—is the food, and it is Bob Kinkead's food, above all, that has made me a steady customer, first at Twenty-One Federal, and for years now at Kinkead's, a few blocks from the White House.

Fish is Kinkead's thing. He takes his inspiration wherever he finds it. His authentic Ipswich fried clams, which always arrive inside a deftly folded napkin, are a real masterpiece, as befits a chef born and trained in New England. Likewise, his clam chowder. But Kinkead has lived in Washington for more than fifteen years, and you can taste the Chesapeake in his sautéed soft-shell crabs and his immorally rich roasted cod stuffed with crab imperial. Central America provided the idea for his pepita-crusted salmon, and Italy suggested his wood-grilled squid with polenta, tomato fondue, and pesto. Read the menu closely, and you'll find hints of Brazil, Sweden, Thailand, and New Orleans, too.

In a mood for something simpler? Kinkead will gladly grill you a piece of salmon or swordfish, or you can order oysters, as many as half a dozen kinds, from the raw bar. My wife, Betsey, likes almost everything Kinkead cooks, but some nights she craves, and gets, his big platter of gorgeous shellfish—oysters, clams, mussels, lobster, shrimp, and crab atop a mountain of shaved ice. Those nights, we feel as if we are in a brasserie in Paris, which is only appropriate, since Bob subtitles his place "an American brasserie."

—*R. W. Apple, Jr.*

Introduction

There are a few assumptions I have made in writing this book: First, that you are interested in learning new ways to prepare fish. Kinkead's is a seafood restaurant; as such, the vast majority of the dishes in this book involve fish or shellfish. We always have two meat or poultry dishes on the menu for non-fish eaters and I have included a few of the more popular of such dishes in this book. Second, that you have a better than basic skill level in cooking. There are some very long and, frankly, complicated dishes in this book; many easy ones as well, but this is not a cookbook for the novice. Finally, that you want more than a mere collection of recipes, that you want a taste of my world, both personally and professionally. Good cookbooks teach; great cookbooks inspire. Use this cookbook as a guidebook. You will never become a great cook by rigidly following recipes. I own approximately 1,200 cookbooks—and with the exception of a baking or pastry recipe, I don't believe I have ever used a single recipe out of any of them.

A Brief History of Kinkead's

January 18, 1993 was a sad day for the employees and many regular customers of Twenty-One Federal, a restaurant on L Street in the nation's capital. A seat in that restaurant had once been among the most coveted in Washington D.C. It was *the* hangout for a good number of the city's movers and shakers and one of the most important power restaurants in town. It was the cafeteria for many of Washington's electronic and print media community. But on that chilly winter day, two days before the first inauguration of President William Jefferson Clinton, Twenty-One Federal closed its doors for the final time after five years of business.

The reasons why a restaurant fails are as numerous as they are complex. One thing is for certain: the deals and decisions made prior to opening will determine a restaurant's success or failure. The terms of the lease, the location, the partners, the rent, the concept, the architect, the cost of construction, the financing, the management, the pricing, the menu, and a hundred other issues are all established before the doors ever open. A bad call in one or two areas might not spell disaster, but a bad call on one or two critical issues and an adverse economic environment can result in bankruptcy. Twenty-One Federal was not immune to the effects of bad decisions or bad timing. None, incidentally, related to poor food, service, or management. It was a good restaurant right to the bitter end.

I was the chef, a partner, and the one responsible for picking up the pieces after we closed. I worked hard to make sure that all the taxes, vendors, and most of all, my employees, got paid. Seeing the handwriting on the wall, I started looking for another situation and another location; I sent out résumés and traveled across the country for job interviews.

I had looked at a number of possible sites and kept gravitating back to an 11,000-square-foot space at

2000 Pennsylvania Avenue on the edge of the urban campus of George Washington University. It was a big saloon restaurant that had been shuttered for two and a half years. It was really too big for my needs, considering that Washington was still in the midst of the early 1990s recession. I felt if I could make the right deal I would be paying the same rent as for many of the sites I saw that were half the size. The University, which owned the building, accepted my proposal and with new partners I opened Kinkead's nine months after Twenty-One Federal closed.

After closing Twenty-One Federal, all I escaped with was my reputation as a good cook. It seemed wise to capitalize on what good will I had established in the community by naming the restaurant Kinkead's, and I settled on cooking something I knew a lot about: fish.

As unfortunate as the closing of Twenty-One Federal was, it became the catalyst for the creation of Kinkead's, one of the most acclaimed and successful restaurants in Washington's restaurant history. In our first ten years we served approximately 1.5 million meals and have been the training ground for at least a dozen of Washington's more notable chefs. Since its opening in September 1993, Kinkead's has established a reputation as one of the premier seafood restaurants in the nation.

How Kinkead's came to be is a story intertwined with my own culinary journey. Its evolution and the philosophies in this book are what I learned along the way in this culmination of a long-held dream. This book is about Kinkead's and some of the personalities who make it work, along with a little of its history and a peek at how a restaurant really operates. Mostly, though, this book is about Kinkead's food.

The Four Essentials

I am a self-taught chef. I have never attended culinary school or had any formal culinary training. What I know about cooking and running a restaurant I learned on the job or from reading books. I learned to cook by experimenting at home and in the restaurants where I was employed. I learned from chefs and coworkers. But mostly I learned from dining in restaurants and cooking, eating, and drinking with friends.

I have worked in pancake houses, roadhouses, bistros, diners, hotels, seasonal resorts, and ultra-luxe restaurants. I once even worked at a ski resort restaurant that served breakfast in the morning and Chinese and Italian food at night (the original Chino-Italiano). I can honestly say that at some time in my career I have worked every single position in the restaurant.

In breaking down the specific skills that make a good cook, I have observed some essential skills that all great cooks must acquire—what I term the Four Essentials:

- **Taste:** The ability to educate the palate and to properly select and season food
- **Fire:** A mastery of fire and how heat affects food
- **Chemistry:** A knowledge of how foods react to and interact with each other
- **Tools:** An accomplished use of kitchen tools, particularly knives

TASTE

Taste encompasses several related skills. Most important is the ability to distinguish whether the flavors of seasoned food are in balance. Is the soup you just made adequately seasoned? Is there enough salt or too much? Are the flavors of a soup's main ingredients in balance? Is there enough acid? A good cook can gain the ability to correctly answer these questions with practice and over time.

Learn the four basic flavors detectable on the tongue: *acid,* generally found in vinegars, citrus juices, verjus, and tart fruits; *sweet,* found in sugars, Karo syrups, fructose, honey, and some alcohols; *bitter,* found in some vegetables and generally a taste one is trying to remove or compensate for; and *salt,* which is probably the most important from a flavor standpoint.

Different combinations of the four basic flavors are what give taste to foods; balance of these four flavors is what makes food taste right. The key is knowing how to truly taste these flavors and note small variants in them. For example, let's take a roasted red pepper soup that you just prepared. It just doesn't taste right. It tastes underseasoned and flat. How do you fix it?

Consistent, balanced use of salt and pepper is one of the most important issues I stress with new cooks at Kinkead's. In particular, learning to use salt correctly is as important a skill as can be learned in a kitchen. The main reason by far that most dishes in restaurants are underseasoned or out of balance is that they are undersalted. More than any other ingredient, salt affects not only how food tastes to us, but also our *ability* to taste food.

Back to your soup. You've added salt and pepper, but the soup still tastes a little flat. One of my favorite flavor enhancers is acid. Acid can be a citrus, such as grapefruit, lime, or lemon juice; a sour fruit like passion fruit juice, tamarind paste, or pineapple; dry white wine or verjus; or, vinegar—balsamic, sherry, red wine, or another type. Any food that imparts a sour taste can, in the right context, work well to add the kick that some foods need. Acids are particularly good in meat- and fish-based sauces, soups, and salads with leafy greens or marinated vegetables.

There are several other reasons your soup could lack flavor: the peppers were not properly roasted, the stock was weak, or too few aromatics were used or they were not properly cooked. Knowing what the potential problem is and then knowing how to correct it is critical. Occasionally, adding more of the base ingredients to the batch can fix the problem. As long as the error is slight, most foods can be brought back into balance. The only taste one cannot eliminate is the flavor of scorched or burned food.

Taste foods during every step of the cooking process. It improves your food and your palate. Never assume a sauce or salad is in balance because you've made it that way twenty times before. Also, get in the habit of having others taste soups, stews, and foods you have made. It confirms your palate development and you might get an ego boost when your victim says, "That's delicious."

A related taste skill is the ability to distinguish a quality food product from a mediocre one. You can't buy a pristine piece of yellowfin tuna if you've never seen or eaten truly fresh tuna. Similarly, you can't tell a truly great meal from a simply good one if you haven't experienced the finest.

Taste also involves knowing which foods complement each other. Classic food matches, like lamb with garlic and rosemary or tuna with olives and tomato, are never out of style. It is important to learn what combinations work and, more important, the ones that don't. One of the great excesses of modern American cooking is when a young chef slams together two or three unlikely ingredients under the misguided impression that pure creativity spawns good food. Reinventing the wheel works only once in a great while; classic food pairings did not become classics for nothing.

THE COUNCIL OF INDEPENDENT
RESTAURATEURS OF AMERICA

In 1974 my good friend Louis Osteen sold his car, a 1973 Chevy Impala he had inherited when his mother passed away, to help purchase his first restaurant, Hart's, in Atlanta, Georgia. He essentially put up everything he owned to have a piece of the American dream. Now the chef and proprietor of Louis's at Pawley's Island in South Carolina, Louis has come a long way, seeing both the highs and lows of becoming an entrepreneurial restaurateur.

In 1980 Michael Foley built his restaurant in Chicago's then-questionable neighborhood of Printer's Row. Michael literally built the restaurant himself. He put a piece of himself into that restaurant, and the much-awarded Printer's Row has helped the neighborhood return to its original vibrancy.

Throughout the United States there are hundreds of similar stories of entrepreneurial chefs and restaurateurs who have risked their life savings and much more. There are several similarities in their stories: a passion for the craft, a love of good food, and a sincere desire both to take care of their customers and to make a good living providing all those things. These men and women want to live and work in a community to help it, and themselves, thrive. Sadly, those days are passing.

In 1987 a national chain paid $1 million to buy out the lease of a two-thousand-square-foot space in Charleston, South Carolina. In Akron, Ohio, and Indianapolis, Indiana, there are but a handful of independent fine dining restaurants left. This scenario is playing out throughout America. Many restaurant operators have been driven out of business by the plethora of national chain restaurants that have opened since the late 1990s. The year 2002 marked the first time in history that chain units outnumbered independent restaurants in our country. Chains have reduced access to prime real estate; depleted the available labor pool; taken the creative ideas of independent operator, without offering remuneration; and sought to homogenize what had been a diverse and exciting culinary heritage. This does not bode well for American cuisine.

If we are to enjoy the foods our grandparents and great-grandparents enjoyed or the new and innovative cuisine of creative individuals, the dining public and especially lovers of good food need to take a stand and support their local, independent restaurants. If we are to experience in the future the authentic ethnic cuisine now available in America, we need to support those independent restaurants that are part of the fabric of our cities and towns.

In 1999 Phillip Cooke and a group of like-minded restaurant owners, including myself, started the Council of Independent Restaurateurs of America (CIRA). We saw an opportunity to create a professional organization that would promote dining in independently owned restaurants and fight for the issues important to independent restaurateurs. We also saw the need for a forum—to exchange ideas, to make business contacts, and to help each other thrive. In an even greater sense, CIRA and its members aim to reintroduce America to what truly good food and gracious service is all about.

In the words of my colleague, Don Luria of Cafe Terra Cotta in Tucson, Arizona, "The independent is about food; chains are about money." Independent restaurateurs have made the culinary reputation of cities like New Orleans, San Francisco, Boston, New York, Seattle, and Chicago. Maine became famous for lobster and seafood because of the independently owned fish restaurants and clam shacks along her coast. Independents have seen the value of locally grown and harvested seasonal food products. Independents are about passion for our food, our business, and our customers' satisfaction. The dining public wants tasty, well-prepared food, served professionally by a waitstaff that cares about them. Independents have the expertise and passion to deliver.

FIRE

The second of our four essential skills is the mastery of fire and how heat affects food. This includes knowing the proper methods of hot food preparation and being able to determine doneness. Braising, sautéing, grilling, boiling, poaching, frying, baking, roasting, broiling, searing—one must be competent with all of these methods to become a great cook. All baking and pastry production depends on precise knowledge of heat and how an oven affects food—primarily flour, yeast and other raising agents, eggs, fats, and sugar. Dry versus moist heat, grill versus sauté, high heat versus moderate heat—knowledge of all is critical.

There are also different types of fire to be mastered. The oven, a gas burner, a flat top, a rotisserie, a grill, a wood oven, and an open-hearth fireplace all involve flame. Some heat sources are intended for different results. Deep-frying in hot oil, steaming under pressure, and microwaving are different ways of bringing heat to food. The main skill to be mastered is how to work with the fire of a live fuel like wood or charcoal versus that of gas, electricity, or steam heat. It can be very different.

With a few exceptions, like boiling pasta and high-heat searing meats, most cooking should be done at a lower temperature, especially when baking or oven roasting. Moderate heat is your friend. It is gentler on the foods and the longer cooking time helps flavors develop better.

CHEMISTRY

The third skill requires a fundamental knowledge of how many basic foods react when heated, aerated, or combined with other foods. Mastery of bread baking and pastry making is impossible without a thorough knowledge of how a few simple foods react. Good cooking, in general, means mastering the chemical properties of foods like eggs, sugar, fats, milk and cream, and acids. Much of this information can be acquired through reading, not just by trial and error.

As it pertains to food chemistry, probably the most important food product is the egg. Eggs are critical to so many foods because of their amazing chemical and physical properties. Mayonnaise, hollandaise, cake batter, soufflés, pancakes, ice cream, custards, and meringues are all impossible without eggs.

Other important chemical reactions are found in food preparation. How do proteins react to heat when concentrated (reduction sauces)? How do fats, oils, and, particularly, butter bond with protein to make or thicken sauces? Bacteria can react both favorably and unfavorably with foods, particularly dairy products—it can help make yogurt, cheeses, and sour cream, and it can spoil milk and make us sick. Learning a handful of useful chemical reactions that occur with foods is essential to becoming a competent cook.

TOOLS

The fourth essential skill is mastery of kitchen utensils. Knives are the most basic and most versatile tools in the kitchen and the importance of good knife skills cannot be understated. The ability to handle, sharpen, care for, and use this tool properly is a skill that will, over a lifetime, save you an enormous amount of time and money.

A good cook must be able to perform many cutting functions. Dicing, cutting, and turning vegetables, and butchering meat, birds, and fish are difficult tasks without good knife skills. Butchering is really more about tearing away the muscle than cutting through it, but knife skills make the job much easier. Here's a little secret: Many chefs I've known find butchering meat a very soothing, stress-relieving task. This is a precious commodity in a professional kitchen, because there is generally a fair amount of tension and stress associated with your average restaurant dinner service. Although it seems much easier for the home cook to have the butcher or fishmonger cut your veal scallops or fillet your haddock, for a change (and to improve your skills), try bringing home a leg of lamb or whole salmon and cutting it yourself.

Cooking is a craft. It is the accumulation of many skills and the acquired knowledge of how food changes and reacts under different conditions. There are artistic aspects to cooking, but I do not consider cooking an art like painting, sculpting, or acting. Great cooking does require talent, however. Part of my job as a chef is to accurately assess the skill level, motivation, and ultimately the potential success of new cooks in my kitchens. My success as a restaurateur depends on it.

Selecting Fresh Seafood

Several years ago I was asked to serve on a panel with a dozen of Washington's better-known chefs to discuss how restaurants purchase fresh seafood. The panel convened as part of a weekend-long seminar on seafood sponsored by the Smithsonian Institute. During that discussion, a question was posed by an audience member: how and where can the home cook buy fish and shellfish of the same quality and freshness as we chefs purchase for our restaurants? Several chefs attempted to answer the question with such advice as how to pick a fishmonger, how to tell the fish is fresh by looking at the gills, how to determine if the fish is fresh by the glint in its eyes, and so on. Frankly, the real answer is this: you can't.

Unless you are extremely lucky on the day you stroll into the fish market, there is little chance you will get a piece of fish of the same quality that a good restaurant gets on a daily basis, for this simple reason: a patron buying two pounds of codfish is never going to have the same buying clout as a restaurant that purchases two thousand pounds of fish a week. Fish wholesalers save their best product for their best and most discerning customers. It is also extremely unlikely that the average fish market consumer is going to be able to inspect seafood the way an experienced restaurant seafood buyer routinely does.

So how can the average consumer maximize his or her chances of getting the best-quality fresh fish? The answer is complex, but it starts with dispelling some of the myths about how fresh seafood actually gets to the table.

One very popular myth, which for some reason is eaten hook, line, and sinker even by food journalists, is the concept of "day-boat" fish—that is, fish caught by fishing boats that go out to sea and return with their catch in the same twenty-four-hour period. The idea is that the fish is only hours out of the water when it reaches the fish wholesaler or restaurant. This would be a wonderful concept if it were true—unfortunately, it is nonsense.

To begin with, the number of day-boat fishermen trawling the waters is minute. Approximately 1 percent of fish brought to market are day-boat fish. These fishermen don't go out every day and they don't go out at all in foul weather. The size of their catch is too small to supply a large amount of fish. The variety and numbers of species caught is also very limited. Generally, only fishmongers in coastal areas get fish the same day and then only if they have good relationships with the fishermen. With the exception of a handful of chefs who are paying truly top dollar, it would be impossible to supply the number of restaurants who claim day-boat fish on their menus.

Let's examine how fish makes its way to your local fish market. The commercial supply chain of seafood is set up to move a glut of a particular species at a particular time of the year. Keep in mind that fish, as opposed to meat or even poultry, is extremely perishable. Moving the product quickly is of paramount importance. Airfreight has completely changed how fish gets to market. Virtually all fish going to noncoastal areas and large urban markets arrives at the fish retailer after traveling through a huge national and international distribution network. A particular species of fish is caught by fishing boats, often as part of a large fishing fleet or a cooperative with many boats generally fishing for that one specific fish. This catch might be brokered to large wholesale shippers who sell that fish to midsize middlemen who broker again to smaller wholesalers and distributors to the final retailer. It might be sold from the

fishing area—say, Trinidad in the Caribbean—directly to a supplier in Washington. It can be a long or short chain and the vast majority of that fish travels by air at some point in the journey.

A big wholesaler in the Washington D.C. area might sell $40 million of seafood a year. That is about eight million pounds of fish and shellfish. The name of the game is moving quality product and consistency for the quality fish wholesaler. Supply and demand determines price and availability. It also determines freshness. Time of year and season makes a big difference in the amount of fish sold and how fresh it is at the retail level. In Washington, spring and fall are the busy times of the year, but in Florida, winter is the busy season when the fish sellers there are moving a lot of product.

The dilemma for a good seafood wholesaler is "How do I provide salmon, tuna, crabmeat, or red snapper to my restaurant and fish store customers who require them nearly year-round?" The smart wholesaler seeks wild products all over the world. He might find tuna running off of Vietnam, red snapper in Trinidad, and genuine blue crabmeat being processed in Venezuela. That same large supplier might have three hundred separate venders for product. Most are species specific; that is, tuna from one supplier, mahi mahi from another, ground fish like flounder, skate, and cod from a third. American red snapper fishing is regulated by our government: it can be commercially caught generally in the first ten days of February, March, April, May, and June. How then, you might ask, is there red snapper available in your fish case on April 20 or for that matter on November 20? One explanation is that the fish is coming from outside American waters. The other is that the red snapper the purveyor is offering is from stock left from the first ten days of April.

Different species of fish are caught in different manners with different types of boats at different times

of year. Rockfish, for example, are commercially caught with gill nets in the fall, pound nets in July, and hook and line in August. Grouper are generally caught by one-, two-, or three-day boats; tuna, by ten- to fourteen-day boats; and there are swordfish boats in the Georges Bank off of Nova Scotia that go out for thirty days.

Fishing is really the last hunter-gatherer occupation left on the planet. It is changing daily. As sad as it might seem, our great-grandchildren will look upon truly wild-caught fish as an expensive delicacy. The vast majority of the seafood they eat will be farmed.

This brings us to the issue of what is truly fresh fish. The most important factor affecting the quality and freshness of fish is the handling procedure demanded by the fishing boat captain. Captains who handle and ice down their catches the best bring in the highest-quality fish. Three- to seven-day trawlers catch most species of fresh seafood brought to the American table.

The larger the fish, the longer it takes to deteriorate. It may take a month for a six-hundred-pound swordfish to begin breaking down (but I wouldn't be buying a fish that old).

Let's look at tuna fishing as an example. Tuna is one of the most popular fish worldwide. Bluefin tuna consistently fetches the highest price per pound, largely due to the Japanese demand for that fatty species. A restaurant like Kinkead's requires grade-A tuna year-round.

Since all varieties of tuna—yellowfin, bigeye, albacore—are in demand year-round, the wholesaler goes where the tuna are. The location of tuna changes with the time of year and migratory patterns of the school. A large fish like tuna can range thousands of miles in a year. Let's say that a particular boat goes out for yellowfin for ten days. The first day and a half is spent getting out to deep waters. It will take that long

HOW TO FIND A QUALITY FISH MARKET

The key to great fish markets and great seafood restaurants is the same: high turnover of product. A bustling fish market is a good one. A first-class fish market should carry a large variety of fresh fish and shellfish, all properly iced and the majority of it whole. Lobster or crab tanks should be clean, with no algae growing, and appear well filtered.

Fish counters and fish markets should smell clean and the fish displayed should smell like the sea. The floors, displays, and counters should be very clean; there should be an employee occupied with cleaning something all the time. If the store smells like old fish or ammonia, go elsewhere.

Although some supermarket fish counters are improving, you should avoid buying fish in a grocery store. The fish is never the best of the lot and the salespeople are generally not well informed. Also, avoid roadside fish stands. You might find the best corn or tomatoes you ever ate at a farm stand; however, roadside or parking-lot fish sellers virtually always disappoint. They do not have the refrigeration and the seafood is almost always poorly handled.

Ice is really the coin of the realm in displaying fresh fish. You should see copious quantities of ice everywhere in a good fish market. There should be no puddles of water or blood mixing with melting ice near the fish. The sales people should always offer to pack your purchase, no matter what size, with crushed ice. Lots of floor drains are a good sign too.

When possible, buy fish near the source. Seafood is almost always better near the water. This makes sense because it is often easier for a local fisherman to sell to a local fish store and pocket the profit than it is to sell to a large broker. Get in the habit of eating local species. Rockfish, sea trout, and crabs near the Chesapeake; Monterey Bay prawns, petrale sole, and Dungeness crab in San Francisco; and so on. If you have the opportunity, eat a lobster in Maine at an "in the rough" restaurant where you pick your lobster and they steam it in a huge tank of seawater. The lobsters are freshly harvested and very alive. You will notice the lobster tastes far superior to those you thought were alive in your local market. It is one of Maine's great dining treats. Feasting on boiled blue crabs with a few beers on a Chesapeake Bay inlet provides a similarly unique dining pleasure.

If your city has an open wholesale fish market or fish pier where many wholesalers sell to the retail trade, stop by. They may sell to the public. The quality is almost always better than at the retail markets. In many cases, they carry fish species that are popular in certain ethnic cuisines. These are often less popular and quite inexpensive fish. Try a few you have never tasted. Experiment; you may find a new favorite. Ethnic fish markets are generally a good place to buy the types of fish popular with that ethnic group. For example, a fish market in downtown New Bedford, Massachusetts, which has a large Portuguese population, will undoubtedly have very good hake, salt cod, scallops, and other seafood popular with that clientele. Conversely, red snapper or grouper (both southern Atlantic fish), if in that store at all, are probably there just for show and don't sell well enough to bother with.

After finding a good fish market, develop a relationship with the salespeople or, better yet, with the proprietor. Ask questions and take suggestions. Find out when deliveries of seafood are scheduled to arrive. Most will come daily, but some special items may be scheduled for certain delivery days. A shipment of super-fresh Alaskan halibut may be coming in on the following two or three Fridays; plan to be there when it arrives. Visit the shop often. As is the case in restaurants, the best customers get the most attention and, in a fish market, that means they get the best and freshest seafood.

to return to port, so that leaves seven days for fishing. But once the fish has been brought back to land, it takes another three or four days to unload the hold, broker the fish, process at the wholesaler, and put the tuna up for sale at the fishmonger's. That means that the "fresh" tuna you buy is quite possibly eleven or twelve days old. Discerning restaurants and fish markets are buying the fish caught in the last day or two, so theirs is probably only four to six days old. The tuna caught in the first day or two is probably going to a processor or an undiscerning buyer for less money.

Another myth is that top-quality fishmongers only purchase "top of the trip" fish—that is, only the fish caught on the last day of the fishing trip before returning to dock. This is misleading on several counts. For argument's sake, let's say that the boat has been out for five days and caught four-fifths of its total catch in the first two days. The remaining fifth was caught on the third day and none was caught on the last two. The supposed "top of the trip" fish is still three days out of the water. It is a classic free-market capitalist system of supply seeking demand. That is why it is sometimes easier in Washington D.C. to get high-quality halibut from Alaska than it is to procure striped bass (or rockfish, as we call it) from the Chesapeake.

Yet another myth of both the seafood and restaurant business is the notion, perpetuated by many chefs and food writers, that all quality purveyors and top chefs are at the docks and fish piers at dawn waiting for the catch to be unloaded to select only the finest fish for their customers. I am sure I am setting myself up for a letter from some chef in Moose Lip, Maine, who will dispute my claim, but here goes: There is no urban chef in America that I am aware of who routinely gets up to personally select seafood for his or her restaurant. Certainly, a few have traipsed down to a fish market at 5 A.M. to inspect

fish as a publicity gimmick, but no chef personally selects his or her fish as a regular part of running the business. This would expand what is normally a twelve-hour day to one of eighteen hours. Every chef and wholesaler I know does his or her fish purchasing over the phone and checks it when it is delivered.

Top-quality restaurant chefs (or, in most cases, stewards or purchasers) compare prices, availability, and quality and make daily buying decisions based on that information. Chefs learn by trial and error which suppliers have the best quality and the fairest prices. Sometimes the best tuna is from supplier A, the best cod from supplier C, and a third supplier is needed for soft-shell crabs. Kinkead's uses from eight to fourteen different seafood suppliers, depending on the time

of year. Training a supplier to select and ship the highest-quality product is an ongoing, daily process. The chef or purchaser must know nearly as much about the seafood coming in the door as the wholesaler. The challenge for the chef is to seek out seafood purveyors who buy well and, more important, handle their product well. The best chefs are continually seeking out new sources for the best products—and jealously guard their knowledge of the ones that deliver.

With a typical seafood delivery, a whole process ensues. The order is placed the previous night and the seafood is delivered to Kinkead's. As the order comes in the door, the purchaser carefully examines the fish and weighs it. All seafood is accepted or rejected based on quality (e.g., bruising, color, freshness or lack thereof), and whether the species and weight of the item is correct. For example, if a wholesaler knows I will reject an order of substandard red snapper and that he will have

to (1) return the inferior product, (2) replace the fish or find an acceptable substitute, and (3) make the same trip back to Kinkead's, he knows it will cost him money to fall short of my expectations. The smart supplier will send the best the first time or at least call ahead to inform us that he does not have snapper of a quality acceptable for service at Kinkead's. Not all fish suppliers are that smart; conversely, not all chefs and purchasers are that discerning. Wholesalers are in the business of moving product. Fish that we find unacceptable will undoubtedly end up at someone else's doorstep.

Knowing all this, how can you better *your* odds of obtaining good seafood? Be informed. Learn the characteristics of really fresh fish and learn to differentiate between similar-looking species. Genuine American red snapper is a medium to large, red-skinned, white-fleshed fish. It is one of the best eating fish in the south Atlantic. Yellowtail snapper has pinker skin with yellow

flecks and a yellow tail. It also has a slightly pink cast to the flesh. While it is a delicious fish, it is more plentiful and not as special as the genuine American red. Red porgy is a generally smaller fish, again with red skin. Its flesh is tough and fairly watery and is much inferior to the other two species for eating. In fact, red porgy is often used as a baitfish. The difference in prices for fillets of these three fish might be $9, $6.50, and $2, respectively. There are over thirty commercial species of snapper, including mutton snapper from the Florida Keys and Gulf, vermilion snapper, and B-Liners, which are one- to two-pound fish of several varieties. You get what you pay for. Though the skin on all these fish is red and might look quite similar, the quality and price differ considerably. The less-than-scrupulous fishmonger may take advantage of uninformed customers by price gouging or using the popular bait-and-switch technique.

So, how can you tell fresh fish? The first and best clues are visual. Whole fish should be packed in ice. Truly fresh fish should look just caught, almost alive. Fresh shellfish *is* alive. The skin of fresh fish should be moist and glistening and in many species has an almost sheer, shimmering film. Fish should be bright-looking with no blood spots, bruises (pink or brown spots), or visible signs of spoilage (browning or graying areas). The gills should be bright red, not maroon, and clean, with no milky residue. Tails and fins should be whole with no signs of dehydration or shriveling. The flesh should be elastic and spring back when touched. If limp or mushy, the fish is not fresh. In most cases clear, bright eyes that look alert and have no blood spots are a good indicator of freshness. Cloudiness in the eyes can be deceptive, especially if all other factors indicate that the fish is fresh. Some species' eyes cloud up or turn red immediately after being removed from the water. This is more common with deep-water species. Other species' eyes stay clear for days, even when the flesh is starting to smell.

Steak fish like tuna, swordfish, and mako shark should be bright colored. Most tuna—yellowfin and bluefin in particular—should be bright red. There should be no cloudiness or brown tint to the flesh. If possible, have your fishmonger cut the steaks from the loin to order, rather than selecting precut slices. Because of the high proportion of flesh exposed to air, deterioration happens quickly.

When possible, buy fish whole. You can more easily determine whether the fish is fresh and, in general, whole fish stay fresh longer. If possible, learn to fillet fish at home. You also have the benefit of being able to cook the fish on the bone, which is better for flavor, texture, and sometimes presentation. If buying fillets or steaks, try to purchase the fish with the skin on. It protects the flesh and is another indicator of freshness. Often the skin either provides a good protective covering when cooking or simply tastes good.

In cut fillets there should be no bands of color or "rainbows" in the flesh, as that is an indicator of older fish. Fillets should look firm and not appear to be falling apart; there should be no hint of discoloration on the edges. Again, the flesh should spring back when pressed. Fillets should be displayed on ice in trays, not embedded in the ice. Never buy fish fillets that have been prepackaged or covered with plastic wrap. You can't really examine the fish and you can't detect "off" smells.

All fish and shellfish deteriorate from the moment they are removed from the water. Even live lobsters are best when removed from the sea for the shortest period. Though they appear to be very alive in tanks you see in the supermarket, once a lobster is removed from seawater it is starting to die. A large fish, depending on

PAIRING WINE WITH FOOD AT KINKEAD'S

When I am asked by guests to recommend wines to accompany their meals, they often begin with the comment, "We're mostly having seafood, so I guess we need a white." There, I have to take a deep breath and quiet that thought running through my head: *Well, if that's all there is to it, why do they need a sommelier?*

I respond with a string of questions: "Can you tell me precisely what you've ordered?" "What kinds of wines do you usually serve at home?" "Do you prefer European wines to domestic ones?" "Full-bodied and rich, or light, fruity, and dry?" I look for clues to the guests' preferences for price range and regional styles by following their finger up and down the wine list. I then draw on the two or three common denominators that thread their way through the guests' dining selections—red meat, red wine sauces, seafood, vinaigrettes, spicy flavors, grilling, citrus, and so on—to make a recommendation or two that should satisfy the greatest number of people at the table.

Happily, for the home cook the scenario becomes greatly simplified, if not altogether effortless. Still, the question remains: what to serve? It would be comforting to take refuge in the axiom "White wine with fish, red wine with meat," but the rules change when it comes to Bob Kinkead's cuisine. I offer as an example his Pepper-Seared Tuna with Flageolets, Grilled Portobello Mushrooms, and Pinot Noir Sauce (page 161). Specifically designed to complement red Burgundy, this dish has yet to find a Chardonnay or Sauvignon Blanc to meet its flavors even halfway. No white wine for this fish, to be sure.

You would do well, then, to remember something I often remind our staff in such matters. Wine should be treated as a sort of *second sauce* rather than a laser-guided beam to the main event, the meat or fish. By matching wine to sauce you'll find as much harmony as the dish possesses in the first place, even within a dizzying array of ingredients and elements.

By this logic, the Halibut with Spring Vegetable Ragoût, Crabmeat Ravioli, and Lemon Butter (page 138), which is served with chervil, would require a citrusy white wine with good, crisp acidity for the lemon, medium body for the butter, and a touch of herbaceousness for the chervil. New World Sauvignon Blanc, Sancerre, dry Loire Valley Chenin Blanc, Austrian Riesling are all good fits for this subtle fare.

On the other hand, Walnut-Crusted Rockfish with Sherry-Beet Sauce and Cauliflower Flan (page 122), far from requiring a full-flavored white wine, suggests something vividly red, with a softly earthy fruitiness, some delicacy, and gentle tannins—good red Burgundy, Chianti Classico Riserva from a ripe vintage, or Oregon Pinot Noir are all strong candidates.

Spicy flavors, to which Chef Kinkead is no stranger, might seem to pose additional challenges. But whether the spice derives from the slow-building heat of chiles, the brassy harmony of ginger with lemongrass, or the incendiary spark of cumin or red pepper, the supporting pillars of fruit, acidity, and even bubbles will stand you in good stead. Southwestern and Central American flavors respond well to Sauvignon Blanc, particularly the pungent gooseberry and lime-inflected Sauvignons from New Zealand's South Island. Asian heat will often like Riesling, with the level of necessary sweetness rising with the fire of the dish. Dry Champagne covers the greatest number of bases, however, with creamy bubbles cleansing and refreshing the palate after each bite.

The order of wine service should preserve the palate while building in the richness and complexity of flavor as you move through the courses. Generally, start light, white, and dry for the apéritif; graduate to fuller, more complex whites; then move on to medium-bodied elegant reds, followed by richer, oakier reds; and finish with a sweet wine.

Champagnes, Cavas, and other New World sparkling wines are ideal starters, as they awaken the taste buds and lighten the mood of the gathering. Sauvignon Blanc, Riesling, Austrian Grüner Veltliner, and Pinot Gris work beautifully in framing shellfish, flaky whitefish dishes, and sauces with citrus and herbs. Fuller, more oak-nuanced Chardonnay, aromatic Viognier, Pinot Blanc, as well as Pinot Noir (or its French counterpart from Burgundy), Barbera, Grenache, and Chianti can fill in nicely for richer seafood or poultry dishes, particularly when there are a few truffles or morels around. Bordeaux, Syrah from the northern Rhône, Spanish Tempranillo, Nebbiolo, and their New World cousins from California, Australia, South Africa, and elsewhere find a place alongside full-flavored meats. For dessert, it's Banyuls or Port for chocolate, and Sauternes, Tokaji Aszú, or late-harvest Riesling for custards and cakes. If it's a refreshing, fruit-inspired tart, fresh berries, or sorbet, try a lovely Muscat Beaumes-de-Venise to round out your meal.

Indulgence, ultimately, is a matter of choice, and the ultimate indulgence may lie in not choosing too strenuously. Are you conflicted between pairing your rack of lamb with the Pomerol or the Peter Michael? Serve both, and let your guests decide. No one ever argues, after all, with an abundance of delicious choices.

—Michael Flynn, Wine Director and Sommelier

species and handling, is in its prime for about four days after leaving the water. It is still good for maybe three more days. After that it goes downhill fast. Smaller fish won't last nearly that long. A medium-sized fish that is noticeably fishy smelling is anywhere from six to ten days out of the water. And all of this assumes the fish has been held under optimum conditions, which is not always the case.

Using your nose to determine freshness is fine, but if you can detect an off smell, the fish is very old and you've probably already figured that out by visual clues. That said, fresh fish, especially whole fish, should smell like the ocean, never ammoniated. This is particularly true around the gills and stomach cavity. Smell can be particularly helpful in determining if the fishmonger you are about to choose is a good one.

Despite the huge amount of money spent to promote the contrary view, good-quality fresh fish is virtually always superior to frozen. That said, a considerable amount of the fish consumed in Japan—a country that clearly appreciates good seafood—is flash-frozen when just caught in large factory freezer fishing boats. In the future, advances in flash freezing and depleting supplies will make frozen fish a more viable alternative to fresh. Unfortunately, in some cases it may become the only option.

Don't shop for fish strictly by price. As with anything else in life, you pretty much get what you pay for. No fishmonger is going to sell you prime, center-cut, harpooned swordfish for a cut-rate price. Plan to pay top dollar—anywhere from $15 to $23 a pound, depending on the location, season, and availability. If you are getting swordfish at $3 a pound less, it is line-caught, older, and a less desirable piece of fish. Fish prices fluctuate due to demand, weather, and availability. You may pay $15 for tuna steaks one week and $19 only days later. It may be of the same or even lesser quality, but demand and, probably, availability have driven up the price.

Finally, be flexible. Build your meals around what's fresh and available rather than following the dictates of a recipe. It is much better to use pristine cod in a recipe than tired halibut. As a general rule, all white, flaky fish (fluke, cod, ling cod, pollock, halibut, haddock, and so on) taste pretty similar; it's usually the texture that is different. Go to the fish market with the idea of purchasing the best-quality seafood in the store, not with the plan that you have to eat swordfish tonight.

Hors d'Oeuvres and Amuses

Sesame Seared Tuna with Seaweed Salad and Wasabi on Fried Wontons ∽ 19

Assorted Oysters with Three Mignonettes ∽ 21

Mushroom Strudels with Virginia Ham ∽ 22

Cherrystone "Stuffies" ∽ 25

Caramelized Onion, Walnut, and Roquefort Tarts ∽ 29

Sesame Seared Tuna with Seaweed Salad and Wasabi on Fried Wontons

This tuna dish makes a tasty amuse or passed hors d'oeuvre, or you can serve several as a first course. It is critical that you use sushi-grade tuna for this recipe, because it features that fish essentially raw. Yellowfin tuna or, if you can find it, bluefin is best for this dish. You can buy fresh wonton wrappers in the produce section of almost any grocery store; look for prepared seaweed salad and sambal at gourmet food stores. Note the preparation time: the tuna must be chilled for several hours or overnight, then marinated, seared, and chilled again before completing the recipe.

TUNA

1-pound loin very fresh, center-cut sushi-quality tuna

1/2 cup soy sauce

4 tablespoons black and white sesame seeds

1/4 cup peanut or other vegetable oil for searing

SOY MIGNONETTE

1/4 cup rice wine vinegar

2 tablespoons minced fresh ginger

1 clove garlic, minced

1 teaspoon cracked black pepper

1/2 teaspoon ground coriander seed

1/2 cup soy sauce

1/2 teaspoon sambal or other hot chile sauce

1 teaspoon freshly squeezed lime juice

1 small shallot, minced

SEAWEED SALAD

3 tablespoons wasabi powder

4 tablespoons water

4 tablespoons pickled ginger

1 cup prepared seaweed salad

1/2 cup tightly packed peeled and julienned daikon

4 radishes, julienned

2 scallions, julienned (about 1/2 cup)

1 small carrot, peeled and julienned (about 1/4 cup)

1 small cucumber, peeled, seeded, and julienned (about 1 cup)

18 to 24 (3-inch) wonton wrappers

3 cups peanut or other vegetable oil for deep frying

Kosher salt

1 cup loosely packed radish sprouts

To prepare the tuna, cut the loin into 2 cigar-shaped pieces, 8 inches long and about 2 inches around. Each will weigh about 7 ounces. Trim the tuna of any sinew. Roll each piece in plastic wrap and twist the ends tightly to make them rounded. Chill for at least 3 hours or overnight.

Remove the tuna from the plastic and marinate in the soy sauce for 45 minutes to 1 hour. Drain and roll in the sesame seeds. In a sauté pan, heat the peanut oil over medium-high heat and sear the tuna on all sides for about 30 seconds. The outer edge of the tuna and the sesame seeds should be brown. Chill for 30 minutes in the refrigerator. You can do this up to 4 hours ahead.

To make the soy mignonette, combine all of the ingredients in a stainless steel bowl.

To make the salad, mix 1 tablespoon of the wasabi powder into 1/4 cup of the soy mignonette and reserve. Put the remaining 2 tablespoons wasabi powder in a small bowl and stir in the water to make a drizzling sauce.

CONTINUED

Julienne half of the pickled ginger; reserve the remaining slices. In a stainless steel bowl, toss the julienned ginger, seaweed salad, daikon, radishes, scallion, carrot, and cucumber with the wasabi-soy mignonette mixture. Let sit for 10 minutes, and then drain and discard the excess liquid.

To make the wontons, cut the wrappers into 2¹/₂-inch circles. In a cast-iron pan or table deep-fryer, heat the peanut oil to 375°F. Fry the wonton wrappers for about 45 seconds, until crisp. Drain on paper towels and lightly salt.

To assemble, slice the tuna into ¹/₄-inch rounds. Place about a tablespoon of the daikon-seaweed salad on each wonton and top with a slice of tuna. Drizzle with wasabi and garnish with a slice of the remaining pickled ginger and some radish sprouts. Serve at once with the remaining soy mignonette on the side for dipping.

Assorted Oysters with Three Mignonettes

At Kinkead's popular raw bar we serve a selection of at least eight oyster varieties daily. For this chilled oyster dish, use any assortment of first-quality fresh oysters that you can find.

A mignonette is a vinegar, shallot, and black pepper condiment traditionally served with oysters in the shellfish stands of France's great brasseries. It has gained much favor with oyster eaters on this side of the Atlantic as well. I am still a big fan of good ol' American cocktail sauce and lots of horse-radish for cooked shrimp, but it doesn't really work with the subtle, elegant taste of a freshly shucked oyster. The tart, peppery sharpness of a well-made mignonette accentuates the briny quality of a freshly shucked chilled oyster.

CLASSIC MIGNONETTE

1/2 cup red wine vinegar

1/4 teaspoon minced thyme leaves

2 tablespoons red wine

1 tablespoon coarse cracked white pepper

2 large shallots, minced

CHAMPAGNE MIGNONETTE

4 tablespoons Champagne (use a good-quality true Champagne)

1/2 cup Champagne vinegar

2 tablespoons coarse cracked white pepper

2 large shallots, minced

1/4 teaspoon kosher salt

GINGER MIGNONETTE

1/4 cup ginger juice (page 262)

1/2 cup rice wine vinegar

2 tablespoons mirin

2 large shallots, minced

1 tablespoon finely grated ginger

1 tablespoon cracked white pepper

1/4 teaspoon kosher salt

Crushed ice for presentation

12 Belon or European flat oysters, rinsed and scrubbed

12 Atlantic oysters (such as Bluepoint, Cotuit, Malpeque, Prince Edward Island), rinsed and scrubbed

12 Pacific oysters (Kumamoto), rinsed and scrubbed

3 lemons, halved

To make the classic mignonette, in a noncorrosive saucepan over medium-high heat, bring the vinegar, thyme, and red wine just to a boil. Remove from heat and let steep for 10 minutes. Strain and let cool to room temperature. Add the pepper and shallots.

To make the Champagne mignonette, combine the Champagne, vinegar, pepper, shallots, and salt in a stainless steel mixing bowl.

To make the ginger mignonette, combine the ginger juice, vinegar, mirin, shallots, ginger, pepper, and salt in a stainless steel mixing bowl.

To serve the oysters, pack lots of crushed ice on 6 large platters. Open all of the oysters and arrange 2 of each variety in a circle in the ice. Garnish with the lemons. For each platter, put 2 tablespoons of each mignonette in ramekins and serve on the side.

Mushroom Strudels with Virginia Ham

his is the oldest recipe in our repertoire. First developed in 1979, it has served us well. There have been many imitators, but this, to my knowledge, is the original. They can be served as a first-course, an hors d'oeuvre, a vegetable accompaniment, or with a salad as a light lunch. They freeze well, so make extra to offer as a quick bite when guests drop in.

Virginia ham is a salt-cured ham from Virginia. It can be bought through mail order if not available in your grocery store; in a pinch, prosciutto with a little extra salt will suffice.

The strudel filling is unique in that it is bound by cream cheese instead of a béchamel sauce, making for both a nicer texture and fewer calories. Not that this is a dish for the weight conscious—the butter, cream, and ham make sure of that.

MUSHROOM STRUDELS

2 tablespoons vegetable oil

$1/4$ cup butter

1 pound mixed wild or exotic mushrooms (chanterelles, trumpets, porcini, oyster, or a mixture of any varieties available), cleaned and sliced

1 pound button mushrooms, cleaned and sliced

4 uncooked bacon strips, diced

3 cloves garlic, minced

3 shallots, finely diced (about 4 tablespoons)

1 tablespoon all-purpose flour

$1/2$ cup Madeira or sherry

$1/2$ cup cream cheese

2 cups veal stock (page 256)

1 cup heavy cream

4 tablespoons Virginia or Smithfield ham, julienned

2 bay leaves

$1/2$ teaspoon chopped fresh thyme leaves

1 teaspoon cracked black pepper

2 tablespoons chopped parsley

1 package frozen phyllo dough

$3/4$ cup clarified butter (page 257)

Kosher salt

VIRGINIA HAM CREAM SAUCE

4 cups veal stock (page 256)

1 tablespoon clarified butter (page 257)

1 tablespoon butter

6 ounces assorted mushrooms, sliced

4 tablespoons bourbon

1 cup heavy cream

Cracked black pepper

6 parsley sprigs or other fresh herb, for garnish

To make the filling, in a large heavy saucepan or braising pan over medium-high heat, heat the vegetable oil and butter. When the mixture is bubbling, add all the mushrooms. Do not overcrowd the pan or the mushrooms will steam instead of browning. If the pan you are using is too small, sauté them in batches. Sauté until they are very brown and almost all the liquid has evaporated. Salt and pepper the mushrooms very lightly, and transfer to a stainless steel bowl.

Wipe out the braising pan. Over medium-high heat, add the bacon and fry until brown and nearly crisp. Add the garlic and 2 tablespoons of the shallots, reserving the rest for the sauce. Cook until transparent. Stir in the flour and cook for 2 minutes. Deglaze with the Madeira and add the

CONTINUED

cream cheese, veal stock, and the heavy cream. Bring to a boil and add 1 tablespoon of the ham (reserving the rest for the sauce), the cooked mushroom mixture, and the bay leaves, thyme, and pepper. Reduce for about 4 minutes, until it is quite thick, the consistency of very heavy cream.

Remove the filling mixture from the heat, stir in the parsley, and spread it evenly on a baking sheet to cool. This part of the recipe can be done a day ahead and refrigerated overnight.

To assemble the strudels, when the filling is cool, unwrap the phyllo dough and cover with a damp cloth to keep the sheets from drying out as you work. Lay 1 phyllo sheet on a cutting board and brush completely with a thin layer of the clarified butter. Top with another sheet and brush with clarified butter. Repeat with a third sheet and butter.

Cut the layered sheets crosswise in fourths. Place a little more than a teaspoon of the mushroom mixture at the bottom of each of the four strips and fold up triangular sections, corner to corner, as you would a flag. Alternatively, to make larger strudels, cut the three layered sheets in half lengthwise. Place 1 1/2 tablespoons of the mixture at the bottom of each half sheet and roll up tightly as you would wrap a submarine sandwich, folding in the sides as you start to roll the strudel so no mixture falls out. Transfer to a baking sheet.

For either size, repeat this process—layering and buttering sets of three sheets, cutting strips, filling, and folding up—until you've used all the mixture and phyllo sheets. Brush the strudels with more clarified butter and refrigerate, or freeze on a baking sheet for 2 hours, or until hard, and transfer to freezer bags for later use.

To make the sauce, in a saucepan over high heat, cook the veal stock until reduced to 1 cup and reserve. Clean the saucepan and heat the clarified butter and whole butter over a medium flame. When bubbling, add the remaining shallots. Sauté and add the remaining Virginia ham. Stir occasionally and cook for 2 minutes. Add the sliced mushrooms and sauté for 3 more minutes. Deglaze with the bourbon. Add the reduced veal stock and the heavy cream and reduce until thick enough to coat a spoon. Add cracked black pepper to taste. No salt should be needed due to the saltiness of the ham.

To bake the strudels, preheat the oven to 400°F. Place the strudels, well separated, on a baking sheet. Bake for about 8 minutes, or until golden brown.

To serve, warm small plates and place 2 to 4 tablespoons of the sauce on each plate. Top with a strudel and garnish with a sprig of parsley, for appetizers. Alternatively, place several strudels on a serving plate with the sauce in the center for dipping, for hors d'oeuvres. Serve warm.

Cherrystone "Stuffies"

"*Stuffie*" *is the Cape Cod and Southeast New England name for a baked stuffed quahog (East Coast hard-shell clam). These are traditionally served as bar food in taverns, pubs, and mom-and-pop restaurants along the coast. They are a particularly prized nosh from Narragansett Sound throughout Cape Cod, where the Portuguese fishermen have influenced the cuisine in many ways. This dish can be made (and correctly so) with larger quahogs, serving 1 or 2 per order. This version uses cherrystones or littlenecks, which make a more appropriate hors d'oeuvre size. Beer is the correct accompaniment. Four cherrystones make an appropriate serving. Stuffies may be made in fairly large batches and frozen for later use.*

4 to 5 slices white or wheat bread, cut into $1/2$-inch cubes (4 cups)

2 cups dry white wine

40 cherrystone clams or 60 littleneck clams

1 cup water

$1/2$ pound Portuguese-style chorizo or linguica

1 cup clam juice

6 tablespoons butter, plus more for baking

4 bacon strips, finely diced

2 cloves garlic, minced

1 small yellow onion, finely diced (about 1 cup)

2 ribs celery, finely diced (about 1 cup)

4 scallions, mostly white parts, finely diced

$1/2$ red bell pepper or pimiento, seeded, deribbed, and finely diced (about $1/4$ cup)

$1/2$ teaspoon dried oregano

$1/4$ teaspoon dried thyme

$1/4$ teaspoon dried red pepper flakes

$1/4$ teaspoon paprika

$1/2$ teaspoon Worcestershire sauce

2 large eggs

1 large egg yolk

1 tablespoon chopped fresh parsley

$1/2$ teaspoon cracked black pepper

$1/2$ teaspoon Tabasco Sauce, plus more for serving

3 lemons, cut into wedges

To make the stuffing, preheat the oven to 375°F. Toast the bread cubes for about 12 minutes, until golden brown.

In a braising pan, combine the wine and water and add the clams. Steam over high heat for 3 to 8 minutes, depending on the size of the clams. Most should open; discard any that do not. Remove from the heat. When cool enough to handle, remove the meat from the shells. Reserve 24 to 30 of the nicest shells; discard the rest. Chop the clam meats (you should have about $2^1/2$ cups) and refrigerate.

Strain the reserved cooking liquid through a fine-mesh sieve and transfer to a saucepan. Add the chorizo and poach for 5 minutes over medium heat. Remove the chorizo from the cooking liquid, strip away the skin, and chop into $1/4$-inch dice; set aside.

Increase the heat to high and cook the liquid until reduced to 2 cups. Add the clam juice and 4 tablespoons of the butter and set aside.

In a sauté pan over medium-high heat, sauté the bacon until crispy. Add the remaining 2 tablespoons butter. When the butter is melted, add the garlic, onion, celery, scallion, red

CONTINUED

pepper, oregano, thyme, red pepper flakes, and paprika. Sauté until the onion is translucent. Set aside and keep warm.

In a stainless steel bowl, toss the bread cubes, clams, chorizo, Worcestershire sauce, eggs, egg yolks, parsley, pepper, and Tabasco. Add the sautéed mixture. Stir and gradually add all of the reserved cooking liquid; the mixture should be moist but not overly wet (like turkey stuffing).

To assemble the stuffies, increase the oven to 400°F. Mound stuffing mixture onto each cherrystone shell. Stuffies should look overstuffed. They can be frozen at this point if reserving for later use. To serve, top each stuffie with a dab of butter and 1 drop of Tabasco. Bake for 7 to 9 minutes, until brown and crispy on top. Serve at once with lemon wedges and extra Tabasco.

THE PRESIDENT COMES TO DINNER

Though not a particularly unusual occurrence in the nation's capital, it's still a big deal when the president of the United States comes to your restaurant for dinner. President Clinton dined at Kinkead's a few times during his administration, but his first visit was a night no one who worked at Kinkead's will ever forget.

Some background is in order. Ris Lacoste is currently the chef of 1789 Restaurant near Georgetown University in Washington. Prior to her tenure at that fine restaurant, Ris (a nickname for Doris) worked in my kitchens for twelve years. I hired her right out of culinary school (LaVarenne in Paris) and she rose through the ranks from garde manger to sous-chef to chef de cuisine. She opened four restaurants with me and has one of the best palates I know.

On the night in question, Ris was "retiring" from Kinkead's to take her new executive chef position at the 1789. We planned to close the restaurant early to have a huge going-away party for her. Many of Washington's notable chefs would be attending, along with food writers, regular customers, coworkers, friends, and family. Late on the morning of the celebration we got the call. The president would like to bring a party of eight to Kinkead's for dinner that night. After the initial panic, we devised a plan. We would close the restaurant early, hold the party as planned in the bar area downstairs, and seat the president and his party in the upstairs private dining room.

For those who have never experienced it, the president's coming to dinner is an ordeal. First, the Secret Service comes to check out the physical plant. They survey egresses, building security, proximity of other buildings, and potential trouble sites. Then they bring in the dogs. Trained dogs sniff for explosives and who knows what. Finally, all the parking on the streets anywhere near the restaurant is cordoned off by police.

Just prior to the president's arrival the real fun begins. In our case, nine Secret Service agents were stationed throughout the premises. When guests arrived for Ris's party, packages and identification were checked. When the president finally did arrive, there was no mistake about it. Lights flashed, sirens blared. First came the police officers on motorcycles, then the police cruisers, a few Suburbans, a full ambulance truck, some more Suburbans, a few limos, and then, the president.

The night was filled with funny incidents. My favorite was when one of the restaurant critics for *The Washingtonian* magazine arrived for Ris's party. He was carrying a nicely wrapped gift box. As he tried to squeeze by the Secret Service agent at the door, he was stopped.

"What's in the box?" asked the agent.

"Oh, I've brought a present for the chef who's leaving. It's a Henkel chef's knife!" Without missing a beat, the agent replied, "Great gift, bad night," then confiscated the package. (Ris got the knife back after the president left.)

The president is allowed to drink only beverages that are unopened. Wine with a cork is fine. His steward, brings a briefcase of bottled water for the president's consumption. He was a very nice man who spent most of the evening watching the food being prepared. I inquired as to whether he had to watch the preparation of the food or in fact had to taste it first. "No," he said, "I like to cook and was hoping to pick up a few pointers. Besides, it's generally very bad for business to be known as the restaurant where the president got poisoned." Touché!

The highlight of the evening was when the president and his party finished dinner. They came to thank the restaurant staff and have the requisite photos taken. At that point, the somewhat tipsy Ris Lacoste decided that while Mr. Clinton may be president, on this night, she was queen. She said, "Mr. President, this is *my* party and I'd be honored if you would walk me down the stairs." And he did! When they appeared, the now well-lubricated crowd downstairs went wild.

Caramelized Onion, Walnut, and Roquefort Tarts

MAKES 24 TO 28 (2-INCH) MINI TARTS OR 13 (4-INCH) TARTS

This recipe was originally developed by Ris Lacoste, our former sous-chef. Ris is currently the chef of 1789 Restaurant in Georgetown.

This tart makes a nice passed hors d'oeuvre or it can be served as a first course with a small salad garnish. The tart can be made in any type of tart pan or sheet pan and cut into portions, or it can be made as mini tartlettes. As a passed canapé, the mini tarts provide a prettier presentation and are easier to eat as finger food. The trick to making this tart successfully is to cook the onions slowly so they become very brown and the natural sugars caramelize. It is the same procedure as for a great onion soup. Store-bought puff pastry can be substituted for the pâte brisée.

1 recipe pâte brisée (page 267)

3 tablespoons butter

2 large yellow onions, halved and cut into julienne (about 7 cups)

1 cup heavy cream

1/4 cup crème fraîche

1 extra large egg plus 1 extra large egg yolk

3/4 cup crumbled Roquefort cheese

1/4 teaspoon kosher salt

1/2 teaspoon cracked black pepper

1 cup walnut pieces, toasted and chopped

Preheat the oven to 325°F. Remove the pâte brisée from the refrigerator and when warm enough to be pliable, roll out to about 1/8 inch thick. Form the brisée into 2- to 4-inch tart molds. Bake the shells for 10 to 12 minutes, until lightly golden. Let cool.

In a sauté pan over medium heat, melt the butter. When bubbly, add the onions. Cook down for 45 minutes, or until the onions are very brown and sweet, stirring from time to time to prevent the onions from sticking. Let cool.

In a stainless steel bowl, combine the heavy cream, crème fraîche, egg, yolk, and cheese to make a custard. Stir in the salt and pepper and set aside. (You may want to use less salt depending on the saltiness of the Roquefort.)

Increase the oven temperature to 375°F. Fill the tart shells about two-thirds full with the cooked onions. Top with the walnuts. Pour the custard mixture over the walnuts and onions. Bake for 10 to 12 minutes, until golden brown. Serve warm or at room temperature.

THE COUNTY FAIR

My big break in the food-service industry came in the summer of 1966, when I was fifteen. Opting for the tried and true, I got my start in the restaurant business washing pots and pans.

A friend who grew up with me was working as a bus girl at the County Fair Restaurant on Cape Cod. She told me there might be an opening. My predecessor in the dish room had "no-showed" for two days. I would like to think I was hired because of my great attitude, professional appearance, and terrific interviewing skills. Truth be known, the dishes and pots were piling up and I was a warm body!

I was interviewed by the blue-haired proprietress, Miss Amelee Teat. After a short interrogation, consisting mainly of how soon I could start and how long into the season I could work, my employment began that day. My starting wage was a whopping $1.25 per hour plus staff dinner.

Amelee was a widow from Jacksonville, Florida, by way of Atlanta, Georgia. In early June each year, she and five of her widowed lady friends would load up the Cadillacs and head north to Cape Cod. The County Fair was a large, converted beach house with several guest rooms where "the girls" would live while they worked through the summer. Each season these charming Southern former debutantes would clean out the cobwebs, do a little touch-up painting, and fire up the stoves to open the eighty-seat restaurant.

Amelee's restaurant served simple home cookin'. The main courses were well made and delicious. Honest food at affordable prices, great for the whole family. The only down side was that the meats and fish, prepared with such integrity, were accompanied by canned vegetables and instant mashed potatoes. The rolls, pies, and cakes were all homemade, though. Evelyn, the baker, made six or eight different pies and four to six cakes or cobblers, from scratch, every day. Her carrot cake and pecan pie remain the standard by which I still judge all others.

Miss Amelee was an imposing woman, nearly six feet tall, with an ample bust and a deep plantation drawl. She ran a tight ship and served as hostess, greeting guests as they entered the restaurant. She could display a charm and Southern hospitality customers would swoon over.

I soon found out that Amelee had one hell of a temper. Especially after she and the girls had polished off a fifth or so of their beloved Jack Daniels.

The usual program, after the customers had been fed, was for the ladies to sit down for their dinner while we local kids, hired for the summer, cleaned up the restaurant. The usual limit was two drinks before and a nightcap after dinner. Even at that, several of the more elderly ladies would have to be helped to their rooms. On occasion, they would get talkin' and drinkin' and soon another bottle would be gone. When Amelee was in her cups, she'd start yelling. Her smooth-as-iced-mint-julep drawl would transform into a piercing, nails-on-the-blackboard screech that went right up your spine. Her tantrums would escalate in intensity and frequency as the summer progressed.

The subject of her rage on any given night might have been one of the ladies from Jacksonville—usually a new recruit who she thought was slacking. More likely, it was directed toward one of the kids, a bus girl, dishwasher, or cook's helper who she felt was not pulling his or her weight. Amelee might go off over the general cleanliness of the place, in which case, all were at fault. Instinctively, all in earshot would busy themselves at some cleaning task, heads low. The ladies generally headed to their rooms or simply kept out of sight until the storm blew over.

Though the job was an eye-opener in many ways, I enjoyed the work, the camaraderie with coworkers, the pace, and the after-work parties. Mostly, I liked learning how to make the delicious food customers raved about. I did not know it then, but I had been bitten by a bug that would turn into a career of more than thirty years and running.

Appetizers

Fried Ipswich Clams with Fried Lemons ∽ 32

Chesapeake Bay Jumbo Lump Crab Cakes with Corn Okra Relish and
Mustard Crème Fraîche ∽ 35

Curry-Fried Soft-Shell Crab with Green Papaya Salad and
Vietnamese Lime Dipping Sauce ∽ 38

Shrimp and Crab *Pupusas* ∽ 40

Broiled Oysters with Celery and Virginia Ham ∽ 42

Grilled Oysters and Pancetta ∽ 45

Shad Roe with Pan-Roasted Shallots and Parsley Salad ∽ 46

Shad Roe with Grits, Virginia Ham, Roasted Onions, and Sorrel ∽ 48

Lobster with Shellbean Succotash and Corn Pudding ∽ 50

Lobster with Savoy Cabbage, White Bean Celeriac Purée, and Truffle Vinaigrette ∽ 52

Grilled Squid with Creamy Polenta and Tomato Fondue ∽ 57

Fried Ipswich Clams with Fried Lemons

This dish has been a signature at Kinkead's since our opening in 1993. Fried clams remind me of summers on Cape Cod; they are typical fare at almost any roadside fish shack on the New England and Mid-Atlantic coasts.

The fried lemons are an unusual, tart accompaniment to the clams. The best way to eat them is to top a fried lemon slice with some tartar sauce and a fried clam, then pop it whole into your mouth. Assembled like this, they also make a nice passed hors d'oeuvre.

The trick to making great fried clams is to use whole belly clams, not strips, and give them plenty of room—don't crowd them, either in the hot oil or after they have been fried. Crisp is the object of the game. The problem with most clam shacks is that they serve their fried clams in cardboard containers, which crowds the clams and steams the crisp coating.

FRIED LEMONS

2 lemons

1/2 cup kosher salt, plus more as needed

1/2 cup sugar

Peanut oil for frying

1 cup all-purpose flour

Freshly ground black pepper

Cayenne

1 cup buttermilk

FRIED IPSWICH CLAMS

Peanut oil for frying (about 4 cups)

48 whole Ipswich or soft-shell clams

2 cups all-purpose flour

Kosher salt and freshly ground black pepper

Cayenne

2 cups buttermilk

3 lemons, for garnish

2 cups Tartar Sauce (page 261)

To make the fried lemons, combine the kosher salt and sugar in a stainless steel bowl. Slice the lemons into 1/4- to 1/8-inch slices and discard the smaller end slices. Toss the lemon slices in this mixture to completely coat them and shake off any excess. Place on a baking sheet and let cure in a cool place for 4 to 6 hours. Spread the lemon slices in a single layer on a baking rack to dehydrate and place in a warm, dry area for about 12 hours. Brush off any excess salt-sugar mixture and pat dry. The slices should be quite dehydrated but not completely stiff. If still very moist, let dry for 12 more hours.

To fry the lemon slices, heat 2 inches of peanut oil in a deep fryer or cast-iron skillet to 350°F. Season the flour with salt, pepper, and a pinch of cayenne. Put the buttermilk in a deep bowl and add the lemon slices. Let them soak for 1 to 2 minutes, then dredge in the seasoned flour. Drop one by one into the hot oil so they do not clump together. Fry for about 2 minutes, then turn and fry for about 1 more minute, until crisp and brown. Remove from the hot oil and drain on paper towels.

To make the fried clams, heat 2 inches of peanut oil in a deep fryer or cast-iron skillet to 350°F. Season the flour with salt, pepper, and a pinch of cayenne. Dip the clams in the buttermilk and then in the seasoned flour. Shake off any excess flour. Drop one by one into the hot oil so they do not clump together. Fry for about 2 minutes, turn, and fry for 1 to 2 more minutes, until crisp and brown. Remove from the hot oil with a slotted spoon and drain on paper towels. Season to taste with salt and pepper and serve immediately with the fried lemon slices, lemon wedges, and tartar sauce on the side.

CLAMS

These bivalves are divided into two categories: hard-shell and soft-shell. Hard-shell clams are generally available year-round; prime season is June, July, and August. Clams are found on both coasts, but the East and Gulf coasts have the greatest commercial production. Small hard-shell clams are now being farmed in Maine and South Carolina. Clams are sold live in the shell, cooked, shucked, and canned or frozen. The meat is then sold whole or as chopped meat. Clam juice, both bottled and frozen, is also readily available.

Named according to size, hard-shell clams are good eaten raw or cooked. Littlenecks, cherrystones, and quahogs are the same hard-shell clam at different ages and sizes. Sized by the bushel, clams that have an expected count of 450 to 650 are called littlenecks; 300 to 325, cherrystones; 160 to 200, mediums; 125 or less, chowders. (Mediums and chowders are grades of quahogs.)

Littlenecks are hard-shell clams that are 1 to 2 inches across. They are best on the half shell or, when very small, steamed with white wine, lemon, and butter. Oddly enough, clams are more readily eaten raw the farther north one goes along the eastern seaboard. You are far more likely to see steamed or cooked clam preparations as you proceed from Maryland south. To a New Englander who has just ordered "steamers" from the menu, it would come as a shock to be served a half-dozen *steamed* hard-shell clams. To a New Englander, steamers are always a pile of soft-shell steamer clams! In contrast, to a native of Charleston, South Carolina, littlenecks would be just what the diner expected.

Hard-shell clams ranging in size from 2 to 2½ inches across the shell are classified as cherrystones. These are slightly bigger than littlenecks and taste just as good. Some people have a harder time swallowing the larger cherrystone whole when eating them on the half shell.

I prefer the cherrystone when used in baked clam preparations like Clams Casino.

Larger clams, or quahogs, are tougher and best suited for chowders and soups after being steamed open and chopped. In addition to being tougher, quahogs have a stronger taste and make a full-flavored broth.

Manila clams have a delicate but hard shell that is almost a cross between a soft and a hard shell in appearance. The Manila is harvested along the Pacific Coast. Manilas cook more like soft-shells and are anatomically more like them as well. They are especially good sautéed or steamed with butter, lemon, garlic, and parsley, and in this country they are favorites for making clam sauce with pasta.

Large, deep-ocean clams are hard-shells; although often mistaken for quahogs, sea clams are a different species. They run about the size of a small hand, with brownish shells. This is the variety commonly used in commercial clam chowder, clam juice, and chopped clams. In the restaurant, we always use sea clams as a base for clam chowder, with quahogs added for flavor.

Note that hard-shell clams are shut tight when alive. Never eat one that is not closed tight. If the shell doesn't open when cooked, the clam is dead and should be thrown away.

Soft-shell clams are thin-shelled clams found on the Atlantic coast and in areas of the Pacific Northwest. Soft-shell clams are generally harvested in muddy tidal areas, whereas hard-shell clams are found by digging on sandbars and in tidal beach areas. Soft-shell clams have a protruding siphon or "neck" and shells that do not close completely. They are far more popular in North America than in Europe. Cooked in the shell, these are the clams prized as steamers. When shucked and deep-fried, they are the star of New England roadside stand cooking: the fried clam.

Chesapeake Bay Jumbo Lump Crab Cakes with Corn Okra Relish and Mustard Crème Fraîche

ike most chefs, I don't get to eat in my restaurant as much as I should (or would like to). On the rare occasions when I do get to, I invariably order this crab cake appetizer before tasting some of the new items on our menu. Crabmeat has a natural affinity for the flavor of mustard and the sweetness and texture of corn, and this simple recipe combines those flavors in a way that other variations I have tried can't seem to beat.

A truly great crab cake has no breadcrumb stuffing and as little filler as possible. Only seasoned mayonnaise to bind the crab morsels is acceptable. Lump, back fin, or body meat tastes fine, but doesn't have the sweetness or, more important, the texture of jumbo lump. A crab cake made with those grades of crabmeat will do in a pinch, but it's not the real deal. No true aficionado of the crab cake would deep-fry them, either. Sautéing or broiling is the only truly acceptable manner of cooking.

Note that the crab cakes require two hours of chilling before you cook them; during this time you can make the relish and crème fraîche.

MUSTARD CRÈME FRAÎCHE

1/2 cup crème fraîche

1/4 cup mayonnaise

2 tablespoons Dijon mustard

2 tablespoons Pommery mustard or other grainy mustard

1 teaspoon honey mustard

1/2 teaspoon kosher salt

1/2 teaspoon freshly ground white pepper

2 drops Tabasco Sauce

CORN OKRA RELISH

1 ear corn, shucked (about 1 cup)

1/2 large red bell pepper, seeded, deribbed, roasted, and peeled, or prepared roasted red bell peppers

2 scallions, chopped

1/2 small yellow onion, diced (about 1/3 cup)

4 pickled okras, sliced into 1/4-inch rounds

1 tablespoon red wine vinegar

1/2 teaspoon kosher salt

1/2 teaspoon sugar

1/2 teaspoon cracked black pepper

1 tablespoon chopped fresh parsley (optional)

CRAB CAKES

2 pounds jumbo lump crabmeat

3 tablespoons butter

1/2 small yellow onion, finely minced (about 1/3 cup)

1/2 small red bell pepper, seeded, deribbed, and minced (about 1/4 cup)

1 extra large egg

1/2 cup mayonnaise

1 tablespoon Dijon mustard

1/4 teaspoon mustard powder

1 tablespoon chopped fresh parsley

Pinch of cayenne

3 drops Tabasco Sauce or other hot sauce, or to taste

Sea salt and freshly ground black pepper

2 cups fresh breadcrumbs, seasoned with salt and pepper

4 tablespoons vegetable oil

Butter for sautéing

CONTINUED

To make the mustard crème fraîche, combine the crème fraîche, mayonnaise, Dijon, Pommery, and honey mustards, salt, pepper, and Tabasco. Store, refrigerated, for up to 4 days. Serve at room temperature.

To make the corn okra relish, blanch the corn and then drain and transfer to a stainless steel mixing bowl. Dice the roasted red pepper and add to the corn along with the scallions, onion, okra, vinegar, salt, sugar, and pepper. Combine and let macerate for 20 minutes. Drain and discard the excess liquid. Add the parsley and toss. Serve at room temperature.

To make the crab cakes, pick *very gently* through the lump crab for shells. In a saucepan over moderate heat, melt 1 tablespoon of the butter and sweat the onion and pepper. Remove from the heat and let cool. In a stainless steel bowl mix the egg, mayonnaise, Dijon mustard, mustard powder, parsley, cayenne, Tabasco, salt, and pepper. Add the cooked onions and peppers and fold in the crabmeat.

Form into cakes about 3 inches across by 1 1/4 inches thick. Pack firmly, but do not crush the lumps; the cake should just hold together. Chill, covered, for at least 1 hour in the refrigerator.

Dredge the cakes in the seasoned breadcrumbs on top and bottom, packing in the breadcrumbs with your hands. Refrigerate for 1 more hour.

To cook the crab cakes, preheat the oven to 400°F. In a sauté pan over medium-high heat, heat 2 tablespoons of the vegetable oil and 1 tablespoon of butter and sauté the crab cakes on one side for about 2 minutes, until brown. Do not crowd in the pan; if serving several cakes at a time, cook in batches, adding 1 tablespoon of butter to the pan for each batch. Turn over and place in the oven for 4 to 5 minutes to heat through.

Serve hot with mustard crème fraîche and corn okra relish.

THE BLUE CRAB

Blue crab is one of the most unique and precious resources in North America. It is caught from Maine to Florida and in the coastal areas of the Gulf of Mexico and is available in some part of the country pretty much year-round. In past years the vast majority were harvested in the Chesapeake during the prime season, from March to October. Now, Venezuela, Brazil, and Asian countries are harvesting them. Due to the Gulf wars and warships from Norfolk emptying their ballast from the Chesapeake into the Persian Gulf, that body of water now has an extensive population of untouched blue crabs. Unfortunately, due to overfishing, pollution, and the economics of aqua culture throughout the world, the production and availability of blue crab from Maryland and Virginia has fallen off in recent years.

The Chesapeake is the largest estuary in America and is the largest producer of blue crabs in the world. The Chesapeake is formed by the confluence of six primary rivers on its western shore: the Susquehanna, Pautuxent, Potomac, Rappahannock, York, and Jamestown. There are a myriad of other tributaries that make up the Bay and its four-thousand-plus miles of coastline. In this watershed are created the brackish outlets and marshes that provide the ideal breeding grounds for the blue crab. More than any of its other flora and fauna, the blue crab represents the best of the Chesapeake's bounty.

Blue crabs are sold by size, with the biggest called whales or slabs. They decrease in size to jumbos, primes, hotels, and finally mediums, which are the smallest. The blue crab provides a variety of crabmeat—whole crabs for boiling, and when molting, soft-shell crabs. For me, the bigger the crab, the better the eating. I find the smaller crabs are too much work for too little reward.

Whole crabs are sold live for crab boils or stews. Around the Chesapeake area there are dozens of mom-and-pop restaurants and crab shacks that specialize in the Chesapeake crab boil. This feast consists of a pile of boiled crabs in the shell, covered with Old Bay or another spicy mix, melted butter, and vinegar, and served with corn on the cob and other side dishes all laid out on newspaper. Each diner is given a wooden mallet to crack the shells and extract the sweet meat. It makes one hell of a mess, but it's a great feed, especially washed down with lots of ice-cold beer.

Most blue crab is sold as picked meat. The crabmeat is also graded by the size of and location on the crab. Lump crabmeat is the large chunks from the body of the crab; "jumbo lump" is the chunks from whale and jumbo sizes. It is the most expensive. As the blue crab population decreases, due to overfishing and pollution, prices are becoming almost outrageous, hitting highs of $22 per pound wholesale in recent years. The next grade is "lump," the same meat from smaller crabs. "Flake" is the meat from smaller cavities; it is in broken-up pieces and generally contains more shell fragments. "Claw" is just what you would expect.

Curry-Fried Soft-Shell Crab with Green Papaya Salad and Vietnamese Lime Dipping Sauce

SERVES 6

reen papayas are a staple of Southeast Asian cooking. A variety much larger than the small papayas we eat ripe as a sweet fruit (1 to 2 feet long and oval shaped) is cultivated for use, primarily while underripe, in savory dishes and as a crunchy vegetable in salads. The flesh is pale green and mild, much like a carrot in texture, though less sweet. If you don't use the papaya within a few days of purchasing, the inner flesh may turn pink near the seeded center, but it can still be used as a green papaya.

PAPAYA SALAD

Juice of 1 lime (about 2 teaspoons)
1/2 green papaya, julienned (about 4 cups)
1 carrot, peeled and julienned (about 1 cup)
1 cucumber, peeled and julienned (about 2 cups)
6 Thai basil leaves, chiffonade
3 scallions, chopped
3 tablespoons coarsely chopped cilantro leaves
2 Kaffir lime leaves, chiffonade (optional)
1 cup Vietnamese Lime Dipping Sauce (page 261)
1/4 cup roasted peanuts or cashews, coarsely chopped
Cilantro sprigs for garnish

CURRY BREADING

11/2 cups tapioca flour
1 cup cornstarch
1 tablespoon Madras curry powder
1/2 teaspoon kosher salt

6 soft-shell crabs (hotel prime)
Peanut oil for frying
2 cups Vietnamese Lime Dipping Sauce (page 261)

To make the papaya salad, toss the lime juice, papaya, carrot, cucumber, basil, scallions, cilantro, lime leaves, and dipping sauce together in a stainless steel bowl. Set aside.

To make the breading, combine the flour, cornstarch, curry powder, and salt in a stainless steel bowl.

To fry the soft-shells, in a cast-iron pan or small deep-fryer heat the peanut oil to 350°F. Drain the soft-shells from the milk bath but do not dry. Toss the crab in the curry breading, shake off the excess, and deep-fry, submerged in the hot oil for about 2 minutes, until brown slightly and are crispy on all sides. Remove with a slotted spoon and drain on paper towels.

To serve, on each of 6 plates place a mound of the papaya salad. Top with chopped peanuts and cilantro sprigs. Surround with the fried soft-shell crab and garnish with more cilantro. Pass a sauceboat or ramekin of the Vietnamese Lime Dipping Sauce.

Shrimp and Crab Pupusas

*P*upusas *are a Salvadoran staple: corn masa cakes generally served with a spicy tomato and vegetable salsa, Salvadoran* crema, *and pickled cabbage. They are similar to the gorditas, or fat corn tortillas, of Mexico, but they differ from tortillas in that they are usually bound with potatoes and other ingredients instead of just masa and lard. Queso fresca, a white Mexican cheese, is available in Latin markets and most supermarkets.* Pupusas *can be stuffed with any number of ingredients, but the authentic filling is cheese, pork, or a combination of the two. At Kinkead's we use them as garnish or as a centerpiece to many dishes. This recipe makes more* pupusas *than you will need for one meal, but they freeze well and make great leftovers.*

SALVADORAN PUPUSAS

1 large Idaho potato, peeled and cut in half-inch dice (about $1/2$ cup)

1 large tomato, peeled and seeded

2 cups dry corn masa harina

1 teaspoon kosher salt

$1/2$ teaspoon cracked black pepper

$1/4$ cup grated Jack cheese

$1/4$ cup peanut or other vegetable oil for pan-frying

SHRIMP AND CRAB

18 medium shrimp (26 to 30 count), peeled, deveined, and split

12 ounces jumbo lump blue crabmeat (or other high-quality crabmeat)

1 cup lobster stock (page 254) or chicken stock (page 255)

1 cup shrimp stock (page 255) or chicken stock (page 255)

1 ancho chile, seeded

Vegetable oil for sautéing

3 cloves garlic, minced (about $1/2$ teaspoon)

$1/2$ small yellow onion, finely diced (about $1/4$ cup)

$1/4$ cup roasted Anaheim chiles (canned is fine), diced

1 large poblano chile, roasted, peeled, seeded, and diced (about $1/8$ cup)

$1/4$ cup butter

3 tablespoons tomato concassé (page 263)

Juice of 1 large lime (about 2 tablespoons)

3 scallions, chopped (about $1/3$ cup)

$1/2$ teaspoon kosher salt

1 bunch cilantro leaves, half coarsely chopped, half whole

2 ounces queso blanco, crumbled

2 tablespoons vegetable oil

To make the pupusas, boil the potatoes in salted water until very tender. Drain, reserving about 1 cup of the cooking liquid in case the mixture is too dry. Grate the potatoes to the consistency of rice. Purée the tomato in a blender and combine with the potato.

In a stainless steel bowl, combine the potato-tomato mix with the masa harina, salt, and pepper. Work the dough by hand until smooth. It should be the texture of loose pie dough but coarse, as if it has sand in it. Form the dough into 18 or 20 balls.

Make a hole in each ball with your finger and stuff a little of the Jack cheese into the ball. Pinch the dough around the cheese and roll into pancakes about 3 inches in diameter and $3/8$ inch thick. Oil the *pupusas* slightly with peanut oil and cook on a cast iron pan or comal over medium heat for 2 minutes, or until golden on both sides.

To make the shrimp and crab, split the shrimp lengthwise and keep chilled. Gently pick through the crabmeat for shells and keep chilled.

In a saucepan over high heat, bring the shellfish stocks to a boil. Add the ancho chile and cook until the stock is reduced by half. Remove from the heat and purée in a blender. Press through a fine-mesh sieve to remove any ancho skin. Keep warm.

In a sauté pan over medium heat, add a little vegetable oil. When hot, add the garlic and onion. Sauté until translucent. Add the Anaheim and poblano chiles and sauté for about 2 minutes. Add the ancho-shrimp stock purée and cook for about 3 minutes, until reduced by half. Whisk in the butter, a little at time, until incorporated. Keep warm.

In a second sauté pan over medium-high heat, heat a little vegetable oil and sauté the shrimp halves on both sides. Add the tomato concassé and the onion-chiles mixture and cook for 1 more minute. Add the crabmeat and gently fold it into the mixture. Remove from the heat and add the lime juice, half of the chopped scallions, the salt, and the chopped cilantro. Keep warm.

To serve, warm 6 plates and place 2 warm *pupusas* on each. Spoon the shrimp, crab, and sauce mixture over the *pupusas.* Garnish with the whole cilantro leaves, the queso blanco, and the remaining chopped scallions.

CRABMEAT

Crabmeat must be picked through for shells before being used. It is very unpleasant to be picking out bits of shell and cartilage every few minutes from your crab cakes or crab imperial. With lump and jumbo lump, it is important to be very gentle when picking through the meat for shells. Do not grind the meat in your hands, as lump crabmeat is delicate and crumbles easily. It is foolish to spend the premium for lump crab and crumble it all up when cleaning. At that point, the flake crab would have been just as good, and it's half the price.

Crab can be frozen, canned, or "pasteurized" (picked through for shells, then canned), but this is not as good as fresh. Some brands of pasteurized crab are quite good and can be used in the winter months when the superior fresh crab is not available.

Broiled Oysters with Celery and Virginia Ham

A nice combination of Chesapeake ingredients—oysters and Virginia Ham. The celery and oysters go together nicely.

24 fresh Chincoteague oysters (or any quality variety)
3 tablespoons unsalted butter
1 shallot, minced
2 stalks celery, diced
1 teaspoon celery seed
1/2 cup dry white wine
2 cups heavy cream
1 small celeriac, peeled and diced
2 stalks Chinese celery, finely diced
3 tablespoons finely diced Virginia ham
Freshly ground black pepper
3 cups coarse sea salt
1 large egg yolk
6 chervil sprigs, for garnish

Shuck the oysters and drain, reserving the liquid. Clean and reserve the deep top shells; discard the bottom shells. Keep chilled.

To make a celery sauce, in a noncorrosive saucepan place 1 teaspoon of the butter over medium heat. Add the shallot and celery and cook for 2 minutes. Add the celery seed and sweat until the shallots are transparent. Add the wine and cook for about 2 minutes, until reduced by half. Add the heavy cream and cook for about 3 minutes, until reduced by half. Add the reserved oyster liquid and bring to a boil. Remove from the heat and strain the solids. Place one third in a small bowl and chill; keep the remaining two thirds warm.

To make a celeriac purée, bring a saucepan of salted water to a boil. Add the celeriac and cook until very tender. Strain and add a little butter and 2 tablespoons of the celery cream. Purée by hand or in a food processor. Strain through a sieve and keep warm.

In a sauté pan, place 1 tablespoon of the butter over medium heat. Add the Chinese celery and cook for 2 minutes, or until transparent. Add the ham and the remaining warm celery cream and bring to a boil. Cook for about 1 minute, until slightly reduced. Add pepper to taste.

Preheat the oven to 375°F. Fill a baking sheet with 1 cup of the sea salt and stick the oyster shells in so that they stand upright. Divide the celeriac purée among the shells and top each with a chilled oyster. Bake for 2 minutes.

Fold the egg yolk into the chilled celery cream to make a glaze. Top the oysters with the hot celery-ham mixture and bake for 1 minute. Turn the oven to broil and brush each oyster with the glaze. Broil for 30 seconds, or until golden.

To serve, place the remaining 2 cups sea salt in the center of each of 6 plates and arrange 4 oysters in a circle on top of the salt on each plate. Garnish with a chervil sprig and serve at once.

Grilled Oysters and Pancetta

This grilled oyster dish is one of the oldest in our repertoire. It has been served in five successive restaurants and can be used as an appetizer or a passed hors d'oeuvre. It is even good as a salad with an assortment of lettuces.

My good friend and one of the best cooks I know, Jimmy Burke, was my predecessor as chef of the Harvest. After Jimmy left to open the Tuscan Grill (and several other Boston-area restaurants), we would often talk about food ideas, particularly ideas for grilled oysters and clams. Jimmy's evolved into a spectacular in-the-shell oyster preparation with cracked pepper. My version, with some revisions over the years, is this recipe.

30 Atlantic oysters (such as Nantucket or Bluepoint)
30 slices pancetta, sliced $1/16$ to $1/8$ inch thick
Coarse rock salt or sea salt
6 rosemary sprigs or other fresh herb, for garnish

OYSTER BUTTER SAUCE
1 teaspoon white wine vinegar
2 tablespoons dry white wine
1 large shallot, minced
6 tablespoons butter
Kosher salt and freshly ground black pepper

BALSAMIC MIGNONETTE
1 teaspoon coarsely ground black pepper
$1/4$ cup balsamic vinegar
4 tablespoons Chianti or Valpolicella

Soak six 7-inch wood skewers in ice water for 1 hour. Shuck the oysters and drain, reserving the liquid. Clean and reserve the deep top shells; discard the bottom shells.

In a sauté pan over high heat, bring about 6 cups of salted water to a boil. Blanch the pancetta for 1 to 2 minutes, drain, and cool. Unroll the pancetta so that it is like strips of bacon. Dry the oysters in a paper towel and roll one strip of pancetta around each. For each serving, double-skewer 5 pancetta-rolled oysters and chill for 30 minutes.

To make the oyster butter sauce, in a noncorrosive saucepan, combine the white wine vinegar, white wine, and $1/4$ of the minced shallots. Bring to a boil over high heat and reduce to almost a glaze. Add the oyster liquor and cook until reduced by half. Whisk in the butter, add salt and pepper to taste, and remove from the heat.

To make the balsamic mignonette, in a bowl, combine the remaining shallots with the cracked black pepper, balsamic vinegar, and Chianti.

To grill the oysters and pancetta, preheat a grill (preferably charcoal or, better yet, wood fired). When hot, grill the skewers on one side until the meat is brown and not sticking to the grill. Turn and grill the other side. The pancetta should be crispy and the oysters still moist. Keep warm.

To serve, spread the rock salt on 6 plates and place 5 of the empty oyster shells on each. Remove the oysters from the skewers. Place a cooked oyster in each shell. Spoon about a half teaspoon of the balsamic mignonette on each oyster. Garnish with the oyster butter sauce and a small rosemary sprig. Serve hot.

Shad Roe with Pan-Roasted Shallots and Parsley Salad

SERVES 6 AS AN APPETIZER, 3 AS A MAIN COURSE

The running of shad in the churning, snowmelt-gorged freshwater streams of late winter is a sign of spring in the Mid-Atlantic states. Diners who know and appreciate its texture and full flavor eagerly await its arrival—the shad generally run in early March, and we usually start getting calls for shad roe at the restaurant by late February.

At Kinkead's, shad roe appetizers tend to outsell shad roe main courses, four to one. Roe sacks come in pairs and are generally sized so that a medium or smaller pair makes a nice main course and one sack of a larger pair makes a nice appetizer. Note that the shad roes must soak in milk for several hours or overnight before proceeding with preparation.

SHAD ROE

3 medium to large pairs of shad roe

2 cups milk

14 large shallots; 12 left whole, 2 minced

4 tablespoons vegetable oil

2 teaspoons balsamic vinegar

1 cup Syrah or other red wine

6 tablespoons butter

Kosher salt and freshly ground black pepper

4 ounces cob-smoked bacon or other high-quality slab bacon

3 cups rich brown chicken stock (page 257)

1/4 cup cream sherry

1/4 cup sherry vinegar

1 teaspoon Dijon mustard

1/4 cup cornmeal

1/4 cup all-purpose flour

1 cup buttermilk

PARSLEY SALAD

1/2 small red onion, sliced

2 cups loosely packed Italian parsley leaves

6 chives, cut into 3-inch lengths

4 scallions, chopped

2 tablespoons tarragon leaves

3 tablespoons chervil leaves

1 tablespoon red wine vinegar

3 tablespoons extra virgin olive oil

Kosher salt and freshly ground black pepper

To prepare the shad roe, wash them in cold running water, being careful not to break the membrane surrounding the egg sack. Soak the roes in the milk, refrigerated, for several hours or overnight (this extracts blood and bitterness).

To roast the shallots, in a sauté pan over medium heat, sauté the 12 whole shallots in 2 tablespoons of the vegetable oil. Brown on all sides and add the balsamic vinegar, Syrah, and 2 tablespoons of the butter. Add salt and pepper to taste and pan-roast for 5 to 10 minutes, shaking the pan and turning the shallots every few minutes. The shallots should be just cooked through. Set aside.

To make a sauce, cut the bacon into 1-inch lardons and sauté in a pan over medium heat until crisp. Strain, reserving the bacon fat, and set aside. Deglaze the pan with the chicken stock and reserve.

Wipe out the pan and add a little of the bacon fat back into the pan. Over medium heat, sauté the minced shallots until they start to brown. Deglaze with the sherry and sherry vinegar. Increase the heat and reduce to almost a glaze. Add back the chicken stock–deglazing liquid and reduce to 1 cup. Add the bacon lardons and the mustard and whisk in the remaining 4 tablespoons butter. Remove from the heat, add salt and pepper to taste, and keep the sauce warm.

To cook the shad roe, remove them from the milk, rinse, and pat dry. Combine the cornmeal and flour and season with salt and pepper. Dip the shad roes in the buttermilk and then into the seasoned cornmeal-flour mixture. In a sauté pan over medium-high heat, heat the remaining bacon fat and vegetable oil and sauté the roes on one side for about 3 minutes, until that side is crispy. Turn and sauté on the other side. The shad roe should be brown and crispy and just pink in the center. Transfer to paper towels on a rack to drain. Set aside on a platter and keep warm. Wipe out the pan and sauté the roasted shallots to warm through.

To make the parsley salad, in a stainless steel bowl, toss the onion, parsley, chives, scallions, tarragon, chervil, red wine vinegar, and extra virgin olive oil. Season with salt and pepper.

To serve as appetizers, warm 6 plates and place 4 tablespoons of the sauce on each. Top each with a cooked shad roe. Divide the parsley salad among the plates, placing it at the 12 o'clock position. Garnish each with 2 shallots and serve at once.

To serve as a main course, warm 3 plates and assemble as above with $1/2$ cup of sauce, a pair of shad roe, and 4 shallots on each plate.

SHAD ROE

Shad roe is the roe sack of the fish shad, a member of the herring family. The roe sacks come in pairs and can be purchased separately from the filets. In fact, they are generally more prized than the fish itself. Shad roe and shad are usually available in the Mid-Atlantic states from early to mid-March through mid- to late May. Do not buy them frozen. Herring roe is an acceptable substitute.

While the strong-flavored, bony shad is quite popular around the Chesapeake area. Its roe sacks are what most gourmets seek. Admittedly, shad roe is an acquired taste. It has a unique, somewhat grainy texture, and a slightly iodine taste that I liken to calf's liver. Preparations for calf's liver work very well with shad roe (and vice versa).

Shad Roe with Grits, Virginia Ham, Roasted Onions, and Sorrel

SERVES 6 AS AN APPETIZER, 3 AS A MAIN COURSE

This is just one of the many dishes I have collaborated on with Jeff Gaetjen—or J. G., as he prefers— my former sous-chef at Kinkead's and now chef of our other restaurant, Colvin Run Tavern. J. G. has been with me for fifteen years; he is my right-hand man, a great friend, and an incredibly talented cook.

Other types of roe, like that of herring or cod, can be used. I find that shad roe has a particular affinity for cured pork products like ham, bacon, or tasso. Sorrel is often seen in old recipes for shad or shad roe, as it's thought that sorrel helps break down the many pin bones found in shad flesh. In any case, its tartness is a great match with the richness of the shad roe.

This dish can be a substantial first course or a luncheon or light supper main course. Note that the shad roes must soak in milk for several hours or overnight before proceeding with preparation.

3 pairs of shad roe

2 cups milk

4 tablespoons garlic oil from confit (page 264), plus more for sautéing

12 boiling onions

1/4 cup butter

2 teaspoons balsamic vinegar

5 cups chicken stock (page 255)

1/2 cup stone-ground grits

Kosher salt and freshly ground black pepper

1 cup dry white wine

1 teaspoon sherry vinegar

2 shallots, minced

1 cup heavy cream

2 tablespoons sorrel leaves, chiffonade

1/2 cup cornmeal

1/2 cup all-purpose flour

1 large egg

6 thin slices Virginia ham or prosciutto (about 3 ounces)

1/3 recipe garlic confit (page 264)

1 teaspoon water

Wash the shad roes in cold running water, being careful not to break the membrane surrounding the egg sack. Soak the roes in the milk, refrigerated, for several hours or overnight (this extracts blood and bitterness).

To roast the onions, in a sauté pan over medium-high heat, heat 2 tablespoons of the garlic oil and sear the onions on both sides. Decrease the heat to low, add 2 tablespoons of the butter and the balsamic vinegar, and caramelize, turning the onions every 2 minutes, or so until golden brown. Keep warm.

To prepare the grits, bring 2 cups of the chicken stock to a boil. Add the grits and stir constantly with a wooden spoon. Stone-ground grits are notoriously variable in the amount of liquid they absorb, so you may need to add more stock or water. Cook for 30 to 40 minutes, until tender and creamy. Stir in the remaining 2 tablespoons butter and add salt and pepper to taste. Keep warm.

To make a sauce, in a saucepan over high heat, combine the white wine, sherry vinegar, and shallots. Reduce to almost a glaze. Add the remaining 3 cups chicken stock and reduce by two thirds. Add the heavy cream and reduce until the sauce coats the back of a spoon. Add the sorrel and add salt and pepper to taste, and keep warm.

To cook the shad roe, remove them from the milk, rinse, and pat dry. Place the cornmeal, flour, and some salt and pepper in a food processor fitted with the metal blade and pulse to incorporate. Transfer to a bowl. Make an egg wash by beating the egg with 1 teaspoon water. Salt and pepper the shad roe, dip in the egg wash, then dip in the seasoned cornmeal-flour to coat.

In a sauté pan over medium-high heat, heat the remaining 2 tablespoons garlic oil and sauté the Virginia ham on both sides until almost brown. Transfer to a dish and keep warm. In the same pan, heat the garlic confit and reheat the onions. Transfer from the heat and keep warm. Add a little more garlic oil and sauté the shad roe on one side for about 3 minutes, until brown, then turn and sauté the other side for about 2 minutes. Do not crowd in the pan; cook in two batches if necessary.

To serve as appetizers, warm 6 plates and place a slice of the ham on each. Top the ham with the grits and surround with the sorrel sauce. Place 1 shad roe on each plate and garnish each with 2 glazed onions and 3 garlic cloves. Serve at once.

Lobster with Shellbean Succotash and Corn Pudding

*T*he ritual of my dad's making his mother's succotash signaled the end of summer vacation. Many summers there was a squall or chilly storm at the family beach house at the end of August—a harbinger of the fall to come. The ten Kinkead children thought that warm succotash tasted mighty good. We surely never had it with lobster.

Accompanied by a late-summer garden tomato salad, this dish can make a great light supper. With the lobster left out, it's an economical side dish or the basis of a unique and delicious soup. At Kinkead's we serve the succotash with a small (1-ounce) timbale of corn pudding.

Unlike the succotash of the South, in which lima or butter beans are used, the New England version features shell beans. The key to this recipe is to use fresh shell beans, which are available in the summer. The use of salt pork is also very typical of New England cookery.

The size of corn kernels and shell beans varies, so make sure you have twice as much corn as shell beans in the final mixture. The succotash can be made up to two days ahead or frozen for four weeks.

6 large ears corn

2 pounds shell beans, removed from their pods (about 3 cups)

2 ounces salt pork, diced very fine

1 yellow onion, diced

2 cups chicken stock (page 255)

2 cups water

1 tablespoon sugar

Kosher salt and cracked black pepper

3 (1-pound) chicken lobsters

1/4 cup butter

To make the succotash, cut the corn off the cob and reserve; you should have about 6 cups. Shell the beans and reserve. In a saucepan over medium-high heat, add the salt pork and render, stirring from time to time, until brown. Add the onion and sauté for about 5 minutes, until starting to brown. Add the shell beans, chicken stock, and enough water to just cover. Cook at a low simmer for 15 to 20 minutes, until the beans are nearly cooked. Add the corn, sugar, 1 teaspoon of salt, and more water to cover. Cook for 8 to 10 more minutes, until the beans and corn are done. Add 1 tablespoon of pepper. If the liquid goes below the surface of the beans, add more water, not chicken stock. The succotash should be the consistency of a thick soup.

To prepare the lobster, in a pot large enough to hold them, bring 1/2 gallon of water and 1/4 cup of salt to a boil. With a sharp knife, pierce the head of each lobster between the tentacles at the mouth. This will kill the lobster instantly. Steam the lobster for 7 to 10 minutes and remove from the water with tongs. When cool enough to handle, remove all of the meat from the lobster. Cut the tails into 3 large pieces. Brush with butter and keep warm. Add the lobster knuckle meat and trimmings to the succotash and reheat.

To serve, ladle into 6 warmed bowls and top each with 2 slices of the tail meat or a slice of tail and a claw. Grind on plenty of cracked black pepper and top with a little butter.

Lobster with Savoy Cabbage, White Bean Celeriac Purée, and Truffle Vinaigrette

This dish is an interesting mix of inexpensive peasant foods (cabbage and beans) and expensive, decadent foods (lobster and truffles). You can omit the truffles if they are too extravagant, but you'll be missing out on most of the impact and flavor. This is a first course to splurge on.

1/2 head savoy cabbage

3 (1-pound) chicken lobsters

3 cups fish, lobster, shrimp, or chicken stock (page 254 or 255)

1 1/4 cups butter

1 tablespoon freshly squeezed lemon juice

Kosher salt and freshly ground black pepper

1 small black truffle

3 tablespoons truffle juice

WHITE BEAN CELERIAC PURÉE

1 small celeriac, peeled and diced (about 2 cups)

2 cups cooked white beans (page 266)

Kosher salt and freshly ground black pepper

1 tablespoon butter

In a stockpot, bring 1 gallon of salted water to a boil. Cut the cabbage in half and blanch in the boiling water for 1 minute. Remove and let cool. Add the lobsters to the boiling water. With a sharp knife, pierce the head of each lobster between the tentacles at the mouth. This will kill the lobster instantly. Cook for 5 minutes. Remove the lobsters with tongs and place in an ice-water bath. The lobster meat will not be completely cooked, only enough to remove it from the shell. When cool enough to handle, crack open the lobster and remove all the meat. Remove the tail in one piece, remove the claws, and extract the large knuckle pieces; reserve these. In a food processor or grinder, chop or grind all the carcasses with the tomalley (greenish lobster liver) and roe to a mushy consistency; reserve.

To make a lobster butter sauce, place the shells and the stock in a noncorrosive pan over high heat and bring to a simmer. Cook for about 10 minutes. Strain, pressing down on the solids. Return the liquid to the pan and reduce to 1 cup. Cut up 1 cup of the butter and whisk it in, a bit at a time, until all is incorporated. Strain again, add the lemon juice, and keep warm.

To finish preparing the savoy cabbage, shred it, discarding the core. In a sauté pan over medium heat, melt the remaining 1/4 cup butter. When it bubbles, add the cabbage and cook for about 8 minutes, until it starts to brown. Add salt and pepper to taste, remove from the heat, and keep warm.

To make the white bean-celeriac purée, in a saucepan with enough salted water to cover, cook the celeriac until tender. Drain and pass it through a ricer, then transfer to the bowl of a food processor fitted with the metal blade. Heat the cooked white beans in a saucepan over medium heat. Transfer to the food processor, reserving the cooking liquid in the pan, and purée with the riced celeriac. The mixture should be a ratio of about two thirds beans to one third celeriac. If the purée is too firm, add a little of the bean cooking liquid. Add about 1/4 teaspoon each of salt and pepper and fold in the butter. Keep warm.

To finish preparing the lobster, in a noncorrosive saucepan over very low heat, poach the lobster tails, claws, and knuckle pieces in the lobster butter sauce for about 10 minutes, until warm and cooked through. Remove the lobster, reserving the lobster butter, and slice each tail into 4 slices.

To make the truffle vinaigrette, with a truffle slicer or a very sharp knife, thinly slice the truffle. In a sauté pan over low heat, combine 2 tablespoons of the lobster butter sauce and the truffle juice. Poach the sliced truffles in this for 2 to 3 minutes, just to warm them through. Add salt and pepper to taste.

To serve, warm 6 soup plates and place 5 to 6 tablespoons of the bean-celeriac purée in the center of each. Surround with the cabbage. Divide the lobster meat evenly among the plates, with each getting 2 slices of tail, 1 claw, and 2 knuckle pieces. Spoon on the truffle vinaigrette. Spoon a little of the lobster butter sauce around the cabbage and the bean-celeriac purée and pass the remaining sauce separately. Serve hot.

LUNCH AT TAILLEVENT

Early in my career, it was my dream to go to France to work and to eat in the famed restaurants I had only read about. In the early 1980s I got my first opportunity when Guy Savoy, now a Michelin three-star chef in Paris, invited me to see how his then two-star restaurant near the Arc de Triomphe operated. I was already the chef of a restaurant in Cambridge, Massachusetts, and Guy had worked with me on a few occasions. For several summers he came to the restaurant I worked at to give cooking demonstrations, host tasting dinners, and get a feel for life in the United States. I stayed in Paris for three weeks and generally got in the way at Chez Guy. I loved it. My French improved and I received a complete immersion in Parisian life and in the mechanics of how a fine restaurant really works.

My then-girlfriend (now my wife), Dianne, was to meet me in Paris. We planned to drive to the Champagne region, then down through Burgundy to Lyons. We would visit wineries, see the French countryside, and sample the justly famous cuisine en route. But before we could leave Paris, it was imperative we eat at Taillevent, a three-star restaurant I had read about and much admired. The only reservation we could get that fit our travel schedule was for lunch on the day that Dianne was to arrive in Paris. She was arriving at 8:30 A.M., so I felt a 12:30 P.M. lunch would work out fine.

At de Gaulle airport, I found Dianne after a longer delay through customs than expected. The bags arrived and we grabbed a cab back to Paris. Big mistake. It was rush hour on a day the union truckers had decided would be just perfect for a strike. They lined the big rigs across all the lanes of the Périphérique (Paris's version of the D.C. Beltway) and drove abreast at five to ten miles an hour. This pretty well held up the traffic behind, especially for the morning commute into the city.

We finally got to our hotel at 12:15 P.M. and hurriedly changed for lunch. Luckily, Taillevent was only a few blocks from the hotel. We literally ran to be on time for our reservation. We got there at 12:50, out of breath and relieved to have made it, and were warmly greeted by the proprietor, Monsieur Jean Claude Vrinat, and a small cadre of hostesses, captains, and managers. We were seated at a beautifully appointed table in a richly paneled dining room filled with fresh flower arrangements. This was the first Michelin three-star we had eaten in and the room and appointments did not disappoint. After settling in, we noticed that we were the only customers in the restaurant. What did we learn that day? That Parisians don't make lunch reservations before 1:00 P.M.!

Monsieur Vrinat approached our table and in perfect English said, "Because Monsieur and Madame are the first to arrive and will be alone in the restaurant for a few minutes, we would like to offer you our special pear cocktail with our compliments." Seemed to me like a good reason for a free drink. Quickly, the eau de vie and fresh pear cocktails arrived. Superb.

The rest of our story makes little sense unless you understand that Dianne does not do well when tired. She gets especially upset when jet-lagged. For this particular lunch, poor Di was exhausted. I take full responsibility for what ensued.

We decided to order the *menu degustation* (tasting menu). We had an *amuse* of goat cheese and herb canapés. Our first course was a small tomato tart with a fresh herb salad. Both were very good. For our third course, we were served a chilled langoustine and fish terrine. When the waiter brought our plates to the table I got a hint of ammonia—the unmistakable smell of spoiled fish. This was something that shouldn't even think of happening in a three-star dining establishment.

I asked for the captain and explained that the fish terrine was old and not servable. He graciously agreed and quickly removed the offending plates. After that, we experienced something I had never seen before nor have I seen since in a restaurant. Literally every person associated with serving food—from the bus boy to the chef to the owner—came to the table to apologize. The chef then replaced the dish, personally serving a sublime dish of sautéed langoustines in a tomato and herb butter. Crisis averted. Unfortunately, by now Dianne was getting very, very tired. And teary-eyed. I tried to assure the captain and waiters that Dianne was just tired and that the food was delicious. I'm sure they thought the spoiled mousse had ruined her entire life.

After Monsieur Vrinat apologized for the second time and saw that Dianne was tearing up, he came by the table and offered her a shawl, draping it over her shoulders, "Because Madame might be cold." At this point, I figured he thought I had brought my wife (or paramour) to a fancy French restaurant to kiss her off. This was the perfect setting for a gentleman to tell his wife he wants a divorce. A setting where she couldn't cause a scene. They probably get a lot of that at Taillevent.

Lunch progressed fairly nicely from there. We had a beautiful Dover sole fillet with seasoned crumbs and a spectacular roast squab with figs and port. Everything was great except for Dianne's almost falling asleep and nearly knocking over the wine decanter. "Everything is so special and delicious, but I just can't stay awake," she whimpered.

Prior to the arrival of the intended tasting dessert, Monsieur Vrinat returned to the table and announced, "Because Madame is upset, we would like to offer you our special house pear soufflés." Worked for me. Even Dianne was starting to perk up. We got the soufflés, which were excellent, and the intended dessert as well. We were finishing our wine and all was becoming right with the world when Monsieur Vrinat returned to the table once again, this time with the Cognac and eau de vie cart. I can say without a hint of exaggeration that there were Cognacs and Armagnacs on that cart that were over 100 years old. The proprietor essentially invited us to take our best shot. Dianne had a Cognac and I, an Armagnac. Both were incredible.

As we left the restaurant, we were bade goodbye by the owner and a throng of employees. As we got out the door, I told Dianne, "Listen, the next time we eat at a three-star, you start crying earlier. This could really work out!"

The point of the story is this: Monsieur Vrinat was and remains the consummate host and restaurant professional. He and his staff were going to make sure that no matter what the circumstances, no guests were going to leave Taillevent anything but extremely impressed and happy. To this day, Taillevent does not open if Monsieur Vrinat is not on the premises. I have eaten there three times since that first visit, and the experience has been excellent on every occasion. In the years that followed I have had a few better meals but have never received service that even approached the graciousness of that lunch.

In this business we all need to take a lesson from Taillevent. As restaurant operators we constantly read about the importance of providing good service and taking care of our customers. Time and again that critical concept is given mere lip service. Monsieur Vrinat takes the idea of providing impeccable service to its highest level. And he does it every day.

Grilled Squid with Creamy Polenta and Tomato Fondue

This dish is probably our most requested appetizer at Kinkead's. I once took it off the menu for two months and regular customers demanded I bring it back, so now it stays on the menu permanently. The tomato fondue recipe makes at least twice as much as you need for the squid. Luckily, it also makes a great sauce for other fish, pasta, or as a base for more complex sauces. For a delicious appetizer, you can use the leftover squid tentacles as a substitute for soft-shell crab in the recipe on page 38.

GRILLED SQUID

6 to 8 fresh squid (about 2 pounds)

2 cups fresh breadcrumbs, plus more as needed

2 cloves garlic, minced

$1/2$ cup Italian parsley, leaves only

$1/2$ teaspoon kosher salt, plus more for seasoning

$1/2$ teaspoon cracked black pepper, plus more for seasoning

$1/4$ cup olive oil

$1/2$ cup extra virgin olive oil

$1/2$ cup clarified butter (page 257)

Olive or vegetable oil for brushing the grill

2 tablespoons pesto drizzle (page 262)

6 basil sprigs, for garnish

CREAMY POLENTA

3 cups milk

$1/3$ cup polenta or cornmeal

$1/2$ cup butter

$1/2$ cup freshly grated Parmesan cheese

$1 1/2$ teaspoons kosher salt

1 teaspoon freshly ground black pepper

TOMATO FONDUE

3 cups (about 18) canned peeled plum tomatoes, coarsely chopped

$1/2$ cup olive oil

4 cloves garlic; 2 minced, 2 very thinly sliced

$1/2$ teaspoon sugar

1 tablespoon red wine vinegar

$1/2$ teaspoon kosher salt, plus more for seasoning

$1/2$ teaspoon cracked black pepper, plus more for seasoning

1 teaspoon fresh thyme leaves

4 tablespoons extra virgin olive oil

2 tablespoons fresh basil leaves, chiffonade

To prepare the squid, soak twelve 9-inch wood skewers in ice water for 1 hour. Wash the squid in cold running water and remove the tentacles and side wings (discard or refrigerate for another use). Remove the cellophane-like inner fiber from the body. Slice the body into $3/8$-inch rounds. Pat dry and double-skewer 6 to 9 rings to make 6 servings. Refrigerate for 1 hour.

To make the polenta, in a saucepan over high heat bring the milk to a boil. Add the polenta and decrease the heat. Simmer, stirring constantly with a wooden spoon, for about 20 minutes, until thick. With the heat still on, stir in the butter, cheese, salt, and pepper. Because of the fat (butter) and the amount of milk, the polenta will be fluffy, not too thick or pasty. Cover and keep warm. Transfer to a water bath if holding for a long period of time.

Remove the squid from the refrigerator. Place the bread crumbs and garlic in a food processor fitted with the metal blade. Coarsely chop the parsley leaves and add to the processor bowl. Add the salt and pepper and the olive oil. Mix until crumbly and moist but not wet. Add more crumbs if needed.

CONTINUED

Combine the extra virgin olive oil and clarified butter in a bowl. Salt and pepper the skewered squid and dip them first in the oil-butter blend, and then in the seasoned crumb mixture to coat on all sides. Refrigerate for at least 1 hour.

To make the tomato fondue, preheat the oven to 375°F. Place 1 cup of the tomatoes in an ovenproof sauté pan and sprinkle with a little of the olive oil. Roast in the oven for 5 to 8 minutes, until the tomatoes are starting to brown and release juice. Transfer to a blender; add the remaining olive oil, the minced garlic, and the sugar, vinegar, salt, and pepper and purée to make a vinaigrette. Reserve.

Place the remaining 2 cups of tomatoes in a stainless steel bowl. Add the sliced garlic, thyme leaves, 2 tablespoons of the extra virgin olive oil, and salt and pepper to taste, and toss together to marinate.

In a sauté pan over medium-high heat, heat the remaining 2 tablespoons extra virgin olive oil. When hot, add the marinated tomatoes. Stir in the roasted-tomato vinaigrette and the basil chiffonade and heat through.

To grill the squid, heat a grill to medium heat and oil it with a little olive or vegetable oil. Lay the squid skewers on the hot grill and cook for 3 to 4 minutes, until they come off the grill easily. Brush with some of the leftover oil-butter mix, turn them just once, and grill for 2 to 3 minutes more. The trick is to handle the skewers gently and minimally so the crumb mixture stays on the squid. Check for doneness by separating a few of the squid rings. If they are opaque, they are cooked.

To serve, warm 6 plates and place ¹/₂ cup or so of polenta in the center of each. Surround with the tomato fondue. Remove the skewers and place 1 skewer's worth of squid on the polenta on each plate. Garnish each serving of squid with pesto drizzle and a basil sprig.

SQUID

Squid is a member of the cephalopod family. Cephalopods are mollusks with no outer shell. It's thought that at one time these creatures had outer skeletons, that disappeared as they evolved. *Cephalopod* means "head foot," as it appears that their tentacles, or "legs," grow from their heads.

Squid have grown tremendously in popularity with American consumers in recent years and represent one of the best values in shellfish. Squid are sold whole or cut up, both fresh and frozen. Like all seafood, squid is better fresh than frozen. Whole fresh squid is almost always sold uncleaned. There are also frozen squid "steaks" on the market: giant squid bodies cut in steak portions.

The squid's tentacles, fins, and cylindrical body are edible. The eye and "head area," outer skin, and small, feathery internal cartilage are discarded. Squid (and cuttlefish) ink is edible, but the ink sac must be removed from the creature intact; it can also be bought frozen in small packets. Squid ink can be used to flavor fresh pasta, sauces, and risottos, such as the famous "Black Rice" of Spain's Catalan coast.

Salads

Seared Rare Tuna with Fennel-Arugula Salad, Pine Nuts, Capers, and Raisins 61

Salad of Bibb and Soft Lettuces with Radishes, Gruyère,
and Mustard-Chervil Vinaigrette 62

Salad of Green and White Asparagus, Leeks, Fingerling Potatoes, and Fried Egg 63

Spring Salad of Asparagus, Ramps, New Onions, Fiddleheads,
and Favas with Pecorino 67

Height-of-Summer Heirloom Tomato Salad 69

Red and Yellow Tomato Salad with Lentils, Basil, and Fresh Goat Cheese 70

Arugula Salad with Haricots Verts, Roasted Beets, and Cambozola 72

Roasted Pear Salad with Gorgonzola, Walnuts, Endive, and Radicchio 75

Salad of Duck Confit, Red Cabbage, Pumpkin, Beets, and Roquefort 76

Lobster, Sweetbread, and Foie Gras Salad 78

Seared Rare Tuna with Fennel-Arugula Salad, Pine Nuts, Capers, and Raisins

This is one of the staple dishes at Kinkead's that customers won't let us take off the menu. It's our version of the now ubiquitous tuna carpaccio. The fennel, raisins, and pine nuts add a Sicilian spin. This dish works as a first course or in a larger version as a main course luncheon salad.

SEARED RARE TUNA

1 (24-ounce) loin center-cut, sushi-quality tuna, skin removed

Kosher salt and cracked black pepper

2 tablespoons vegetable oil

1/4 cup port

1/4 cup dried currants or raisins

3 tablespoons freshly squeezed lime juice

2 tablespoons extra virgin olive oil

1 clove garlic, minced

1/4 cup capers, drained

1/4 cup pine nuts, toasted

6 large basil leaves, chiffonade, plus extra sprigs for garnish

Coarse sea salt

FENNEL-ARUGULA SALAD

2 fennel bulbs, sliced very thin (about 4 cups loosely packed)

2 cups arugula leaves (preferably young leaves)

1 small red onion, sliced (about 1 cup)

2 teaspoons red wine vinegar

2 tablespoons extra virgin olive oil

Kosher salt and freshly ground black pepper

To prepare the tuna, cut the loin into 3 log-shaped pieces, each 4 inches long and about 2 inches thick. Place each in plastic wrap and twist the ends tightly to form a rounded, sausage shape. Chill for several hours. They will keep the round shape when unwrapped.

After chilling, unwrap the fillets, salt and pepper them, and let them rest for 1 minute. In a sauté pan over medium-high heat, heat the vegetable oil and sear the tuna on all sides, except the ends, for a few seconds. Place in the freezer for at least 10 minutes, then slice into 1/8-inch-thick-pieces. This works best with an electric slicer, but you can use a sharp, serrated carving knife.

On the centers of the 6 chilled plates, place the tuna slices in rows.

In a saucepan over medium-high heat, combine the port and currants and simmer for 4 to 6 minutes, until the currants are plumped. Strain the currants.

In a small stainless steel bowl, combine the lime juice, extra virgin olive oil, minced garlic, and some pepper. With a pastry brush, paint the tuna with the mixture. Divide the capers, pine nuts, currants, and basil chiffonade over the tuna plates. Sprinkle with coarse sea salt and grind some cracked black pepper over the top.

To make the fennel-arugula salad, in a stainless steel bowl, toss the fennel, arugula, and onion with the vinegar and extra virgin olive oil. Add salt and pepper to taste.

To serve, surround the tuna with the salad. Garnish with basil sprigs and serve at once.

Salad of Bibb and Soft Lettuces with Radishes, Gruyère, and Mustard-Chervil Vinaigrette

This very simple, light dinner salad is a nice alternative to a mixed green or mesclun salad. Use as many of the Bibb or butterhead varieties of lettuce as you care for. As an alternative to the Gruyère, try a generous sprinkling of a blue cheese like Roquefort, Blue d'Auvergne, or Maytag. Soft lettuce heads vary wildly in size; you will need 2 to 2½ cups of mixed lettuces per person.

1 head Boston Bibb lettuce

2 heads Kentucky Bibb lettuce

2 heads butterhead lettuce

1 head curly butterhead lettuce

3 scallions, chopped

½ cup Mustard-Chervil Vinaigrette (page 262)

Kosher salt and freshly ground black pepper

8 French breakfast radishes (or any type), sliced

1 cup finely shredded Gruyère cheese

1 teaspoon chopped chives, for garnish

Chill 6 to 8 salad plates. Core and separate the lettuces. Wash thoroughly and dry in a lettuce spinner or with paper towels. In a stainless steel bowl, toss the lettuces with the scallions, vinaigrette, and salt and pepper to taste. Divide onto the chilled plates, top with the radish slices, and sprinkle on the Gruyère. Garnish with the chopped chives.

Salad of Green and White Asparagus, Leeks, Fingerling Potatoes, and Fried Egg

SERVES 6

*C*hervil defines the flavors of spring and works very well with the mustard in the vinaigrette. This salad is also very nice with the addition of crisp pancetta rounds or strips of cob-smoked or other thick smoked bacon.

New baby leeks look like large scallions and come bundled in bunches of 4 to 6. Fresh white asparagus is much easier to find these days, but if it is not available, all green is fine. For my money, when it comes to asparagus, bigger is better. Find the jumbo-sized stalks and be sure to peel them. The peels and scraps can be used to make soup or purée for a sauce. You can even deep-fry them and use them as a garnish. If you are using thin or pencil-sized asparagus, don't bother peeling, and add more to the recipe.

12 large white asparagus stalks, peeled and trimmed

18 jumbo green asparagus, peeled and trimmed

12 small new-season leeks, bottoms trimmed

2 tablespoons butter, plus more for cooking eggs

12 fingerling or other new potatoes

1/2 small red onion, sliced (about 1/2 cup)

1 large head frisée, cored and broken up

1/2 cup Basic Vinaigrette (page 262)

Kosher salt and freshly ground black pepper

12 slices country-style or other coarse bread

6 large eggs

2 tablespoons extra virgin olive oil

4 scallions, chopped (about 1 cup), for garnish

2 tablespoons chervil leaves, for garnish

CHAMPAGNE VINAIGRETTE

1 large shallot, minced (about 3 teaspoons)

2 cloves garlic, minced

1/4 cup Champagne or white wine vinegar

1/4 cup Champagne

2 tablespoons Dijon mustard

1/2 teaspoon kosher salt

1/2 teaspoon white pepper

1/2 cup extra virgin olive oil

1 tablespoon Italian parsley leaves, chopped

To prepare the asparagus, preheat a grill. Chill 6 salad plates. Blanch the white and green asparagus in a shallow pan of boiling salted water. This should take about 3 minutes after the water returns to a boil. When just cooked, refresh in an ice-water bath. Drain the asparagus and reserve.

Blanch the leeks in a sauté pan with a little water and the 2 tablespoons butter. Cook, turning frequently, until tender. Refresh in an ice-water bath.

In a saucepan of salted water over high heat, cook the fingerling potatoes until tender. Drain and, when cool, slice lengthwise into 1/4-inch slices. In a stainless steel bowl, toss the potato slices with the red onion, frisée, and basic vinaigrette. Salt and pepper the dressed potatoes and reserve.

To make the champagne vinaigrette, purée the shallot, garlic, vinegar, Champagne, mustard, salt, pepper, and oil in a blender. Remove from the blender and stir in the parsley.

CONTINUED

Brush the bread with oil and grill over a hot grill or toast in a broiler or large toaster until toasted on both sides. Keep warm.

Place a little butter in a small sauté pan over medium heat, and cook the eggs one at a time, sunny side up.

To serve, dress the asparagus, leeks, and potatoes in the Champagne vinaigrette. Salt and pepper the vegetables and arrange them on the chilled plates in this order: leek, green asparagus, white asparagus, green asparagus, white asparagus, green asparagus, leek. At the 6 o'clock position on the plate, place some of the potato-frisée salad. Top each asparagus and leek arrangement with 2 slices of grilled bread and a fried egg. Garnish with the scallions, and chervil.

Spring Salad of Asparagus, Ramps, New Onions, Fiddleheads, and Favas with Pecorino

This salad is something of an "old-world classic meets the Appalachian Trail." Spring farm vegetables like asparagus, favas, and leeks combine with the spring wild bounty from Virginia: ramps (wild leeks), "rareripes" (new spring onions), and fiddlehead ferns. Fiddleheads are new-season, immature ferns that have just sprouted and are harvested before they unfurl and grow. The name comes from the curled head, which resembles the spiral head of a violin or fiddle. The younger and smaller the fiddlehead, the better; as they get older they become woody and are harder to clean.

18 to 24 large asparagus, peeled and trimmed

4 pounds whole fava beans, shelled from the pod (about 2 cups)

24 fiddlehead ferns, trimmed

18 ramps, with greens

12 new onions with bulbs, red or white

8 scallions (about 1 1/2 bunches)

6 tablespoons extra virgin olive oil

2 cloves garlic, minced

2 tablespoons chervil leaves, plus extra for garnish

2 teaspoons white wine vinegar

Kosher salt and freshly ground black pepper

2 ounces Pecorino Romano cheese, shredded with a vegetable peeler

HERB VINAIGRETTE

1 teaspoon chopped tarragon leaves

2 teaspoons chopped chervil leaves

3 teaspoons chopped Italian parsley leaves

4 large basil leaves, chiffonade and chopped

1 large shallot, minced

Juice of 1 lemon

Grated zest of 1 lemon

1/4 cup Champagne or white wine vinegar

1 1/2 tablespoons Dijon mustard

1/2 teaspoon kosher salt

1/2 teaspoon ground white pepper

3/4 cup extra virgin olive oil

Chill 6 salad plates. Blanch the asparagus in a shallow pan of boiling salted water. When just cooked, refresh in an ice bath. Drain and reserve. Blanch the favas and fiddleheads in separate pans of boiling salted water for about 2 minutes, until a little firm. Refresh in separate ice-water baths. (Boiling them separately allows for different cooking times and keeps the flavors separate.) Peel the outer skin off the favas and discard; reserve the beans.

Trim the bottoms off the ramps and cut the greens from the white parts. Set aside the white parts; cut the greens into chiffonade.

Trim the green top parts from the new onions (leaving about a 2-inch top) and the scallions. Chop the greens. Cut the bulbs in half.

In a sauté pan over medium-high heat, heat 2 tablespoons of the olive oil and sauté the ramp whites, onion bulbs, and whole scallion bottoms for 2 to 3 minutes, until they start to brown. They should be cooked but still crunchy. Transfer from the heat and reserve.

CONTINUED

To make a purée of the greens, wipe out the pan and place it over medium heat. Sauté the ramps, scallion, and new onion with the garlic in 2 more tablespoons of the olive oil. When cooked, purée in a blender with the 2 tablespoons chervil, the white wine vinegar, and the remaining olive oil. Add salt and pepper to taste.

To make the vinaigrette, in a small stainless steel bowl combine the tarragon, chervil, parsley, and basil. In another stainless steel bowl, whisk together the shallot, lemon juice, lemon zest, vinegar, mustard, salt, and pepper. Add the olive oil in a stream, whisking until completely incorporated. Whisk in the fresh herb mixture. Dress all of the vegetables in the vinaigrette.

To serve, spoon the purée onto the center of the chilled plates. Salt and pepper the dressed vegetables and arrange on top of the purée, giving each plate an equal amount of asparagus, favas, fiddleheads, scallions, ramps, and new onions. Garnish with the cheese and chervil.

GROWING TOMATOES

Late each spring, my wife, Dianne, and I pick out ten to twenty tomato varieties to grow in our backyard. Dianne likes to garden and does pretty much all of the work of growing the crops. I pretty much just pick 'em and eat 'em. Since we grow tomatoes just for the fun of it and could not possibly consume all we grow, the restaurant is the beneficiary of this tomato windfall.

Then there is the matter of Chuckie, our thirty-pound woodchuck "tenant." He (or she) and his (or her) two offspring dine extremely well on our tomatoes, beans, and squash throughout the summer. Unfazed by the wire mesh fence surrounding the garden, Chuckie and the brood flatten out and slide under, generally grazing on several varieties at each meal. God forbid they find one they like and eat all of it. No, they have to sample by taking a single bite out of two or three different tomatoes. Despite the costs and the troublesome varmints, growing heirloom tomatoes is an enjoyable project. We get terrific salads at home most of the summer and into the fall. You can't go wrong with a sandwich of vine-ripened tomato and red onion, either.

For those who have the space, I recommend growing a crop of your own. If nothing else, it provides a great feeling of accomplishment, self-satisfaction, and a sense of connecting with the earth. Whether you grow your own or buy them in a farmers' market, heirloom tomatoes are a culinary treat.

Height-of-Summer Heirloom Tomato Salad

This salad remains one of the true seasonal food treasures we have left. You can get asparagus in December, apples in the spring, and melons year-round. But you can really only get a good tomato in the summer. Simply dressed and correctly seasoned, a ripe tomato salad is one of the wonders of gastronomy.

Using different combinations of cherry, grape, currant, red, purple, yellow, green, striped, and orange tomatoes, and different variations of vinegars, citrus, and oils, the possibilities are daunting. Some of my favorite tomato varieties are Cherokee purple, Zebra stripe, yellow currant, Brandywine, and lemon drop.

3 to 4 pounds assorted heirloom tomatoes, at least 10 varieties, and a nice assortment of shapes, colors, and sizes

1 large red onion, sliced

10 large basil leaves, chiffonade, plus 6 sprigs for garnish

8 large opal, purple, or other basil leaves, chiffonade

2 cloves garlic, minced

4 tablespoons red wine vinegar

1/2 cup fruity extra virgin olive oil

1/2 teaspoon kosher salt

1/2 teaspoon cracked black pepper

Chill 6 large plates. Cut the larger tomatoes into various shapes. Cut some in rounds, some smaller ones in half, and others in wedges. Leave any cherry or currant tomatoes whole.

In a stainless steel bowl, toss the chopped tomatoes with the remaining ingredients. Let marinate for 3 to 5 minutes. Drain and artfully arrange on the chilled plates. Garnish with the basil sprigs.

Red and Yellow Tomato Salad with Lentils, Basil, and Fresh Goat Cheese

SERVES 6

In the fall, when tomato season is coming to an end, we prepare a variation on this salad, substituting roasted red and yellow peppers and grilled red onions.

Montrachet is an imported French goat cheese. If not available, any full-flavored and slightly aged soft goat cheese will do. When cutting the Montrachet or any soft cheese, it is best to use a hollow knife or a knife dipped in very hot water. It makes slicing much easier and keeps the cheese rounds whole.

3 large ripe red tomatoes (Brandywine, Cherokee purple, or other variety)

3 large ripe yellow tomatoes

1 cup French lentils

1 tablespoon vegetable oil

1/3 cup finely diced celery

1/3 cup finely diced yellow onion

1/3 cup finely diced carrot

3 cups chicken stock (page 255) or water

1 cup red lentils

2 cloves garlic, minced

6 tablespoons extra virgin olive oil

4 tablespoons red wine vinegar

Kosher salt and cracked black pepper

9 basil leaves, chiffonade, plus 6 sprigs for garnish

1 red onion, thinly sliced

1/2 teaspoon sugar

1 (9-ounce) log Montrachet or other goat cheese

1/4 cup toasted walnuts, finely chopped

3 tablespoons aïoli (page 259)

BASIL VINAIGRETTE DRIZZLE

1 cup packed fresh basil leaves

1 tablespoon freshly squeezed lemon juice

1 teaspoon red wine vinegar

1 tablespoon vegetable oil

Kosher salt and freshly ground black pepper

To prepare the tomatoes, bring 8 cups salted water to a boil. Core the tomatoes and score the bottoms with a paring knife. Plunge the tomatoes into the boiling water for 1 minute. Refresh in an ice-water bath. When cool, peel the tomatoes and reserve, discarding skins.

To prepare the lentils, bring a quart of salted water to a boil and add the French lentils. Cook for 10 minutes, and then drain. In a saucepan over medium heat, combine the vegetable oil and the diced vegetables and sweat for 3 minutes. Add the French lentils, 1 cup of the chicken stock, and 1 cup water and bring to a boil. Cook for another 12 to 15 minutes, until tender but not mushy. Drain and place in a stainless steel bowl.

Bring the remaining 2 cups chicken stock to a boil and pour it over the red lentils. Let stand for 10 minutes. Drain and reserve. Add to the French lentils. Stir in the garlic, 4 tablespoons of the olive oil, and 2 tablespoons of the red wine vinegar. Add salt and pepper to taste.

Chill 6 salad plates. Cut the skinned tomatoes in wedges. Combine the remaining 2 tablespoons olive oil and 2 tablespoons red wine vinegar and half of the basil chiffonade. Add the tomato wedges, red onion, sugar, and salt and pepper to taste and toss. Let sit for about 10 minutes.

To make the vinaigrette, in a saucepan of boiling water, blanch the basil leaves for 10 seconds. Refresh in ice water and drain. Purée in a blender. Blend in the lemon juice, vinegar, and vegetable oil. The consistency should be like a pourable mayonnaise. Add salt and pepper to taste.

Preheat the oven to 375°F. Roll the Montrachet log in the walnuts and cut into six 1¹/₂-ounce rounds, each about 1¹/₂ inches thick. Place the rounds on a baking sheet and warm in the oven for 2 to 3 minutes.

To serve, divide the lentil salad onto the chilled plates and top with alternating red and yellow tomato wedges in overlapping circles. Top each with some of the remaining basil chiffonade and a round of warm goat cheese. Garnish with a basil sprig and drizzle with the aïoli.

Arugula Salad with Haricots Verts, Roasted Beets, and Cambozola

I am a huge fan of beets and they appear in many different forms throughout the year on Kinkead's menus. In fact, there is never a menu that does not have beets on it in some form. This is a spring salad but it could be served almost any time of year. It uses beets in two forms: first, as a thin-sliced beet salad—almost a carpaccio—to complement the arugula and green beans; second, as a diced beet tartare that highlights the seasonal varieties of vegetable and serves as a pedestal for the round of goat cheese. The contrast of the cool beets with the slight pungency of warm goat cheese is a bistro classic. Any high-quality domestic or imported soft goat cheese will work.

The vinaigrette recipe makes 1 cup, about 1/4 cup more than what you'll need. The extra is nice to have on hand for salads and dressing vegetables.

6 red beets (about 3 inches in diameter), scrubbed

2 small red or pink beets, scrubbed

2 small yellow beets, scrubbed

2 small Chiogga or other striped beets, scrubbed

1 pound haricots verts, ends picked

12 ounces Cambozola, cut into 1-inch-thick wedges

1 pound arugula, trimmed

1 red onion, sliced

Kosher salt and freshly ground black pepper

1 tablespoon extra virgin olive oil

WALNUT OIL VINAIGRETTE

1 large shallot, minced

2 cloves garlic, minced

1 tablespoon chopped Italian parsley leaves

1 tablespoon balsamic vinegar

1/4 cup red wine vinegar

1/2 teaspoon kosher salt

1/2 teaspoon freshly ground black pepper

2 tablespoons walnut oil

1/2 cup extra virgin olive oil

To prepare the beets, preheat the oven to 350°F. In a sheet pan, roast the red beets for 10 minutes. Add the rest of the smaller beets and cook for 15 minutes, or until tender. When cool, peel all the beets. Slice the large beets into 1/8-inch-thick rounds. Dice the smaller beets into 1/3-inch cubes or cut them into 6 wedges. Keep the oven on.

Blanch the haricots in boiling salted water for about 2 to 3 minutes, until just done but still with a little crunch. Refresh in an ice-water bath. Drain, cut into 3-inch lengths and chill.

To make the vinaigrette, in a stainless steel bowl, combine the shallot, garlic, parsley, vinegars, salt, and pepper. In a separate small bowl, combine the oils, and then add them to the other ingredients in a slow stream, whisking constantly, until incorporated.

Place the Cambozola on a baking sheet and warm for 1 minute in the oven. Set the sheet on the stovetop to keep warm.

To assemble the salads, wash the arugula in 2 or 3 changes of water. In a large stainless steel bowl, toss the sliced beets in 1/4 cup of the vinaigrette. On each of 6 large chilled plates, form a ring of overlapping beet slices, leaving a 3-inch-diameter space inside. Add salt and pepper to taste. Drizzle with the olive oil. In a stainless steel bowl, toss the haricots verts, onion, and arugula with $1/4$ cup of the vinaigrette. Add salt and pepper and toss to coat evenly. At the 12 o'clock position on each plate, arrange this salad so that some of the beets are covered, but do not cover the 3-inch center space.

In a stainless steel bowl, toss the diced beets with a $1/4$ cup vinaigrette just to coat. Add salt and pepper to taste. For each serving, tightly pack a 3-inch mold with the diced beets and tip out into the center, on top of the ring of sliced beets. Place 2 Cambozola wedges on top of each diced-beet "pedestal." Serve at once.

Roasted Pear Salad with Gorgonzola, Walnuts, Endive, and Radicchio

f you have ripe Bosc pears, you can use them as is. If the pears are not good and ripe, you will need to poach them. Feel free to use another variety of pear like Anjou, Comice, or Bartlett. Another option is to use little Seckel pears; for this salad you will need two per person. These can be kept whole, with the cores removed in a tube, like a baked apple, and the center filled with cheese mixture. They make a nice presentation.

40 walnut halves (about 1¹/₂ cups)

3 ripe Bosc pears

Juice of 1 lemon

2 tablespoons sugar (optional)

1 teaspoon kosher salt (optional), plus more as needed

4 ounces Gorgonzola or Roquefort cheese

4 tablespoons cream cheese

3 heads endive, 24 outer leaves reserved for garnish, the rest julienned

1 head radicchio, cored and julienned

¹/₄ teaspoon cracked black pepper

PORT VINAIGRETTE

1 shallot, minced

4 tablespoons red wine vinegar

2 tablespoons port

¹/₄ teaspoon kosher salt

¹/₄ teaspoon cracked black pepper

¹/₄ teaspoon honey

6 tablespoons olive oil

4 tablespoons walnut oil

2 tablespoons grapeseed oil

1 teaspoon chopped chives

Preheat the oven to 375°F. Spread the walnut halves on a baking sheet and toast in the oven for 6 to 8 minutes, or until starting to brown. Transfer to a rack and let cool, leaving the oven on. Reserve 24 walnut halves for garnish; chop the rest.

To prepare the pears, peel and cut in halves. Add the lemon juice to a bowl or pan of water deep enough to cover the pear halves and submerge them in it. If the pears are not fully ripe, peel them, leaving them whole. In a saucepan, bring enough water to cover the pears to a simmer. Stir in the sugar and salt. Submerge the pears and poach for 3 to 4 minutes, until tender. Drain and let cool, then cut in halves.

In the bowl of a mixer fitted with a paddle attachment, place the Gorgonzola, cream cheese, and chopped walnuts and mix until incorporated and slightly aerated.

Drain and dry the pear halves and cut out the center seeds. Place on a baking sheet, cored side up, and cover with the Gorgonzola mixture. Bake for about 8 minutes, until the pears are tender and the Gorgonzola mixture is melting.

To make the vinaigrette, whisk all of the ingredients together in a stainless steel bowl.

In a separate stainless steel bowl, toss the endive, radicchio, kosher salt, pepper, and remaining walnuts with the vinaigrette. On each of 6 plates, place 1 warm pear half. Divide the salad among the 6 plates and garnish each with 4 whole endive leaves and sprinkle with walnut halves.

Salad of Duck Confit, Red Cabbage, Pumpkin, Beets, and Roquefort

This is a nice autumn main course salad. Actually, calling it a salad may be a misnomer—this is one of those dishes that takes a broad reading of the concept of salad. Making the confit is a lot of work—and takes several days—but it can be used for many recipes.

You can replace the pecans with walnuts, and any type of beet or combination of beets works with this dish. For a less pungent taste, try replacing the Roquefort with a milder blue cheese, like Bleu de Bresse, or even a goat cheese. You may also forego adding the bacon fat to the vinaigrette for a lighter dressing.

6 red or Chiogga beets

$1/2$ recipe duck confit (page 265)

4 bacon strips, cut into lardons

1 large red cabbage, cored and finely shredded (about 12 cups)

6 tablespoons red wine vinegar

4 tablespoons dark brown sugar

Kosher salt and freshly ground black pepper

60 haricot verts, ends picked

2 tablespoons vegetable oil

1 small pumpkin or butternut squash, peeled and cut into $1/4$-inch slices

24 pecan halves, toasted

6 ounces Roquefort or other mild blue cheese, such as Cambozola

2 heads endive; 18 whole leaves reserved for garnish, the rest julienned

1 red onion, julienned

WALNUT OIL–BACON VINAIGRETTE

2 oranges

2 cloves garlic, minced

1 small shallot, minced

2 tablespoons raspberry vinegar

1 tablespoon red wine vinegar

2 teaspoons Dijon mustard

6 tablespoons peanut oil (or canola or grapeseed)

4 tablespoons walnut oil

$1/2$ teaspoon kosher salt

$1/2$ teaspoon cracked black pepper

To prepare the beets, preheat the oven to 375°F. Roast the beets for about 2 hours. When cool enough to handle, peel and dice into $1/2$-inch cubes. Set aside.

To prepare the duck legs, sear them in a cast-iron pan over medium heat until crisp. Remove the meat from the legs and trim off any tendon or sinew. Keep warm. Wipe out the pan and return it to medium-high heat. Sauté the bacon lardons until crisp. Remove from the fat and keep warm. Reserve the fat for the vinaigrette.

To prepare the cabbage, place the cabbage in a stainless steel bowl. In a small saucepan over high heat, bring the red wine vinegar and brown sugar to a boil, and then pour over the cabbage. Salt the cabbage with about $1/2$ teaspoon kosher salt. Toss and let marinate for 20 minutes. Drain excess liquid and discard.

In a saucepan of boiling salted water, blanch the haricots verts and shock in an ice-water bath.

In a sauté pan over medium heat, heat the vegetable oil. When hot, add the pumpkin slices and brown on both sides, 2 to 3 minutes per side. Add salt and pepper and keep warm.

Chop half of the pecan halves and place on a plate, reserving the remaining halves for garnish. Crumble the Roquefort into a bowl and set aside.

To make the vinaigrette, section the oranges; save the juice and reserve the sections. In a stainless steel bowl, combine the garlic, shallot, vinegars, and mustard. Whisking constantly, add the peanut oil, and then the walnut oil in a slow stream. When incorporated, whisk in the salt, pepper, reserved orange juice, and reserved bacon fat. This makes 1/2 cup.

To assemble, warm 6 plates. Toss the julienned endive, red onion, and blanched haricots verts together in the vinaigrette. Place 3 endive leaves at the 12 o'clock position on each plate. Portion out the marinated cabbage. Surround with diced beets, orange sections, and slices of pumpkin. Top each salad with confit, chopped pecans, and crumbled Roquefort. Garnish with the pecan halves.

Lobster, Sweetbread, and Foie Gras Salad

Truly a heart attack on a plate, this rich, decadent salad is delicious nonetheless. Many variations on this type of "Millionaire's" salad have been prepared on both sides of the Atlantic. One of the more notable was Salade Pere Maurice, served by Gerard Boyer at Les Crayeres in Reims, France. It was a perfect foil for the elegant Tête de Cuvée rosé Champagnes of the region.

Preparing this main-course salad from scratch is an all-day project—not to mention the considerable expense of assembling all the high-end ingredients. If one has the time and enough extra cash for a car payment, the dish is worth the effort. It is sure to elicit "Wows" from your guests. The foie gras is what really makes this salad special.

3 (1¼-pound) lobsters

1 lobe Grade A foie gras

Kosher salt and cracked black pepper

2 teaspoons Armagnac

2 tablespoons extra virgin olive oil

2 shallots, sliced

6 ounces sweetbreads, blanched and trimmed (page 264)

All-purpose flour for dredging

3 tablespoons butter

½ teaspoon chopped tarragon leaves

6 large fresh artichoke bottoms

6 hearts of palm (fresh or glass-jar preserved)

1 pound haricots verts, ends removed

3 ripe plum tomatoes, cut into wedges

½ red onion, sliced

1 head frisée (about 3 cups)

1 head butterhead lettuce, torn into bite-sized pieces

1 cup mesclun mix

3 scallions, diced

1 tablespoon chopped chives

2 tablespoons Basic Vinaigrette (page 262)

TRUFFLE VINAIGRETTE

1 black truffle, peeled (peelings reserved)

1 tablespoon black truffle oil

1 clove garlic, chopped

2 tablespoons walnut oil

5 tablespoons good-quality olive oil

1 tablespoon sherry vinegar

4 tablespoons truffle juice

¼ teaspoon kosher salt

¼ teaspoon freshly ground black pepper

½ shallot, minced

To prepare the lobsters, in a large stockpot over high heat, bring 16 cups of salted water to a boil and cook the lobsters, covered, for 8 to 10 minutes. Plunge them into an ice-water bath. When cool, extract all of the meat and cut the tail into 4 or 5 medallions. Refrigerate with the claws and body meat. Reserve the shells for lobster stock or another use—they freeze well.

To prepare the foie gras, season with salt, pepper, and Armagnac. Refrigerate for 1 hour.

In a cast-iron pan over high heat, add 1 tablespoon of the olive oil and sear the lobe on all sides until brown. Place the sliced shallots in a roasting pan and place the foie gras on top of the shallots. Roast the foie gras for about 10 minutes, until just set. The internal temperature should be about 100°F. Remove from the heat and let rest for 5 minutes. Refrigerate for 1 hour.

CONTINUED

To prepare the sweetbreads, slice them into medallions about 1/2-inch thick. Salt and pepper the sweetbreads, and dredge in flour. Shake off excess. In a sauté pan over medium-high heat, heat the remaining 1 tablespoon olive oil and 1 tablespoon of the butter. Sauté the medallions until very crisp. Turn and do the same to the other side. Drain on a paper towel and keep warm.

In a sauté pan over low heat, melt the remaining 2 tablespoons butter and stew the lobster meat until warmed through. Add the tarragon leaves and toss. When just warm, slice the tail meat into medallions and keep the rest warm.

To make the vinaigrette, mince the truffle and set aside. In a blender, purée the truffle peelings, truffle oil, garlic, walnut and olive oils, vinegar, truffle juice, salt, and pepper. Transfer to a small stainless steel bowl. Stir in the minced truffle and the shallot. This makes 3/4 cup; the salad requires only 1/2 cup, so save the extra 1/4 cup for other salads.

To make the salads, cut the artichoke bottoms and hearts of palm in half. Blanch the haricot verts in boiling salted water and then shock in an ice-water bath. In a stainless steel bowl, toss the haricots, tomato wedges, onion, artichoke bottoms, and hearts of palm with 4 tablespoons of the truffle vinaigrette. Add salt and pepper to taste.

In another stainless steel bowl, combine the frisée, butter lettuce, and mesclun. Add salt and pepper and toss in the scallions and half of the chives. Dress with the basic vinaigrette.

To serve, arrange the dressed lettuces on 6 large chilled plates. Divide the truffle vinaigrette–dressed vegetables and warm sweetbreads evenly among the plates. Divide out the lobster pieces, making sure each gets several tail medallions, some knuckle meat, and a claw. Slice the foie gras into 1/2-inch-thick slices and portion out among the plates. Drizzle with the remaining truffle vinaigrette and sprinkle with the remaining chives.

Soups, Chowders, and Stews

Chesapeake Chowder

This dish represents our attempt at Kinkead's to feature the bounty of the Chesapeake Bay all in one bowl. Obviously, it would be impossible to include all of the wonderful food products grown and harvested on the Delmarva Peninsula, but this chowder does include some of the more notable products: Chesapeake fish, crabmeat, and shellfish, Silver Queen corn, and Virginia ham. You can leave out the cream if you like and replace it with more fish stock or water. It will not be as rich but the flavor will be fine.

The concept with this chowder is to utilize local food products, so you can substitute Chincoteague oysters for our Bluepoints, or Kumimoto, or even use clams. Cod, halibut, or even salmon can replace the rockfish. Use whichever products are local, fresh, and in season.

18 oysters, any variety

4 tablespoons butter

1 leek, white part only, diced

1 yellow onion, diced (about 1 cup)

3 shallots, minced

1 tablespoon fresh thyme

5 bacon strips, diced

1 tablespoon all-purpose flour

3 cups fish stock (page 254)

2 cups clam juice

1/2 cup dry white wine

2 large potatoes, peeled and diced (about 2 cups)

2 ounces Virginia ham, finely diced

2 cups Silver Queen or other fresh-shucked corn kernels

2 cups heavy cream

1/4 cup sherry

4 drops Tabasco Sauce

16 ounces rockfish or striped bass fillets, skinned and cut into 1-inch cubes

16 ounces jumbo lump crabmeat, picked through for shells

Cracked black pepper

2 tablespoons chopped chives for garnish

Shuck the oysters and strain the liquor through a fine-mesh sieve. Reserve the oysters and liquor separately.

In a sauté pan over medium-high heat, melt the butter until bubbling. Add the leek, onion, shallots, and thyme and cook until the onion is transparent. Transfer from the heat. In a separate large saucepan over medium-high heat, cook the bacon until crisp. Lower the heat, add the flour, and cook the roux for 3 to 4 minutes. Add the fish stock, clam juice, oyster liquor, wine, potatoes, and ham. Add the leek-onion mixture and simmer for about 5 minutes, until reduced by one quarter. Add the corn and cook for 2 minutes. Add the cream, sherry, and Tabasco Sauce and cook for 2 more minutes, stirring so as not to scorch. Add the rockfish, crabmeat, and reserved oysters and cook for 1 minute. Add pepper to taste.

To serve, ladle into in 6 warm soup terrines and garnish with the chives.

Shrimp Bisque with Ricotta and Spring Pea Agnolotti

SERVES 8 (MAKES 2¹/₂ QUARTS)

This is a true bisque in that it is thickened with rice. The recipe calls for shrimp but works well with lobster shells and lobster stock. I like the subtler, sweeter flavor of the shrimp. This soup can be made with or without the agnolotti and, either way, it makes a great main course for lunch. It's a fair amount of work and would be impractical to make in a smaller batch. Note that you can make the base a day or two in advance.

SHRIMP BISQUE

2 pounds medium shrimp (26 to 30 count)

2 tablespoons vegetable oil

3 cloves garlic, minced

1 shallot, minced

1 small fennel bulb, chopped (about 2 cups)

1 leek, white part only, minced (about ¹/₂ cup)

1 yellow onion, diced (about 1¹/₂ cups)

1 stalk celery, diced (about ¹/₂ cup)

10 tablespoons butter

1 level teaspoon kosher salt

¹/₄ teaspoon red pepper flakes

2 bay leaves

1 cup Arborio rice

2 tablespoons tomato paste

4 cups lobster stock (page 254)

4 cups shrimp stock (page 255)

¹/₂ cup cream sherry

2 tablespoons freshly squeezed lemon juice

3 cups half-and-half

4 cups heavy cream

¹/₂ teaspoon Worcestershire sauce

5 drops Tabasco Sauce

1 scallion, chopped diagonally, for garnish

1 teaspoon chervil leaves for garnish

RICOTTA AND SPRING PEA AGNOLOTTI

¹/₂ cup ricotta cheese

1 tablespoon butter

1 clove garlic, minced

¹/₂ shallot, minced

4 medium shrimp (26 to 30 count), peeled and diced

¹/₄ cup fresh-picked English peas, blanched

1 teaspoon chopped chervil leaves

¹/₂ teaspoon kosher salt

¹/₂ teaspoon cracked black pepper

1 large egg

2 teaspoons water

¹/₃ recipe pasta dough (about 9 ounces) (page 266)

Peel and devein the shrimp, reserving the shells for the bisque. Chop 10 of the shrimp and set aside.

To make the bisque base, in a braising pan over medium-high heat, heat the vegetable oil, add the garlic and shallot, and cook for 1 minute. Add the fennel, leek, onion, celery, and 2 tablespoons of the butter and sweat until the onions are transparent. Add the salt, red pepper flakes, bay leaves, and rice and cook for 2 to 3 minutes. Add the tomato paste, lobster stock, shrimp shells, chopped shrimp, and 4 tablespoons of the sherry. Bring to a boil, and then lower the heat to a simmer. Cook for 20 to 30 minutes, stirring frequently, until the liquid is reduced by half. Purée in a blender and strain through a fine-mesh sieve. You should have about 7 cups of base.

Slice the whole peeled shrimp in half lengthwise. In a saucepan over medium heat, melt 2 tablespoons of the butter and sauté the shrimp for 2 to 3 minutes, or until opaque. Transfer from the saucepan and keep warm.

To finish the bisque, add the bisque base to the saucepan and stir in the remaining sherry, the lemon juice, half-and-half, heavy cream, and the Worcestershire and Tabasco. Bring to a simmer and whisk in the remaining butter. Cook for 2 minutes, or until the flavors meld.

To make the agnolotti, press the ricotta through a fine-mesh sieve and set aside. In a sauté pan over medium heat, melt the butter. When bubbling, cook the garlic and shallots for 2 minutes, or until soft. Add the diced shrimp and cook for 1 minute, or until opaque. Transfer to a stainless steel bowl. Add the ricotta, peas, chervil, and salt and pepper and mix together. Refrigerate for about 30 minutes.

Make an egg wash with the egg and 2 teaspoons water.

Roll out the pasta dough into 2 thin sheets. Cut the dough into 12 (or more) 4-inch squares. Place 2 tablespoons of the filling in the center of each pasta square. Brush around the filling with the egg wash. Fold the square in half to form a triangle. Wrap the triangle around your index finger to form a ring. Brush the tips of the agnolotti with the egg wash to make the ring stick together. Chill for at least 30 minutes. When ready to serve the soup, cook the agnolotti in a pot of boiling salted water until they float to the top.

To serve, divide the shrimp halves and cooked agnolotti among 6 warm pasta bowls or, if serving family style, place in a large soup terrine. Pour the hot bisque over and garnish with the scallions and chervil. Serve hot.

Tautog and Nantucket Bay Scallop Chowder with Celeriac

SERVES 6 (MAKES 9 CUPS)

*T*his chowder is a nice marriage of two Nantucket bay species, the firm but sweet tautog and the prized bay scallop. Tautog, also called blackfish or sheepshead, is commonly found close to shore along the North Atlantic coast of the United States. It is a slow-moving fish; when I was growing up on Cape Cod, we often caught them with spear guns.

Tautog's very firm flesh is great for chowders, soups, and stews. Its toughness also makes it fine for braising but less desirable for roasting, grilling, or sautéing. If tautog is not available, any firm-fleshed fish like rockfish (striped bass), monk, wolf fish, or halibut is fine. Likewise, sea scallops are fine if Nantucket bays are not available; the chowder, however, will not have as much natural sweetness.

6 cups fish stock (page 254)

1 cup dry white wine

1 pound Nantucket Bay scallops, connector muscle "feet" separated and reserved

2 ounces salt pork, minced

1/2 cup butter

1 small yellow onion, diced (about 1 1/2 cups)

2 ribs celery, diced (about 1 cup)

3 tablespoons all-purpose flour

2 cups clam juice

1 small celeriac, peeled and diced in 1/2-inch cubes (about 1 1/2 cups)

1 large Idaho potato, peeled, diced, and kept in cold water

2 cups heavy cream

1 teaspoon sea salt

1/2 teaspoon cracked white pepper

1 pound tautog (blackfish) fillets, skinned and cut into 1/2-inch cubes

2 tablespoons coarsely chopped parsley leaves

2 teaspoons chopped fresh dill

2 scallions, chopped

In a saucepan over high heat, bring the fish stock and white wine to a boil. Add the reserved scallop "feet" and cook for 3 to 4 minutes. Strain the broth and reserve.

In a saucepan over medium-high heat, cook the salt pork until brown. Add 4 tablespoons of the butter and the onion and celery. Sauté until the onion is translucent. Add the flour and cook for 3 to 4 minutes to make a roux. Add the fish stock–scallop broth, clam juice, celeriac, and potato and bring to a light boil. Lower the heat and simmer for 5 minutes. Add the heavy cream, salt, pepper, and tautog, and simmer for 2 minutes. Add the scallops and simmer for 1 more minute.

To serve, stir in the remaining butter, the parsley, and dill, and season to taste with salt and pepper. Ladle the chowder into 6 warm bowls and garnish with the scallions.

Lobster Stew with Spring Vegetables and Chervil

obster stews vary wildly, from a simple pan roast of lobster meat, butter, sherry, and light cream to buttery extravagances made with exotic vegetables and truffles. This version lies somewhere in between.

One of the beauties of the simpler versions is that the lovely marriage of sweet lobster meat and pure cream is not lost. Using lobster stock for this dish is not recommended, as it results in a stew that tastes too strongly of lobster shells. The trick is to enhance the lobster flavor without masking it.

3 (1-pound) chicken lobsters

3/4 cup butter

1/3 cup finely chopped yellow onion

1/3 cup finely chopped carrot, plus 1 cup diced

1/3 cup finely chopped celery, plus 1 cup diced

4 tablespoons Cognac or brandy

1 cup cream sherry

2 cups milk

4 cups heavy cream

1 cup quartered button mushrooms

1 cup chopped leeks, white part only

6 scallions, white part only (reserve the greens for another use)

1 cup haricot verts, cut into 1-inch lengths and blanched

1 cup shelled, blanched, and peeled favas

Sea salt

1/4 teaspoon cracked black pepper

1 tablespoon fresh chervil leaves, stems reserved

1 tablespoon chopped chives

In a stockpot, bring 6 quarts of salted water to a boil. Cook the lobsters for about 3 minutes. Remove and run under cold water. Remove all of the meat from the bodies and set aside (it will be slightly raw). Cut the tails into 5 or 6 rounds and leave the claws and knuckle meat intact. Break up the shells and add to a food processor along with the tomalley (lobster liver) and any roe. Pulse several times to coarsely chop.

In a saucepan, melt 2 tablespoons of the butter, add the onion, 1/3 cup finely chopped carrots, and 1/3 cup finely chopped celery, and cook for about 5 minutes over medium heat. Add the chopped lobster shells and cook for 10 minutes, stirring from time to time. Add the Cognac, sherry, chervil stems, milk, and heavy cream and bring to a simmer. Cook for about 40 minutes, until pink. Strain, pressing on the solids, and reserve about 8 cups of lobster cream.

In a sauté pan, melt 2 tablespoons of the butter and cook the mushrooms for about 4 minutes, until browned on all sides. Keep warm.

In a small sauté pan over medium heat, melt 2 tablespoons of the butter, add the diced carrots, diced celery, and leeks, and sweat until soft. Add the scallions and cook for 3 minutes. Add the lobster cream and sautéed mushrooms and bring to a simmer. Add the lobster meat, haricots verts, favas, salt to taste, and the pepper. Cook for about 1 minute more, until the lobster is cooked through. Transfer from the heat and keep warm.

To serve, divide the lobster meat among 6 soup plates and ladle on the stew. Garnish with the chervil and chives and the remaining butter.

Tuna and Tomatillo Soup Yucatan Style

This is a made-to-order soup that utilizes products and flavor combinations of Mexico. It is similar to the Spanish coastal tuna soup called marmitako, *but it uses the chiles, cilantro, and lime of the Yucatan. Although this is not a particularly spicy dish, you can adjust the heat by adding more or less jalapeño to the recipe—or pass around some lime wedges and chopped jalapeño or serrano chiles when you serve it.*

The process in making this dish is to prepare two purées, which are blended together with chicken stock at the final heating. This preserves the color and the freshness of the flavor.

4 tablespoons vegetable oil, plus 3 cups for frying

10 to 12 tomatillos, husks removed, washed, and cut in half

2 large poblano chiles

1 jalapeño, seeded and minced

1 white onion, thickly sliced

2 cloves garlic, minced

1 small can Anaheim or other mild green chiles

1 bunch scallions (about 6), white and green parts diced separately

2 cups loosely packed cilantro leaves

3 cups chicken stock (page 255)

4 (5-inch) corn tortillas, cut in 1/2-inch julienne

1 shallot, minced

16 ounces bluefin, yellowfin, or albacore tuna, skin removed, cut into 1-inch cubes

1 tablespoon freshly squeezed lime juice

1/2 teaspoon kosher salt

1/2 teaspoon freshly ground black pepper

6 tablespoons sour cream

To make the tomatillo purée, in a cast-iron pan over medium-high heat, heat 2 tablespoons of the vegetable oil and add the tomatillo halves, cut side down. The pan should be very hot. Sear on one side until they start to brown, then turn them—very carefully, or they will disintegrate—and cook for 1 more minute on the rounded side. Transfer from the pan and place in a blender.

Wipe the pan dry. Over high heat, toast the poblanos and jalapeño until the skin blisters. Place them in a paper bag and when cool enough to handle, peel off the skins and remove the seeds and stems. Cut into 1/4-inch dice and add to the blender.

Wipe out the cast-iron pan again. Over high heat, toast the onion slices on both sides until charred. Add them to the blender and purée, then pour out into a bowl and reserve. This should make about 2 1/2 cups of tomatillo purée.

To make the cilantro purée, without rinsing the blender canister, add the garlic, the Anaheim chiles, the scallion greens, and 1 1/2 cups of the cilantro leaves. Purée and reserve. This makes about 1 cup.

In a saucepan over medium heat, bring the chicken stock to a boil. Transfer from the heat and keep warm.

Wipe out the cast-iron pan a fourth time and heat the 3 cups vegetable oil over medium heat. Add the tortilla strips and fry until crispy. Drain on paper towels and salt lightly. Strain and reserve the oil for another use.

In a sauté pan over medium heat, heat the remaining 2 tablespoons vegetable oil and sweat the shallot.

Add the diced tuna and brown on two sides. Add the warm reserved chicken stock, the tomatillo purée, and the cilantro purée. Bring to just a simmer. Add the scallion whites, lime juice, and salt and pepper. The lime juice must be added just before serving; if allowed to sit for any amount of time, it will turn the soup an olive drab color.

To serve, portion out the soup into 6 large warm soup plates. Top each with tortilla strips, some sour cream, and the remaining cilantro leaves.

Jasper's Steamer Clam Soup

My friend Jasper White is the proprietor of the Summer Shack restaurants in Cambridge and Boston, Massachusetts. Among his many accomplishments over a long career, Jasper is a James Beard Award winner, chef, and cookbook author of considerable national reputation. Considering he is from New Jersey, Jasper knows as much about New England cooking as anybody. His book Cooking from New England *is probably the definitive tome on the subject.*

Several years ago, Jasper agreed to participate in a charity fundraising dinner when I moved to Washington to open Twenty-One Federal. He did a version of this dish that was his take on a James Beard recipe, Steamer Clam Soup That Cures. It is one awesome soup, giving the diner all the flavor of a bowl of piping hot steamed clams and drawn butter with none of the work. Fortunately for me, Jasper didn't put the recipe in his book. He was kind enough to let me steal it. Here it is, with a little Kinkead's spin on it.

48 to 60 steamer (soft-shell) clams

2 cups water

2 cups dry white wine

1 cup butter cut into $1/2$-inch cubes, plus 2 tablespoons, and extra for the crackers

3 large stalks celery, cut in $1/4$-inch dice (about 2 cups)

1 small celeriac, peeled, diced, and kept in acidulated water (about $1^1/2$ cups)

1 yellow onion, cut into $1/4$-inch dice (about $1^1/2$ cups)

1 cup clam juice

Common crackers, for garnish

3 tablespoons freshly squeezed lemon juice

2 tablespoons chopped fresh parsley

2 tablespoons chervil leaves

$1/2$ teaspoon cracked black pepper

Sea salt

Wash the clams and place them in cold, lightly salted water for 2 hours to purge sand and any impurities. Drain and place in a stockpot over high heat. Cover with the water and wine and steam over high heat for 4 to 6 minutes. Most should be open; discard any that are not. Strain the clams, reserving the liquid. When cool enough to handle, pull the meats from the shells and remove the tough neck skin from the siphon. Discard the skin and shells. Rinse the meats in the reserved cooking liquid and keep warm. Strain the cooking liquid through cheesecloth into a saucepan and reserve. You should have about 9 cups.

In a sauté pan over medium heat, melt the 2 tablespoons of butter. When bubbling, sweat the celery, celeriac, and onion. Add the clam juice and reduce by one quarter.

Meanwhile, preheat the broiler. Top the crackers with the extra butter and toast under the broiler.

Add the reduced pan contents to the reserved cooking liquid. Bring to a simmer and whisk in the 1 cup of cubed butter and the lemon juice. Add the reserved clams and the parsley, chervil, and pepper, and salt to taste.

Serve at once, garnished with the toasted crackers.

Harvest Oyster Stew

The Harvest was a visionary restaurant opened in Cambridge, Massachusetts, in 1975 by noted architect Ben Thompson and his wife, Jane. It was one of the first restaurants in the country to focus on regional American cooking, local American food products, and American growers. It was also the training ground for many now-famous American chefs.

It was at the Harvest that I began to really define a personal cuisine. In many ways, being chef of the Harvest was the best job I ever had. It was also the last pure cooking job I would have. The irony of the restaurant business is that as one proceeds up the food chain, going from chef to executive chef to chef owner, one does precious little of what it was that drew you to the profession in the first place.

The recipe for Harvest Oyster Stew was a favorite of Mr. Thompson. Ben was an extraordinarily creative guy with a unique perspective. Sadly, Ben Thompson passed in the fall of 2002.

The julienne of vegetables in this stew should be very fine—almost filaments of vegetable. You will need about 3 cups, loosely packed.

36 Atlantic oysters (such as Wellfleet, Bluepoint, Nantucket)

1 cup Sauvignon Blanc or other dry white wine

1 large shallot, minced

1 teaspoon Champagne vinegar

2 cups fish stock (page 254)

3 cups heavy cream

2 cups half-and-half

3 tablespoons butter

3 cups loosely packed very fine julienne of vegetables (equal parts onion; celery; carrots; leeks, white part only; celeriac; fennel; and zucchini peelings)

2 teaspoons freshly squeezed lemon juice

1/2 teaspoon fine sea salt

1/2 teaspoon white pepper

1 tablespoon chopped chives for garnish

Shuck the oysters and drain the liquor through a fine-mesh sieve. Chill the oyster liquor and oysters separately. In a noncorrosive saucepan over high heat, combine the wine, shallots, and vinegar and reduce to a glaze. Add the fish stock and cook for 6 to 8 minutes or until reduced by half. Add the heavy cream and half-and-half and cook for 3 to 4 minutes or until reduced to the consistency of heavy cream, or about 5 cups. Keep warm over very low heat.

In a sauté pan over medium heat, melt 2 tablespoons of the butter and, when bubbling, add the vegetables. Sauté until the onions are translucent. Add the oyster liquor and bring to a boil. Lower the heat, add the raw oysters, and poach for about 1 minute.

To serve, place 6 poached oysters in each of 6 warm soup plates, reserving the poaching liquid. Add the cream mixture to the oyster-poaching liquor and bring to a boil. Stir in the lemon juice and salt and pepper and ladle the stew over the oysters. Garnish with the chives and remaining 1 tablespoon butter and serve at once.

Scandanavian Salmon Stew with
Mushrooms and Dill (see page 94)
with Dill Crackers (see page 224)

Mussel, Carrot, and Saffron
Soup with Aïoli and Croutons
(see opposite page)

Mussel, Carrot, and Saffron Soup with Aïoli and Croutons

*T*his is a hearty fall or winter shellfish soup with lots of garlic. It takes its inspiration from the saffron- and tomato-based soups of the Riviera and Marseille. The carrots provide some thickness for the soup and their sweetness harmonizes with the natural sweetness of the mussels. Unlike the Italians, the French have no problem with the concept of serving shellfish with cheese.

48 mussels scrubbed and debearded (Prince Edward Island cultivated are fine) (about 2 pounds)

2 cups dry white wine

1 large shallot, sliced

1/4 cup olive oil

1 yellow onion, diced (about 1 1/2 cups)

1 small leek, white part only, diced (about 1/2 cup)

1/2 teaspoon dried thyme

1/2 teaspoon red pepper flakes

3 carrots, peeled and sliced (about 3 cups loosely packed)

3 cups water

1 teaspoon kosher salt

1/2 teaspoon cracked black pepper

1/4 teaspoon saffron

2 cups vermouth

6 cups fish stock (page 254)

2 cups tomato concassé (page 262) (about 6 plum tomatoes)

4 tablespoons garlic confit (page 264)

Zest and juice of 1 lemon (about 1 1/2 tablespoons of juice)

24 slices baguette

1/2 cup freshly grated Parmesan cheese

1 teaspoon chopped parsley, for garnish

6 to 8 tablespoons aïoli (page 259)

To prepare the mussels, place them in a stockpot with the white wine and the shallot and steam over high heat for 4 to 7 minutes. Most should be open; discard any that are not. Strain and reserve the cooking liquor. When cool enough to handle, pull the mussel meats from the shell and reserve. Discard the shells.

To make the soup base, in a braising pan over medium-high heat, heat 2 tablespoons of the olive oil and sauté the onion, leek, thyme, and red pepper flakes. Cook, stirring occasionally, until the onion starts to brown. Add the carrots and water. Bring to a boil, add the salt and pepper, and cook for about 20 minutes, until the carrots are very tender. Purée in a blender and return to a saucepan.

In a separate saucepan, combine the saffron, vermouth, fish stock, tomato concassé, and garlic confit and bring to a boil. Cook for about 5 minutes, and then add the mussel cooking liquor and the lemon zest and juice. Cook for 2 minutes. Purée in a blender until smooth.

To finish the soup, add the tomato-garlic purée to the saucepan with the carrot purée and bring to a boil. Add salt and pepper to taste. Add the reserved mussel meats. Heat through but do not reboil.

To make the croutons, preheat the oven to 375°F. Brush olive oil onto the baguette slices and top with Parmesan. Bake on a baking sheet in the oven until brown and crisp.

To serve, warm 6 soup plates and, using one third of the aïoli, place a small dollop on the bottom of each. Divide the soup among the soup plates, making sure to divide the mussels evenly (there should be 8 per bowl). Place 2 croutons on each and top with another dollop of aïoli, and a sprinkling of Parmesan and parsley. Pass the remaining croutons, aïoli, and Parmesan separately.

Scandinavian Salmon Stew with Mushrooms and Dill

*M*ost of the best ideas that chefs come up with for new dishes result from trying to use the leftover or less desirable cuts of one product or another. Profitability in a restaurant comes from the total utilization of every food product that arrives at the back door. Chefs are particularly pleased with themselves when they come up with a dish that fulfills three key criteria. First, it uses up a by-product of another dish. Second, it is delicious (and preferably not labor-intensive). Third, it sells well.

When preparing Scandinavian stew (pictured on page 94) at the restaurant, we use the trimmings and smaller cuts of the salmon fillet. This made-to-order stew is a sensational seller, a rich, filling and delicious soup for a cold winter day.

12 ounces salmon fillets (preferably Atlantic), skinned, pin bones removed

3 cups fish stock (page 254) or 2 cups clam juice

1/4 cup dry white wine

4 bacon strips

3 tablespoons butter

2 shallots, minced (about 4 tablespoons)

12 button mushrooms, quartered (about 2 cups)

2 cups heavy cream

2 Yukon gold or other waxy potatoes, peeled and diced (about 2 cups)

1 small yellow onion, finely diced (about 1 cup)

1 small leek, white part only, minced

1 teaspoon sea salt

1/2 teaspoon cracked white pepper

2 tablespoons chopped fresh dill

2 tablespoons chopped chives for garnish

2 dill crackers (page 224), broken up, for garnish

Cut the salmon into 2 by 1/2 by 1/2-inch pieces and refrigerate. In a saucepan over medium heat, combine the fish stock and wine and reduce by one third. In a sauté pan over medium-high heat, cook the bacon until crispy.

Transfer to paper towels to drain. Add 1 tablespoon of the butter to the bacon fat and add half of the shallots and the mushrooms. Sauté until well browned. Transfer to a bowl and wipe out the pan.

In a large saucepan over high heat, combine the reduced fish stock–wine mixture with the cream and bring to a boil. Add the potatoes and cook for about 5 minutes, until tender. Strain the potatoes and return the fish stock–cream mixture to a boil to reduce.

In a saucepan over medium heat, melt 2 the remaining tablespoons butter and sweat the onion, leek, and remaining shallots. Stir in the remaining mushrooms, the bacon, cooked potatoes, and reduced fish stock–cream mixture. Add the salmon. Decrease the heat to medium and simmer for 1 minute and add the salt and pepper to taste.

To serve, stir the dill into the hot stew. Divide the stew among 6 warm soup plates and garnish with the chives and dill crackers.

Tomatillo Gazpacho with Spot Prawns and Radish Salad

or this gazpacho, I like to use a sweet prawn like the Monterey Bay prawn. These are somewhat hard to find, but they are available on the West Coast around February. Alaskan or Pacific Coast spot prawns also work well; that is what we use in Washington D.C. But any high-quality shrimp will do.

8 to 10 large tomatillos, husks removed, washed and
   cut in half

1 cucumber, peeled

1 small yellow onion, diced

2 cloves garlic, minced

2 canned Anaheim chiles, diced

6 scallions, diced

1 serrano chile or jalapeño, minced

1 small bunch cilantro, leaves only (about $^1/_2$ cup packed)

$1^1/_2$ teaspoons kosher salt

$^1/_2$ teaspoon cracked black pepper

2 teaspoons olive oil

4 tablespoons freshly squeezed lime juice

12 spot prawns or other medium shrimp
   (26 to 30 count)

$^1/_2$ teaspoon coriander seeds

1 teaspoon chile powder

2 tablespoons basic vinaigrette (page 262)

RADISH SALAD

4 large red or French breakfast radishes

$^1/_4$ (2-inch-thick) round daikon, peeled

1 teaspoon red wine vinegar

Kosher salt and freshly ground black pepper

On a hot grill or in a cast-iron pan over high heat, sear the tomatillos, cut side down. When starting to blacken, turn very gently and cook for 1 more minute. Remove from the heat and cool.

Julienne the cucumber with a mandolin. Reserve the inner seeds. Dice the julienne into fine dice. Transfer the seared tomatillos and cucumber seeds to a blender and add half the onion, the garlic, Anaheim chiles, scallions, serrano chile, two thirds of the cilantro leaves, $^1/_2$ teaspoon of the salt, and the pepper. Purée in the blender. Add the olive oil. Chill for at least 2 hours. Fold in the diced cucumber, the remaining onion, and the lime juice.

In a saucepan over high heat, add the prawns with enough water to cover, the remaining 1 teaspoon salt, and the coriander seeds. Bring just to a boil. Drain the prawns, discarding the liquid, and chill in an ice-water bath. When cold, drain and peel devein the prawns. Toss at the last minute in a stainless steel bowl with the chile powder and vinaigrette.

To make the radish salad, slice the radishes and daikon into $^1/_8$-inch slices, and then julienne into uniform $^1/_8$-inch matchsticks. In a small bowl, toss the vegetables with the vinegar and salt and pepper to taste.

To serve, ladle the tomatillo gazpacho into 4 chilled bowls. Garnish each with 3 spot prawns, divide the radish salad into the center of each, and garnish with the remaining cilantro leaves.

Minnesota Wild Rice Soup with Pheasant

One day many years ago, when I was chef on Nantucket at Twenty-One Federal, one of our cooks, David Johnson, made this soup as a special. It was his grandmother's recipe and we loved it. It was so American and besides, it goes great with day-after-Thanksgiving turkey sandwiches. Though it has been through a number of alterations over the years, it is still essentially his recipe. I do not know what David has been up to lately, but I hope that, through its appearance here, his grandmother's soup will gain a wider following.

You can substitute chicken or duck for the pheasant, and any combination of mushrooms works fine.

1 (2- to 2¹/2-pound) pheasant or small (2¹/2- to 3-pound) chicken

2 small ham hocks, split

12 cups chicken stock (page 255)

6 bacon strips

1 tablespoon vegetable oil

1 small yellow onion, finely diced (about 1¹/2 cups)

1 small carrot, peeled and diced (about ¹/2 cup)

2 stalks celery, diced (about 1 cup)

1 leek, white part only, diced (about ³/4 cup)

¹/2 teaspoon chopped thyme leaves

4 tablespoons butter

4 tablespoons all-purpose flour

1 cup dry white wine

2 bay leaves

¹/4 cup diced Virginia ham

1 parsnip, peeled and diced (about ¹/2 cup)

¹/3 cup wild rice

¹/2 pound button mushrooms, cleaned and cut in quarters

¹/2 pound chanterelles or other mild mushroom, cleaned and sliced

¹/2 cup dry sherry

1 cup heavy cream

1 teaspoon chopped chives, for garnish

¹/4 cup slivered almonds, toasted, for garnish

Preheat the oven to 400°F. Eviscerate the pheasant, leaving the breasts whole and reserving the giblets (except the liver). Separate the drummers from the thighs. Keep the breast and thighs together. Chop the wings, neck, and drummers. Place these in a roasting pan, along with the carcasses and giblets, and roast for about 40 minutes, until very brown.

Transfer the cooked pheasant meat and bones to a stockpot, add the ham hocks, and cover with the chicken stock. Bring to a boil and reduce by one quarter. Transfer the hocks from the liquid and reserve. Strain the liquid and discard the bones.

In a large soup pot over medium-high heat, cook the bacon until crisp. With a slotted spoon, transfer the cooked bacon and reserve. Add the vegetable oil, onion, carrot, celery, leek, and thyme to the pot and sauté for 2 to 3 minutes, until they start to brown. Stir in 2 tablespoons of the butter and the flour and cook for 2 minutes. Deglaze with the wine and cover with 8 cups of the chicken-pheasant stock. Add the ham hocks, bay leaves, Virginia ham, parsnips, and reserved bacon strips. Bring to a simmer and add the wild rice. Cook for about 40 minutes, until the rice has bloomed.

In a sauté pan over medium-high heat, melt the remaining 2 tablespoons of the butter and sauté the domestic mushrooms and chanterelles for 3 to 4 minutes, or until brown on all sides. Deglaze with the sherry and add the heavy cream. Bring to a boil and add all to the soup pot.

In a saucepan over high heat, bring the remaining stock to a boil. Add the pheasant breast and thighs and reduce the heat to a simmer. Poach the pheasant for about 6 to 8 minutes, or until cooked through. Remove from the stock and pour the stock into the soup pot. Julienne the meat and discard any bones or cartilage from the thigh. Keep warm.

Remove the hocks and bay leaves from the soup. Pick off the meat from the hocks and dice. Return to the soup.

To serve, divide the pheasant meat among 6 large warm soup bowls. Ladle the soup over it and garnish with the chives and toasted almonds. Serve hot.

New Bedford Portuguese Fisherman Stew with Chorizo and Romesco Sauce

Nearly every fishing area around the world has developed some type of seafood soup or stew; this one celebrates the stews of the Portuguese fishermen of southeastern New England. The mixing of pork products and shellfish is a very Portuguese culinary concept quickly adopted by the fishermen of New Bedford and Provincetown, Massachusetts.

Use any type of fish you prefer. Firmer species like monk and wolf fish stand up better than more delicate spices like flounder or scrod. For a real treat, add some lobster to the dish.

Also, use Portuguese-style chorizo in this recipe—Mexican-style chorizo is too crumbly and is often spicier than the dish requires. Linguica or even smoked polish sausage is a better substitute.

6 ounces salt cod fillets

PORTUGUESE STEW BASE

2 Portuguese-style chorizo sausages (about 1 pound)

4 tablespoons olive oil

2 ounces salt pork, finely diced

1 small yellow onion, finely diced (about 1 1/2 cups)

4 cloves garlic, minced

1 teaspoon dried oregano

1/2 teaspoon dried thyme

2 celery stalks, finely diced (about 1 cup)

1 large carrot, peeled and finely diced (about 3/4 cup)

1 small leek, white part only, minced

1 small fennel bulb, finely diced (about 1 cup)

3 bay leaves

1 cup dry white wine (such as Albariño)

3 tablespoons tomato paste

4 cups peeled, diced plum tomatoes and their juice

2 cups clam juice

2 teaspoons red wine vinegar

Juice of 1 orange

Zest of 1 orange

1/2 teaspoon sea salt

1/2 teaspoon cracked black pepper

2 teaspoons freshly squeezed lemon juice

2 tablespoons chopped Italian flat-leaf parsley

STEW

4 tablespoons olive oil

4 cloves garlic, minced

2 shallots, minced

18 littleneck clams, washed

1 cup clam juice or fish stock (page 254)

1 cup vermouth

12 mussels, scrubbed and debearded

4 anchovy fillets

8 ounces cleaned squid, cut into rings

1/4 cup Madeira

8 ounces haddock fillets, skins removed

6 ounces monkfish fillets

8 ounces wolf fish or cod fillets

Sea or bay scallops (about 6 ounces)

12 large shrimp, peeled

4 tablespoons chopped Italian flat-leaf parsley

1 cup freshly grated Parmesan

18 large slices French baguette

2 cups romesco sauce (page 260)

Soak the salt cod for 4 hours. Change the water, then soak overnight. Cut into 2 by 1/2-inch pieces and reserve.

CONTINUED

To make the Portuguese stew base, bring 6 cups of water to a boil. Poach the chorizo for about 2 minutes. Remove from the water and discard the cooking liquid. Peel the outer skin off the chorizo and dice in 1/2-inch cubes.

In a large saucepot over medium-high heat, heat the olive oil. When hot, add the salt pork and fry until brown. Add the chorizo and the onion. Cook for 2 minutes and add the garlic, oregano, and thyme. Cook for 1 to 2 minutes and then add the celery, carrot, leek, fennel, and bay leaves. Sweat for 2 to 3 minutes, stirring from time to time. Deglaze with the white wine and add the tomato paste. Cook for 2 minutes and add the diced tomatoes and their juice, the clam juice, red wine vinegar and the juice and zest of the orange. Bring to a simmer and cook for 8 to 10 minutes. Add the salt and pepper. Cook for 2 minutes, or until the stew base is starting to thicken. Add the lemon juice and parsley and transfer from the heat. This base can be refrigerated for up to 2 days.

To make the stew, in a saucepan over medium-high heat, heat 2 tablespoons of the olive oil. Add the garlic and half of the chopped shallots and sweat the shallots for 2 to 3 minutes. Add the littleneck clams, clam juice, and vermouth. Cover and steam for 3 minutes. Add the mussels, cover, and steam for 3 more minutes. Transfer from the heat and strain the liquid through a fine-mesh sieve.

Discard any clams or mussels that remain unopened. Reserve, keeping shellfish and liquid separate.

In a separate pan, heat the remaining 2 tablespoons olive oil. Add the remaining shallots and sweat until transparent. Add the anchovies and cook for about 2 minutes, until they disintegrate. Add the squid and sauté on both sides. Deglaze with the Madeira and reserve.

In a braising pan over high heat, add the salt cod to the Portuguese stew base. Bring to a boil. Reduce to a simmer and add the reserved clams and mussels, the haddock, monk, wolf fish, scallops and shrimp, and the reserved squid mixture with its cooking liquid. Cook for 2 minutes. Adjust the salt and pepper. At the last minute, add the parsley.

To make the croutons, sprinkle the baguette slices with Parmesan, then bake on a baking sheet in the oven until brown and crisp.

To serve, with a slotted spoon, spoon equal portions of the seafood into 6 large warm pasta bowls. Ladle the remaining stew over the fish and shellfish. Serve immediately with the toasted baguette topped with some romesco sauce. Serve any remaining Parmesan and romesco sauce on the side.

Finnan Haddie Chowder with Johnnycakes

*J*ohnnycakes, once a staple of southern New England cooking, are cornmeal cakes made from a special coarse-ground meal, a New England version of grits. Kenyon Corn Meal Company in Rhode Island still mills it the way it has done for over a century. This method for cooking the cakes has nothing to do with healthy—it's just delicious. Traditionally, johnnycakes were cooked in lard or bacon fat. If you must, cook them in butter or vegetable oil (weenie!).

Finnan haddie is smoked haddock made famous in Scotland centuries ago, in the years when cod was king.

This dish can be served either as a traditional chowder, with the johnnycakes on the side, or as a kind of fricassee, served over the johnnycakes. The amount of cream and clam juice determines the consistency.

FINNAN HADDIE CHOWDER

1 pound center-cut finnan haddie fillets

2 cups milk

8 to 10 bacon strips

2 green bell peppers, seeded, deribbed, and julienned (about 1 cup)

1 yellow onion, julienned (about 1 1/4 cups)

3 tablespoons butter

1 large potato, peeled and diced (about 1 cup)

2 small parsnips, peeled and diced (about 1/2 cup)

3 cups clam juice, chicken stock (page 255), or water

4 cups heavy cream

1/2 pound fresh haddock or cod

1/2 pound baby Maine shrimp (or any other small shrimp)

Sea salt and freshly ground black pepper

JOHNNYCAKES

1/2 cup water

1 cup milk

1 cup johnnycake meal or any other coarse stone-ground cornmeal

1 teaspoon sugar

1/2 teaspoon kosher salt

1 teaspoon butter, plus more for serving

2 tablespoons bacon fat, butter, or vegetable oil

Trim and cut the finnan haddie into medallions or large chunks. Make sure to remove any pin bones. In a saucepan over medium-high heat, bring the milk to a simmer and poach the finnan haddie for 2 to 3 minutes. Drain, reserving the fish and milk separately.

In a sauté pan over medium-high heat, fry the bacon until crisp. Crumble about 4 slices and reserve for the garnish. Save the rest for a BLT or, better, a bacon sandwich on toast with mayonnaise. (Why not? Bacon is so good it's its own food group.) Save the bacon fat for the johnnycakes!

In a braising pan over medium heat, sweat the peppers and onion in 2 tablespoons of the butter for 2 to 3 minutes. Add the potatoes and parsnips. Cover with the fish poaching milk, clam juice, and heavy cream and bring to a simmer. Cook for about 5 minutes, until the potatoes are tender. Add the haddock chunks and cook for 2 minutes. Gently strain out the solids; reserve and keep warm.

CONTINUED

Place the liquid over high heat and reduce to the thickness of light cream. At the last minute, add the shrimp and cook for 1 minute. Add salt and pepper to taste and finish with the remaining 1 tablespoon butter.

To make the johnnycakes, in a saucepan over medium-high heat, bring the water and milk to a boil. Add the cornmeal, sugar, and salt and stir to form a medium thick batter. If you like them thinner, add more boiling milk. Stir in the butter. In a sauté pan over medium heat, heat the bacon fat. Drop tablespoonfuls of the batter into the pan to form cakes about 3 inches in diameter and $1/2$ inch thick. Cook for 6 minutes on each side. Do not crowd the pan. Monitor the heat so it is not too hot, or they will scorch. Cook until nicely browned. Drain on paper towels and keep warm.

To serve, divide the finnan haddie, haddock, and vegetables into 6 large warm soup plates. Pour the chowder over and garnish with the crumbled bacon. Serve the warm johnnycakes on the side with lots of butter.

TOM AND THE GOVERNOR

Tom Kahoe has been a waiter at Kinkead's for several years. Though extremely professional and efficient, Tom is one of those special individuals who make the restaurant fun for staff and guests alike. Restaurant work can be very demanding and stressful, so workers who are quick witted, can tell a good story, and most importantly, laugh at themselves are held in high esteem.

Tom Ridge, our first Secretary of Homeland Security, dines at Kinkead's from time to time. Prior to Congress elevating the new department to cabinet status, Governor Ridge and his wife were dining with another couple at the restaurant. Tom Kahoe was their server. After presenting menus and taking cocktail orders, Tom returned to the table to explain some menu items and answer questions about the night's offerings. After he'd answered all of their questions, Kahoe inquired, "Governor Ridge, I have a question for you. I can understand why you are not addressed as Mr. Secretary right now, since yours is not officially a cabinet level appointment. But why are you addressed in the print and electronic media as Governor, when you are no longer the governor of Pennsylvania?"

Governor Ridge replied, "Good question. When the president asked me to take the job of Director of Homeland Security, he asked me which title I would prefer. I stated that the last elected position I had held was governor and that I was comfortable with that title." To which President Bush replied, "Fine, Governor it is." Governor Ridge finished his story by saying, "But frankly, I prefer to be called just Tom." Not missing a beat, Kahoe replied, "That's funny, my name is Tom, too, but I prefer to be called Governor!"

Pasta and Rice

Sweet-Potato Gnocchi with Pancetta, Chanterelles, Walnuts, and Sage

SERVES 6

*G*nocchi is a food that generally elicits either raves or sneers. My Italian grandchildren are a good example. Izzy, who is ten, hates 'em. But he doesn't like polenta, either. It's a texture thing with him. Elisa, my eight-year-old granddaughter, can't get enough of them. I have seen her eat a plate of maybe two dozen large gnocchi in one sitting. And then ask for more.

Jeff Gaetjen, my chef at Colvin Run Tavern, has been with me for 15 years, through three restaurants. JG is the type of cook who will work at a dish he wants to master until it is perfect. The trick to this version is to sauté the gnocchi after they are boiled. It adds lots of flavor and diminishes that dough-ball texture problem you have with some gnocchi. Deep-fried sage makes a good garnish.

2 large Idaho potatoes

1 Yukon gold potato

1 large sweet potato

1 cup all-purpose flour, plus more as needed

3 egg yolks

2 tablespoons kosher salt, plus more as needed

1/2 teaspoon cracked black pepper, plus more as needed

1/4 cup Parmigiano-Reggiano cheese

1/4 cup butter, melted, plus 1/4 cup at room temperature

1 cup olive oil

2 ounces pancetta, cut in 1/4-inch dice

1/2 pound chanterelles, cleaned and sliced if necessary

1 small shallot, minced

1/4 cup coarsely chopped walnuts

1 cup chicken stock (page 255)

6 large sage leaves, chiffonade, plus 6 whole leaves, for garnish

2 tablespoons shredded Parmigiano-Reggiano

Preheat the oven to 400°F. Place the Idaho and Yukon potatoes and sweet on a baking sheet and bake for 60 to 75 minutes, until tender and dry.

Place the flour on a clean work surface and form it into a bowl. While the potatoes are still hot, split them and scrape out the flesh. With a potato ricer, rice all of the potatoes into the flour. Make a well in the center and add the egg yolks, salt, pepper, cheese, and the melted butter. Using your hands, work in to make a dough that is moist but not sticky. If too sticky, add a little flour.

On a floured sheet pan or surface, roll the dough into 1/2- inch-wide cylinders and cut the cylinder into 1/2-inch pieces. Roll the pieces into 1/2- inch balls; try to keep them all the same size. Using a gnocchi paddle or a fork, roll the balls along the length of the paddle or fork tines with your fingers to make a small grooved oval shape.

When all are done, bring a pot of salted water to a boil. Cooking in batches, cook the gnocchi for 1 or 2 minutes, until they float to the top. Using a slotted spoon, transfer to a parchment-lined baking sheet, and drizzle with a little olive oil. At this point you can refrigerate them for up to 1 day.

In a sauté pan over medium-high heat, heat a little olive oil, add the pancetta, and sauté until crispy. Remove the pancetta, add the chanterelles, and sauté until they are tender and starting to brown. Add the shallot and walnuts and sweat for 1 to 2 minutes. Add the stock and return the cooked pancetta to the pan. Reduce by one third and then whisk in the butter and the sage chiffonade. Add salt and pepper to taste. Pancetta is salty, so you won't need much salt. Keep warm.

Wipe out the sauté pan, and over medium-high heat, heat olive oil and sauté the cooked gnocchi, in batches, until brown and a little crispy on both sides. Keep warm. When all are cooked, portion out the gnocchi among 6 warm plates and top with the pancetta and chanterelles. Garnish each with a sage leaf and Parmigiano-Reggiano.

Cavatappi with Sausage, Mushrooms, Garlic, Sage, and Cream

*W*hen my first grandson was born, my wife and I flew to Italy to see the new arrival. Aside from the extraordinary joy of seeing this cute little fellow, Isidoro, for the first time, it was also Christmas time.

In Italy, at the Christmas Eve dinner seven fishes are traditionally served. For this special Natale dinner, just one would suffice. Before the cod fish main course, we had spaghetti arrabbiata, with tomato, pancetta, hot pepper flakes, and traditional sheep's milk pecorino cheese; ravioli al pana (with cream and Parmesan); and a spaghetti variation on this cavatappi with sausage and mushrooms. Since that first visit we have eaten in well over a hundred restaurants all over Italy, but that meal remains one of the finest I've eaten in the country. In light of the circumstances of Izzy's birth that Christmas season, it was certainly the most memorable.

I often cook this pasta dish at home. This version uses cavatappi—a long, curly, thick macaroni with ridges that holds the sauce well—but really, any shape will work. The sauce freezes well, so make extra.

2 cups veal or beef stock (page 256)

4 to 5 large dried porcini slices

1 pound sweet Italian sausage (preferably with fennel)

3 tablespoons olive oil

2 tablespoons butter

4 large porcini mushrooms (frozen can be used, or another wild mushroom)

18 button mushrooms, washed and quartered (about 1 1/2 pounds)

4 cloves garlic, minced

1/4 cup Madeira

2 cups heavy cream

4 sage leaves, chiffonade

Kosher salt and freshly ground black pepper

1 1/2 pounds cavatappi or other high-quality dried spiral pasta

3 tablespoons Parmigiano-Reggiano cheese

In a small saucepan, over high heat, bring the stock to a boil and add the dried porcini. Decrease to a simmer for 3 to 4 minutes, and then transfer from the heat and let steep until the dried mushrooms soften. Strain the porcini-flavored stock and reserve. Chop the rehydrated porcini.

Cut the membrane off the sausages and discard it; crumble the sausage by hand. (If the sausage does not have fennel, add the fennel). Slice the fresh porcini and reserve. In a heavy-sided sauté pan over medium heat, heat 2 tablespoons of the olive oil and cook the sausage until brown. Drain off the fat and reserve the cooked sausage meat.

Wipe out the pan and add the remaining 1 tablespoon olive oil and 1 tablespoon of the butter. Over medium heat, sauté the fresh porcini and button mushroom quarters in the oil-butter mixture. When they start to brown, add the garlic and the remaining butter and cook until all are browned. Deglaze with Madeira and let the liquid in the pan reduce to a glaze. Transfer to a saucepan. Add the porcini-flavored stock and rehydrated porcinis and reduce by half. Add the cream and reduce until it starts to thicken. Add the sausage. Season with salt and pepper to taste.

Meanwhile, cook the pasta in a large pot of boiling salted water for about 11 minutes, or according to the package's directions, until al dente. Drain and return to the pot, leaving about 1 tablespoon of the cooking water in the pot.

To serve, toss the cavatappi with just enough of the sausage cream sauce to coat. Serve in 4 to 6 pasta bowls and garnish with the Parmesan-Reggiano.

Wild Mushroom Ravioli with Mushroom Broth, Creamed Leeks, Porcini, and Frigo Parmesan

This is a fairly complicated and time-consuming dish, but the results are well worth the effort. It was Tracy O'Grady's swan song to Kinkead's and one of the best dishes she ever came up with. She would have won the Bocuse d'Or with this baby. The ravioli are terrific by themselves and can be used with any number of traditional pasta sauces. In this porcini broth, they are sublime.

Frigo is a dish found in many bars in the Friuli region of Italy; it is served in the frigo bars to accompany wine and drinks. They use many kinds of cheese, most often Montasio. In this recipe we use Parmesan, baked until crisp and broken up over the ravioli instead of traditional shredded Parmesan. It provides a delicious flavor and textural contrast.

RAVIOLI

1/2 pound pasta dough (page 266)

3/4 cup veal stock (page 256) or other meat stock

2 tablespoons butter

2 cloves garlic, minced

2 shallots, minced

12 ounces domestic button mushrooms, cleaned and sliced

4 ounces wild mushrooms (such as chanterelle, or morels, but not shiitakes)

3 to 4 slices of dried porcini, soaked in warm water for 30 minutes to rehydrate and soaking liquid reserved

1/4 cup cream sherry

1/2 teaspoon tomato paste

2 teaspoons chopped Italian flat-leaf parsley

1/4 cup heavy cream

1/4 cup cream cheese

1/2 teaspoon kosher salt

Cracked black pepper

3 tablespoons ricotta cheese

1 large egg

1/2 cup cornmeal

MUSHROOM BROTH

3 tablespoons olive oil

1 small yellow onion, sliced

3 cloves garlic, sliced

2 pounds button mushrooms, sliced

1 cup Madeira

3 or 4 sprigs thyme

2 sprigs rosemary

6 to 10 slices dried porcini

2 cups chicken stock (page 255)

2 cups water

1 teaspoon kosher salt

1/2 teaspoon cracked black pepper

2 leeks, green part only

CREAMED LEEKS

1 tablespoon butter

2 leeks, white part only, minced

1 cup heavy cream

Kosher salt and freshly ground black pepper

1 tablespoon olive oil

1 clove garlic, minced

6 fresh porcini or other fresh wild mushrooms, cleaned and sliced

1 cup grated Parmigiano-Reggiano cheese

1 teaspoon chopped chives, for garnish

To make the ravioli dough, let the pasta dough come to room temperature.

CONTINUED

In a saucepan over high heat, cook the veal stock for 3 to 4 minutes, or until reduced by two thirds.

In a sauté pan over medium heat, melt the butter. When hot, sweat the garlic and shallots. Add the domestic and wild mushrooms and rehydrated porcini and sauté until they are brown and most of the liquid is reduced. Add the sherry, tomato paste, and parsley and cook to a glaze. Add the veal stock reductions, the strained liquid from soaking the porcini, and the cream, cream cheese, salt, and pepper. Reduce to the thickness of heavy cream. Remove from the heat and let cool. Transfer to the bowl of a food processor and pulse several times, to the consistency of coarse duxelles. Fold in the ricotta and chill for 20 to 40 minutes.

To make the broth, in a braising pan over medium-high heat, heat the olive oil. When hot, add the onion and garlic and cook until they just start to brown. Add the mushrooms and sauté until they are brown and almost all of the liquid is evaporated. Deglaze with the Madeira and add the thyme, rosemary, dried porcini, stock, water, salt, pepper, and greens. Bring to a boil and reduce by one quarter. Pass through a coarse strainer, pressing on the solids to extract the mushroom liquid. Discard the solids and strain again through a fine-mesh sieve. Keep warm.

To make the ravioli, make an egg wash with the egg and a little water. Using a pasta roller, roll out a sheet of the pasta dough. The sheet should be almost thin enough to see through. Every three inches or so, place a hefty teaspoon of the mushroom filling mixture on the sheet. Dip your finger into the egg wash and make a circle around the filling to create a seal for the ravioli. Make as many ravioli as the pasta will allow. You can freeze extras for later. When all of the filling is used, cover with another thin sheet of pasta. With your hands, press the top layer of pasta around the mushroom filling. Do not tear the pasta. Cut out each ravioli with a 3-inch round cutter (or a square cutter if you prefer). Check that each ravioli is completely sealed on all sides. Place on a parchment-lined sheet pan and sprinkle with cornmeal. Refrigerate. These ravioli must be used within 24 hours or frozen.

To prepare the leeks, in a sauté pan over medium heat, melt the butter and sweat the leeks. Do not brown. Add the cream and reduce until most of the liquid is evaporated. Add salt and pepper to taste and keep warm.

In a sauté pan over medium-high heat, heat the olive oil and sweat the garlic. Add the porcini slices so they do not overlap. Sauté until brown on both sides. Add salt and pepper to taste and keep warm.

Preheat the oven to 300°F. Sprinkle the Parmesan cheese in a single layer on a silpat or greased baking sheet and bake for 15 to 20 minutes, until all is melted, like a giant lace cookie. Remove from the oven and let cool. With a metal spatula, scrape up the cheese. It should break up. You want it crumbly.

To cook the ravioli, place in a large pot of simmering salted water and cook for 1 to 2 minutes, until they pop to the surface.

To serve, portion out the creamed leeks in the centers of 4 large pasta bowls. Place 3 ravioli around the leeks and pour about 1/2 cup of the mushroom broth over the ravioli. Garnish with the sautéed porcini, a sprinkling of the Parmesan, and chopped chives.

Lobster and Macaroni Gratin

This dish can be used as a first course or as an accompaniment to a main-course lobster or fish dish. Though any small macaroni pasta shape can be used, it seems to work best with little shells or ditalini (little tubes). You can make this dish in one large gratin dish or in six 10-ounce individual ovenproof baking dishes. The recipe calls for roasting and peeling red bell pepper, but canned pimientos— or better, Piquillo peppers—are an acceptable alternative.

2 (1 1/2-pound) lobsters

1/4 cup vegetable oil, plus more for sautéing the peppers

1/4 cup butter, plus more as needed

1 clove garlic, minced

2 teaspoons all-purpose flour

1/2 cup cream sherry

2 teaspoons tomato paste

2 cups heavy cream

2 cups milk

1 cup crème fraîche

Kosher salt and freshly ground black pepper

2 red bell peppers

1 pound ditalini or other shape of small, high-quality dried pasta

1/2 cup shredded Gruyère cheese

1/4 cup shredded Parmesan cheese

1 cup breadcrumbs

To prepare the lobsters, bring a stockpot filled with 4 inches of salted water to a boil. Steam the lobsters for 4 minutes and remove. They will still be uncooked in the center. Break off the claws and steam for another 4 to 5 minutes. When cool, remove all tail, claw and body meat and chill. Chop the shells and legs or pulse them in a food processor.

In a large, noncorrosive saucepan over high heat, heat the 1/4 cup oil and 1/4 cup butter. When hot, add the chopped shells and cook until they start to brown. Add the garlic and sauté for 1 minute. Add the flour and cook for 2 more minutes. Deglaze with the sherry. Add the tomato paste, cream, milk, and crème fraîche and bring to a boil. Lower the heat to a simmer. Stirring frequently, let cook for about 15 minutes, until thick enough to coat the back of a spoon. Add salt and pepper to taste and strain through a sieve, pressing on the shells to extract all the juices. Strain again through a fine-mesh sieve.

Dice the lobster tail and knuckle meat and one claw. Slice the remaining claws in half lengthwise. You should have 6 half claws for garnish. In a saucepan, bring 2 cups of the lobster cream to a simmer over medium-low heat. Add the diced lobster meat, except the claws, and simmer for 2 to 3 minutes. Remove from the heat.

In a cast-iron pan over high heat, sear the red peppers in a little oil until blackened on all sides. Alternatively, you can grill the peppers. Transfer to a bag and let sit for 10 minutes. When cool enough to handle, peel and seed the peppers and dice them into 1/4-inch cubes.

Meanwhile, to prepare the pasta, bring a pot of salted water to a boil. Add the *ditalini* and cook, per package directions, until al dente. Do not overcook. Toss the pasta in the remaining butter to coat and reserve; do *not* refrigerate!

CONTINUED

Preheat the oven to 400°F. In a mixing bowl, combine the cooked pasta, diced pepper, most of the Gruyère, and the 2 cups of lobster cream with the added lobster meat. Mix thoroughly and check the salt and pepper balance. Butter 1 large gratin dish or 6 individual ovenproof gratin dishes. Place the mixture in the dish or dishes and top with the remaining lobster cream and Gruyère, Parmesan, and breadcrumbs. Dot with butter and bake in the oven for 10 to 15 minutes, until brown and bubbling. Warm the reserved lobster claws and use as garnish. Serve hot.

MADAME BELLINI

In 1987 I moved to Washington D.C. to open my former restaurant, Twenty-One Federal. Bill Collison was the second person I hired, and he has been working in my restaurants ever since. Bill is a meticulous server. When we have a party that absolutely, positively, must have perfect service, whose guests must be well taken care of, Bill is our man.

In addition to being a great waiter, Bill will always go the extra mile to help the restaurant or give support to a charity function. He played Santa Claus for the kids at our annual Christmas party. One year he even dressed as the Easter Bunny for a charity event. Everyone was quite relieved that he thought better of appearing on New Year's Eve at Kinkead's as a diaper-clad baby. A very scary thought, indeed!

Billy's finest portrayal, however, was at a carnival we put on to defray the medical expenses of a coworker who had been in an automobile accident. We had carnival rides, a yard sale, and the ever-popular dunk tank. Billy's contribution was to set up a booth as the carnival's fortune teller.

Jaws hit the ground when Madame Bellini, Billy's alter ego, arrived in full Hungarian gypsy regalia. Small children cowered behind their mothers. This was not just Billy in drag, but Billy in total gypsy persona. He had so much makeup on we all thought he would need a chisel to remove it. Carnival attendees didn't know what to think—especially those who did not work with Billy.

Madame Bellini had a steady line outside "her" little tent and folding card table for four straight hours. Madame read palms and told fortunes, all in her thick Eastern European accent. He—er, she—was the hit of the event. The most amazing part was that the vast majority of those whose palms were read believed the gypsy was for real. We overheard many conversations about how remarkably accurate and clairvoyant Madame Bellini was! Those palm readings raised several hundred dollars that day.

A sad postscript to the Madame Bellini story is that a few years later, she took her props on a trip to New York City. Her set of giant fake boobs was stolen from the car. Nothing else was missing, just the prosthetics. Billy is still upset about the loss of those falsies. Sadly, we have never seen the return of Madame Bellini.

Clam, Cockle, and Parsley Risotto with Lemon and Garlic

SERVES 4

ockles are actually several separate species, some clams, some not. All are hard-shelled mollusks found on both Atlantic and Pacific coasts and now starting to be harvested commercially. The cockles being harvested off the Rhode Island coast are delicious, with a more delicate flavor than littlenecks, and the shells have an algae-green tint. In the British Isles and parts of the Mediterranean, cockles are highly prized. Generally 1 to 2 inches across, they can be prepared like littlenecks or Manila clams. Expect to see cockles gain in popularity. If you cannot find fresh cockles, any kind of clam or other shellfish will be just fine.

24 littleneck clams

36 cockles

1 bunch Italian flat-leaf parsley, stems and leaves separated

4 cups fish stock (page 254)

3 cups chicken stock (page 255)

$1/2$ cup dry white wine

2 tablespoons olive oil

8 cloves garlic, sliced

$1/4$ cup butter

1 small yellow onion, diced (about 1 cup)

2 cups Arborio or canaroli rice

Grated zest and juice of 1 lemon

$1/2$ teaspoon kosher salt

$1/4$ teaspoon cracked black pepper

1 tablespoon chopped chervil

Wash the clams and cockles in cold water. In a saucepan over high heat, heat the parsley stems, 2 cups of the fish stock, and the wine until steaming. Add the clams and cockles, cover, and cook until the shells are steamed open. Remove the clams and cockles from the broth. Discard any that did not open. Strain the broth, add it to the remaining fish stock, and bring to a boil. Reserve the parsley. In a separate saucepan, bring the chicken stock to a boil, then decrease the heat to a simmer.

Remove the clam meats from the shells and discard the shells. Remove all but 12 of the cockle meats from the shells; reserve these for garnish.

In a large noncorrosive saucepan over medium-high heat, heat the olive oil and sauté the garlic, stirring, until it is just starting to brown. Remove the garlic and set aside. Add 3 tablespoons of the butter. When hot, add the onion and sweat for 3 minutes. Increase the heat to high, add the rice, and sauté for about 3 minutes, until all the grains are coated with the hot butter and oil. Add the simmering chicken stock and cook, stirring frequently, until almost all of the liquid has been incorporated into the rice. Add 2 cups of the boiling fish-clam stock and cook, stirring gently, until the liquid has been mostly absorbed into the rice. Add the remaining boiling fish-clam stock, the sautéed garlic, the lemon zest and juice, and the salt and pepper and stir until creamy and the rice is just a hint al dente. Coarsely chop the parsley leaves and stir them into the risotto along with the chervil and the remaining 1 tablespoon butter. Serve in warm soup plates. Garnish with the opened cockles.

Crabmeat Risotto with Favas, Asparagus, and Arneis

SERVES 4

There are a few things you need to know to master the fine art of risotto making. First, use high-quality, fresh rice. The two main types generally available in this country are arborio and carnaroli. Either is fine for this recipe, but I prefer the smaller-grained carnaroli. Second, be sure to coat the rice with the hot oil or butter so it seals each grain. Finally, use boiling stock in each of the three stock additions. Boiling stock extracts the maximum rice starch; this gives risotto its creamy texture.

This risotto, like the one on page 113, has no Parmesan. Italians are very fussy about the concept that fish and seafood should never be accompanied by cheese. Arneis is a dry white wine from the Piedmont region of Italy.

1 cup shelled fava beans

1 bunch large (not jumbo) asparagus, peeled

1 pound jumbo lump crabmeat

2 1/2 cups chicken stock (page 255)

2 cups lobster stock (page 254)

2 tablespoons olive oil

5 tablespoons butter

1 large shallot, minced

2 cups Arborio or canaroli rice

1 cup Arneis or Sauvignon Blanc

1 teaspoon kosher salt

1/4 teaspoon white pepper

2 tablespoons chopped chervil

2 tablespoons chopped chives

1 teaspoon chopped tarragon

Juice and zest of 1 lemon

Blanch the fava beans in boiling salted water for about 3 minutes, until just firm. Refresh in an ice-water bath and peel off the outer skin. Bring a braising pan of salted water to a boil. (If you are blanching a lot of asparagus it is best to tie them in bundles, but for small quantities like this it isn't necessary; it's more work than it's worth.) Blanch the asparagus for 2 to 3 minutes, until just tender. Shock in an ice-water bath and drain, reserving about 1/2 cup of the cooking water. Cut off the bottom third of the asparagus stems, chop, and place in a blender with enough of the cooking water to make a purée; you may not need all of it. Purée, strain through a fine-mesh sieve, and set aside. Cut the remaining asparagus stalks diagonally into 1 1/2-inch lengths.

Pick gently through the crabmeat for shells and then refrigerate. Place the chicken and lobster stocks in separate saucepans and bring to a boil.

In a large noncorrosive saucepan over medium-high heat, heat the olive oil and 3 tablespoons of the butter. When hot, add the shallot and sweat for 2 minutes. Add the rice and sauté for about 2 minutes, until all the grains are covered with the hot fat. Add the Arneis and 1 1/4 cups of the boiling chicken stock and cook, stirring frequently, until almost all of the liquid is incorporated. Lower the heat to medium, add the boiling lobster stock, and cook, stirring, until the liquid is mostly incorporated. Add the remaining boiling chicken stock, the asparagus purée, the cut asparagus, favas, and salt and pepper, and stir until creamy and the rice is just a hint al dente. Stir in the chervil, chives, and tarragon, the lemon juice and zest, and the remaining 2 tablespoons butter. Serve in warm soup plates.

Cherry Tomato, Artichoke,
Pancetta, and Basil Risotto
(see page 116)

Crabmeat Risotto with Favas,
Asparagus, and Arneis
(see opposite page)

Cherry Tomato, Artichoke, Pancetta, and Basil Risotto

SERVES 4

The small tomatoes in this recipe can be any kind you like, but try for a mix of sizes, shapes, and colors—the more varieties, the better. This risotto takes a little more liquid than the previous two because the Parmesan tends to tighten the risotto more.

4 tablespoons olive oil

4 ounces pancetta, diced into 1/4 inch cubes

1 pint various vine-ripened cherry and currant tomatoes

6 cups chicken stock (page 256), vegetable stock, or water

12 baby artichokes, halved

1/4 cup butter

1 small yellow onion, diced (about 1 cup)

2 cloves garlic, minced

2 cups Arborio or carnaroli rice

1/2 cup dry white wine

1/2 cup shredded Parmigiano-Reggiano cheese

1 teaspoon lemon juice

1 teaspoon lemon zest

1 teaspoon kosher salt

1/2 teaspoon cracked black pepper

12 large basil leaves, chiffonade

1 tablespoon chopped fresh parsley

In a sauté pan over medium-high heat, heat 2 tablespoons of the olive oil and cook the pancetta until crispy. Transfer the pancetta onto paper towels to drain. Reserve the rendered fat and oil mixture.

Slice the larger cherry tomatoes in half; leave the currant tomatoes whole.

In a saucepan, bring the chicken stock to a boil, then decrease the heat to a simmer.

Place 4 of the artichokes (8 halves) and a little water in a blender and purée. Strain and reserve.

In a sauté pan over medium-high heat, heat the remaining 2 tablespoons olive oil and sauté the artichoke halves, cut side down, until golden. Turn and heat through. Keep warm.

To prepare the rice, in a separate large noncorrosive saucepan over medium-high heat, heat the rendered fat and oil mixture and 3 tablespoons of the butter. When hot, add the onion and sweat for 2 minutes. Add the garlic and sweat 1 more minute. Increase the heat to high, add the rice, and sauté, stirring, until all the grains are coated with the hot fat, about 2 minutes. Deglaze with the white wine and add 2 cups of the boiling stock. Cook the rice, stirring frequently, until almost all of the liquid is incorporated. Lower the heat to medium and add 2 more cups of the boiling stock and the reserved cooked pancetta. Keep stirring and cook until the liquid is almost fully incorporated. Add the remaining boiling stock, half of the cheese, the artichoke purée, the lemon juice and zest, and the salt and pepper and stir until creamy. The entire three-step cooking process should take between 16 and 18 minutes. The rice should be just a hint al dente.

To serve, stir in the halved cherry tomatoes, warm artichoke halves, basil, parsley, and the remaining 1 tablespoon butter, and divide into 6 warm soup plates. Sprinkle on the remaining cheese and serve immediately.

Finfish

Pepita-Crusted Salmon with Chiles, Corn, and Shrimp Ragoût

his dish is without question the best-selling preparation served at Kinkead's. It is our signature dish. Customers have told servers at Kinkead's time and time again that this was the best salmon dish they have ever eaten.

Though there are a lot of ingredients, it is really a very simple dish to put together. We've found it's easiest to garnish the dish with drizzles of cilantro and ancho crema when the creams are in plastic squeeze bottles.

ANCHO CREMA

1 ancho chile

1 tablespoon freshly squeezed orange juice

1/4 teaspoon kosher salt

1/2 cup Salvadoran crema or sour cream

CILANTRO CREAM

1/4 teaspoon kosher salt

1 cup loosely packed cilantro leaves

1 scallion, chopped

2 tablespoons mayonnaise

4 tablespoons sour cream

SALMON

Kernels from 2 ears corn (about 2 cups)

1/2 cup pepitas, toasted

1 cup tortilla chips

Sea salt and cracked black pepper

30 ounces salmon fillets, skinned and cut into 6 portions

1 cup buttermilk

SHRIMP RAGOÛT AND TOMATO RELISH

1/2 cup peanut or vegetable oil

1 small yellow onion, diced (about 1 cup)

2 cloves garlic, minced

1/4 cup dry white wine

4 scallions, diced

2 poblano chiles, roasted, peeled, and diced

5 fresh tomatillos, diced

2 russet potatoes, peeled, diced, and blanched (about 2 cups)

3 tablespoons freshly squeezed lime juice

6 plum tomatoes, peeled, seeded, and diced (about 2 1/2 cups)

1 cup (2 sticks) butter

18 medium shrimp (26 to 30 count), peeled, deveined, and cut into large dice

Kosher salt and freshly ground black pepper

1 bunch cilantro, leaves only (about 3/4 cup loosely packed)

8 ounces jumbo lump crabmeat (picked for shells)

1 teaspoon olive oil

To make the ancho crema, in a saucepan over high heat place the ancho with enough water to cover. Bring to a boil and cook for about 5 minutes, until soft. Strain and dry. Remove the seeds and stems. In a blender, combine the softened ancho, orange juice, and salt. Purée to a paste. If too dry, add a little water. In a stainless steel bowl, mix the purée into the Salvadoran cream. The crema should be thick but pourable. Refrigerate for up to 2 days.

To make the cilantro cream, in a small saucepan bring 2 cups of water and 1/8 teaspoon of the salt to a boil. Blanch the cilantro leaves and scallion for 1 minute and refresh in an ice-water bath. Strain and squeeze dry. Transfer to a blender and purée. Place the purée in a stainless steel bowl,

CONTINUED

add the mayonnaise, sour cream, and remaining salt, and mix well. Refrigerate for up to 2 days.

To make the salmon, preheat the oven to 375°F. Blanch the corn in salted, boiling water for 4 minutes, or until tender. Strain and reserve.

In a food processor, place the pepitas and tortilla chips and pulse to a medium coarse mixture.

Salt and pepper each salmon fillet and dip into the buttermilk on one side only. Next, dip each fillet into the pepita-tortilla mixture. Let rest in the refrigerator for 5 minutes.

In a sauté pan over medium-high heat, heat 2 tablespoons of the peanut oil. When hot, sauté the fillets, coated side down, for 3 minutes or so, until they start to brown. Carefully turn over and place in the oven for 4 to 6 minutes, until just barely cooked in the center. You will most likely need to do this in two batches for 6 portions.

To make the shrimp ragoût, in a sauté pan over medium-high heat, heat 2 tablespoons of the peanut oil and sauté the onions until transparent. Add the garlic and cook for 2 minutes. Deglaze with the white wine and add the blanched corn, scallions, poblanos, tomatillos, potatoes, 2 tablespoons of the lime juice, and half of the diced tomatoes. Cook for about 2 minutes and whisk in the butter, 1 tablespoon at a time. Add the shrimp and cook for 1 to 2 minutes. Chop half of the cilantro leaves and set some aside for garnish. Add salt and pepper to taste. Transfer from the heat and stir in most of the chopped cilantro leaves and crabmeat.

To make a tomato relish, combine the remaining tomatoes with the olive oil, the remaining chopped cilantro, and the remaining 1 tablespoon lime juice.

To serve, divide the shrimp ragoût onto 6 warm plates. There should be slightly more than 3/4 cup on each. Top with a fillet of salmon. To garnish, drizzle on the ancho crema and cilantro cream. Top each fillet with the tomato relish and sprinkle with the whole cilantro leaves.

Portuguese Fisherman–Style Baked Haddock with Clams and Chorizo

This hearty dish, perfect for late fall or winter, was inspired by the cooking of the fishermen who work the waters off New Bedford and Fall River in southeastern New England. Though clearly far more complex than the simple fare those fishermen would prepare, it retains the pork and shellfish combination still popular in that Portuguese community. In days gone by, their ancestors prepared hearty meals for the crew upon returning to the docks with the days' catch. Cod was king, so they used the fish caught in the nets with the cod or by catch to make their stews and one-pot meals. What we would now call "trash fish" were whatever species they landed that could not be sold.

We have served many variations of this dish over the years. Haddock, a relative of cod, is used here, but monkfish and wolf fish work very well with this preparation. While clams and haddock, or cod and pork, may seem to be odd combinations, it is a wonderful mix popular with Portuguese cooks on both sides of the Atlantic.

6 ounces salt cod

36 ounces haddock fillets, skinned, bones removed (at least 30 ounces cleaned)

2 cups cracker crumbs

1/2 teaspoon paprika

Kosher salt

1/2 teaspoon freshly ground black pepper, plus more as needed

1 tablespoon butter, melted

1/2 cup buttermilk

1/4 cup olive oil

1 small yellow onion, finely diced (about 1 cup)

4 cloves garlic, minced

4 anchovies

1/4 teaspoon dried oregano

4 ounces Portuguese-style (not Mexican-style) chorizo or linguica, skin removed, sliced

2 cups diced tomatoes (canned are fine)

1/2 teaspoon saffron

2 tablespoons tomato paste

2 cups clam juice

2 cups fish stock (page 254) or water

24 littleneck clams

1 cup Albariño or other dry white wine

18 new potatoes

Juice and zest of 1 lemon

4 or 5 piquillo peppers or pimientos, diced

2 tablespoons chopped Italian flat-leaf parsley

1/2 cup romesco sauce (page 260)

Soak the salt cod for at least 24 hours, changing the water every 6 hours. Cut into 2-inch pieces.

To prepare the haddock, cut the fillets into six 5-ounce portions and chill. In a bowl, mix the cracker crumbs with the paprika, some salt and pepper, and the melted butter to form a slightly moist meal. Salt and pepper the haddock pieces and dip in buttermilk on one side only. Press them onto the seasoned cracker crumbs to coat. Refrigerate for about 1 hour.

To make a sauce, in a saucepan over medium heat, heat the olive oil and sauté the onion, garlic, and anchovies until

CONTINUED

the anchovies disintegrate. Add the oregano, chorizo, and tomatoes and cook for 2 to 3 minutes. Add $1/4$ teaspoon of the saffron and the tomato paste, clam juice, fish stock, and salt cod. Cook for about 45 minutes, until reduced by one third.

In a sauté pan, place the littlenecks and wine and steam, covered, over high heat for 5 to 7 minutes. Discard any that have not opened. (Cooking the clams separately ensures that if any are bad, they will not spoil the entire batch of sauce.) Add the clams with the shells and broth to the sauce.

In a saucepan, add the potatoes and remaining saffron to 2 to 3 cups boiling salted water, or just enough water to cover. Cook until tender. Drain, reserving the liquid, and return the potatoes to the liquid to keep warm.

To bake the haddock, preheat the oven to 375°F. Drizzle some olive oil over the crusted haddock. Place on a baking sheet and bake for 6 to 8 minutes, until cooked through. The cracker crust should be nice and brown. Remove from the oven and set aside in a warm area.

Add the lemon juice and zest, the piquillo peppers, and about 1 cup of the saffron potato water to the sauce and return it to a boil. Add the parsley, the $1/2$ teaspoon black pepper, and salt to taste. Note that it will probably not need any salt due to the saltiness of the salt cod and clams.

To serve, in each of 6 large warm pasta bowls place 4 of the clams and 3 of the potatoes. Divide the chorizo slices among the plates and place a healthy ladleful of the tomato sauce in each bowl. Top each with a haddock fillet. Garnish with romesco sauce or pass separately.

SALT COD

Salt cod is usually found whole, split, and salted, with the head on and bones removed. It is usually as hard as cardboard and must be soaked for 24 hours before using to extract the salt and make it pliable. When using salt cod, it is helpful to change the water every 6 hours or so to extract the maximum amount of salt. After soaking, the cod must be poached. The flesh becomes flaky, tender, and a bit fishy tasting. Salt cod, also known as *bacalao,* can be found in ethnic markets, particularly Italian, Spanish, and French, and in very well-stocked fish markets and gourmet stores.

Walnut-Crusted Rockfish with Sherry-Beet Sauce and Cauliflower Flan

SERVES 6

This preparation is one of our most popular in the fall and winter months. The beets and horseradish have a natural affinity for each other; the combination is reminiscent of borscht. The sauce color stays bright purple-red but is mellowed by the butter, which also gives it richness. This type of vegetable butter can be made with many vegetables, but carrots, celeriac, and other root vegetables seem to work best. Roasted onions or baby carrots make a nice accompaniment to this dish.

CAULIFLOWER FLANS

1/4 small head cauliflower, cut into small florets (about 1 cup)

1/4 cup heavy cream, plus more if necessary

1/4 cup milk

1 clove garlic

1/8 teaspoon kosher salt

1/8 teaspoon white pepper

2 large eggs plus 2 large egg yolks

2 tablespoons grated Parmigiano-Reggiano cheese

Vegetable oil spray

SHERRY-BEET SAUCE

1 cup butter, cold

6 large button mushrooms, sliced (about 1 cup packed)

1/2 small yellow garlic, diced (about 1 cup)

2 cloves garlic, minced

1/2 teaspoon fresh thyme

1 shallot, minced

1/2 cup sherry

1/4 cup sherry vinegar

1/2 cup Pinot Noir or other light red wine

1/2 teaspoon black peppercorns

4 cups beet juice

2 cups chicken stock (page 255)

Kosher salt

ROCKFISH

1 1/2 cups walnuts, toasted

1 cup breadcrumbs

2 tablespoons fresh grated horseradish or 4 tablespoons prepared horseradish, squeezed dry

1/4 cup butter, melted, plus 1 tablespoon butter, at room temperature

Kosher salt and freshly ground black pepper

6 (5-ounce) pieces rockfish (striped bass) or skate, snapper, fluke, or mahi mahi, skin and bones removed

1/2 cup buttermilk

2 tablespoons grapeseed or other vegetable oil

2 tablespoons walnut oil

3 cups Horseradish Creamed Spinach (page 222)

To make the flans, in a noncorrosive saucepan over high heat, bring the cauliflower, cream, milk, garlic, salt, and pepper to a boil. Add a little more cream if necessary to completely cover the cauliflower. Cook for about 8 minutes, until the cauliflower is very tender. Drain, reserving the liquid, and return the liquid to the pan. Reduce to 1 cup. Remove from the heat and let cool completely. Purée the cauliflower and its cooking liquid in a blender until very smooth. Add the eggs, yolks, and cheese. It should make about 2 cups. The flan mixture can be prepared to this point a day ahead and refrigerated.

Preheat the oven to 275°F. Spray nine 1-ounce flan molds, plastic cups, or mini muffin tins with the vegetable oil

CONTINUED

spray. Fill the molds four-fifths of the way to the top and place in a water bath. Bake for 1 hour, or until a toothpick inserted into the flans comes out clean.

To make the beet sauce, in a noncorrosive sauté pan over medium-high heat, melt a little of the butter and sauté the mushrooms, onion, garlic, thyme, and shallot. Add the sherry, sherry vinegar, red wine, and peppercorns and cook until reduced by half. Strain through a fine-mesh sieve.

In a separate pan over medium heat, cook the beet juice until reduced by one third.

In a third saucepan, cook the chicken stock until reduced to almost a glaze. Pour the contents of the three pans into one large sauté pan and reduce over very low heat until it starts to thicken. Transfer to a blender. Add the remaining butter, and salt to taste. Purée and strain through a fine-mesh sieve. The sauce should be the consistency of heavy cream. If too thin, add more butter. Keep warm.

To prepare the fish, preheat the oven to 400°F. In a food processor, pulse the walnuts until coarsely ground. Add the breadcrumbs and horseradish and pulse until somewhat coarse. Add the melted butter and salt and pepper to taste and pulse to incorporate. Transfer from the food processor and place on a large plate for breading the fish.

Salt and pepper the rockfish and dip the top side only into the buttermilk, then dip that side of the fillet into the walnut-horseradish mixture. Chill for 6 to 8 minutes or up to 1 hour.

To cook the fish, preheat the oven to 350°F. Bring an oven-proof sauté pan to medium-high heat. Add the grapeseed and walnut oils and when hot, place the rockfish fillets in the pan, breaded side down. Sauté for 2 to 3 minutes, until brown and crispy. Turn and place in the oven for 3 to 4 minutes, until just done.

To serve, place 4 tablespoons of the sherry-beet sauce on each of 6 warm plates. Place a quenelle of the creamed spinach at the 11 o'clock position. Place 1 rockfish fillet on the sauce. Invert the flan molds and pop out the flans. Garnish each fillet with a flan at the 1 o'clock position.

ROCKFISH

This fish is not to be confused with the Pacific Coast rockfish, a separate species. In the Mid-Atlantic area, rockfish is the name given to striped bass. These can be freshwater or saltwater fish, depending on where they are raised. They are great sport fish in either habitat. Salt sea bass can grow quite large, up to 20 pounds or more. In the '80s there was a fishing moratorium on "stripers" all along the East Coast and the Chesapeake. Since that time, with restrictions on sport anglers and professional fishermen, the species is well on its way to making a comeback. This is great news for fish lovers, as it is one of the finest eating fish on this side of the Atlantic. Rockfish like to swim along the rocky coastlines and eat smaller fish and, in brackish waters, baby crabs. Some postulate that the downturn in the Chesapeake crab population in the past several years is due, in part, to the return of the rockfish.

Mustard-Glazed Salmon with Crabmeat and Tomato-Basil Butter

SERVES 6

I learned the basic premise of this dish many years ago while helping to prepare a lecture and tasting dinner with Paula Wolfert, noted food lecturer and cookbook author. As I was to learn later, the dish was originally from the repertoire of my friend Jean Louis Palladin, who toiled for years in Washington D.C. at the famed Restaurant Jean Louis in the Watergate Hotel. Jean Louis was an extraordinarily creative and gifted cook with an enormous appetite for life. Sadly, he passed away far too young. His friends and the entire food service community miss him tremendously.

Any thin, flaky fish like flounder, halibut, sea bass, haddock or cod can be used. Full-flavored, oily fish like salmon, char, bluefish, or striped bass are particularly good. When pounding the fish, plastic freezer bags work best; they are thicker and can withstand more abuse than plastic wrap or waxed paper.

DEEP-FRIED LEEKS

1 to 2 cups vegetable oil for frying
2 large leeks, white part only, julienne
Kosher salt

SALMON

1 side of salmon, skin and pin bones removed (about 2$^{1}/_{2}$ pounds)
1 cup crème fraîche
3 tablespoons pommery or other grainy mustard
Sea salt and freshly ground white pepper

TOMATO-BASIL BUTTER

2 teaspoons olive oil
1 large shallot, minced (about 4 teaspoons)
$^{1}/_{2}$ cup tomato concassé (page 263)
1 tablespoon tomato paste
$^{1}/_{4}$ cup dry white wine
1 tablespoon Champagne vinegar
3 tablespoons heavy cream
$^{3}/_{4}$ cup (1$^{1}/_{2}$ sticks) butter, chilled and cut into cubes
Kosher salt and freshly ground black pepper

CRABMEAT

$^{1}/_{2}$ cup jumbo lump crabmeat, picked for shells
$^{1}/_{4}$ cup loosely packed basil chiffonade

To make the deep-fried leeks, in a cast-iron pan, heat 2 inches of the vegetable oil to 375°F. Fry the leeks in the hot vegetable oil for about 1 minute, until golden and crispy. Transfer from the oil and drain on paper towels. Season with salt and keep warm.

To prepare the salmon, trim any dark flesh from the bottom of the salmon fillet. Cut the fillet lengthwise into 2 halves. Cut each fillet into 3 portions and pound them slightly between 2 plastic freezer bags to about $^{1}/_{2}$-inch thick. Trim each piece as neatly as possible into a rectangular paillard. Keep chilled. Reserve any trimmings for a fish mousse or the Scandinavian Salmon Stew (page 94).

In a stainless steel bowl, mix the crème fraîche and mustard. Salt and pepper the salmon on both sides and coat with the crème fraîche–mustard mixture on the top only. Chill for 20 minutes.

To make the tomato-basil butter, in a noncorrosive saucepan over high heat, heat the olive oil and when hot, add the shallot and cook until transparent. Add the tomato concassé and tomato paste and sauté for 1 to 2 minutes. Add the white wine and vinegar and reduce until most of the liquid is evaporated. Add the heavy cream and reduce by one quarter. Whisk in the butter cubes, a few at a time, until all are incorporated. The sauce should be thick enough to coat the back of a spoon. Add salt and pepper to taste and keep warm.

To make the crabmeat, in a sauté pan over low heat, place the crabmeat and a little of the butter sauce and warm through. Add the basil chiffonade to the sauce and keep warm.

To cook the salmon, preheat the broiler. Place the salmon rectangles on a Teflon or oiled baking sheet and place 6 to 8 inches from the broiler. Broil for 2 to 3 minutes, until the crème fraîche is bubbling and golden brown.

To serve, divide the sauce among 6 warm plates and top each with a salmon rectangle. Garnish each with a stack of the deep-fried leeks.

Brazilian-Style Grouper with Cashews and Coconut Shrimp Curry

SERVES 6

This is a Brazilian-inspired seafood dish in the style of the Bahia region of that country. Grouper, a large fish found in warm waters on both sides of the equator, is one of the best values in fresh fish anywhere. Its firm white flesh can be used in virtually every manner of preparation. Alternatives for this dish, if you choose to splurge, are rock lobster tails or very large shrimp. Monkfish is also a very nice substitute.

18 medium shrimp (26 to 30 count), peeled and chilled, shells reserved for curry sauce

BRAZILIAN COCONUT CURRY

Shrimp shells from 18 peeled shrimp

2 tablespoons vegetable oil or palm oil (dende), if available

1 clove garlic, minced

1 small yellow garlic, diced (about 1 cup)

3 tablespoons masaman Thai yellow curry paste

1 tablespoon Madras curry powder

1/4 cup peeled, grated fresh ginger

1 (10-ounce) can coconut milk

1/2 cup mango juice

1 tablespoon freshly squeezed lemon juice

1/4 cup cream sherry

1 cup fish stock (page 254) or water

1/2 teaspoon kosher salt

GROUPER

1/2 cup cashews, toasted

1 cup breadcrumbs

1 extra large egg

2 tablespoons coconut milk

1/2 teaspoon kosher salt

1/2 teaspoon white pepper

6 (6-ounce) pieces grouper, trimmed

1/4 cup all-purpose flour

2 cups peanut oil or vegetable oil

1 small yucca, peeled into shavings with a vegetable peeler (about 1 1/2 cups)

2 teaspoons butter

1/4 teaspoon paprika

1/4 teaspoon chile powder

1/2 cup loosely packed, cilantro leaves, for garnish

4 scallions, chopped (about 1/2 cup), for garnish

Peel and devein the shrimp and reserve the shells for the curry sauce. Refrigerate the peeled shrimp.

To make the curry sauce, in a saucepan over medium heat, heat 1/4 cup of the vegetable oil. When hot, add the garlic and onions. Sauté until just starting to brown. Add the curry paste and curry powder and sauté for 2 to 3 minutes, stirring frequently. Turn the heat to high and add the ginger, the coconut milk, mango juice, lemon juice, sherry, stock, and salt. When it comes to a boil, lower the heat to a simmer and cook until reduced by one third. Transfer the sauce to a blender and purée. Strain through a fine-mesh sieve and keep warm.

To prepare the grouper, place about three quarters of the cashews in a food processor, leaving the rest whole for garnish. Add the breadcrumbs and pulse to form a coarse meal.

Make an egg wash with the egg and coconut milk. Salt and pepper each piece of grouper. Dredge in the flour and shake off the excess. Dip in the coconut egg wash and then in the cashew–breadcrumb mixture. Refrigerate for about 1 hour.

Preheat the oven to 375°F. In a sauté pan over medium-high heat, heat 1/4 cup of the peanut oil. Sear 3 pieces of the breaded grouper until brown on all sides, and then place on a baking sheet. Repeat with the remaining grouper fillet. Bake for 5 to 7 minutes, until cooked through. Keep warm.

In a cast-iron pan sauté pan over medium heat, heat 1 1/2 cups of the peanut oil. When hot, fry the yucca shavings for 3 to 4 minutes, until crisp. Transfer to drain on a paper towel; add salt to taste. Place the butter in a saucepan and when hot, add the paprika, chile powder, and shrimp. Sauté on both sides. Transfer from the pan and keep warm.

To serve, divide the curry sauce onto 6 warm plates or large pasta bowls. Place 1 piece of grouper and 3 of the shrimp in each. Garnish with the whole cashews, cilantro, scallions, and crispy fried yucca.

BUTTERY CHARDONNAY

Gaby Pantano has been a waiter at Kinkead's for about six years. He is what is considered, in the business, a real pro. Like many others who work in the front of the house at Kinkead's, he is also quite a character. Gaby is originally from Brazil, so whenever we put a dish on the menu that is inspired by the cuisine of that country, we check with Gaby to make sure the flavors are *authentico.* Gaby loves to cook and has brought many of his creations to sample during staff meals. He even bottles his soon-to-be-famous Brazilian salsa verde, a spicy green sauce that goes very nicely with grilled meats and fish.

This story belongs in the "customers never cease to amaze" category. One evening, a dining couple asked Gaby to recommend a wine to accompany two dishes that they were contemplating ordering. He asked several questions to ascertain the kinds of wines they preferred. The gentleman said that they liked white wines and that he was interested in trying something new from California. Gaby suggested a Chalone Pinnacles Chardonnay, which he described as "a dry wine with good fruit and a fair amount of oak—what might be termed a very 'buttery' Chardonnay." Upon hearing that, the woman at the table stopped Gaby and gasped, "Well, we can't have that—I'm lactose intolerant!"

Arctic Char with Creamed Leeks, Asparagus, and Carrot Butter

*L*ike salmon, arctic char and its cousin, the Dolly Varden char, are anadromous fish: they breed in fresh water and can live in salt water. Some species of char live entirely in fresh water. L'omble chevalier, *the most prized of the char, is one such fish.*

Whole char generally run between 2 and 4 pounds but can be bigger. Char flesh can range in color from very pale pink—almost white—to bright orange, like salmon. It is a sweet-tasting fish, almost like a cross between salmon and trout. It has good fat content, so it stays moist, but it is not as strong-tasting as salmon.

Preparations that work for salmon are generally very good for char as well. To be really luxurious, top each char fillet with a slice of cucumber topped with beluga caviar.

18 large green asparagus, peeled

12 large white asparagus, peeled

1 cup butter

2 leeks, white part only, chopped (about 2 cups)

1 cup heavy cream, plus more if necessary

Sea salt and cracked white pepper

12 French bunch carrots (round), peeled and cut in half lengthwise

2 teaspoons cardamom seeds, crushed and toasted

1 cup fresh carrot juice

1 teaspoon cumin, toasted

1 star anise

1 tablespoon sherry vinegar

6 (5-ounce) pieces arctic char (preferably Pomble chevalier) fillets, skinned

2 tablespoons olive oil

1 tablespoon chopped chervil leaves

12 French breakfast radishes

6 new onions with bulbs, cut lengthwise

2 tablespoons water

2 tablespoons chopped chives, for garnish

Kosher salt

To prepare the asparagus, bring a saucepan of salted water to a boil. Cook the green and white asparagus for about 2 minutes, until just tender. Shock the asparagus in an ice-water bath and drain. Dry on paper towels and trim the ends so all are of even length.

To make the creamed leeks, in a small saucepan over medium heat, melt 2 tablespoons of the butter. Sweat the leeks for 3 minutes and add the cream. Cook for about 5 minutes, until reduced by half. If too thick, add a little more cream. Add salt and pepper to taste and keep warm.

To make the carrot butter, in another saucepan over medium heat, melt 2 tablespoons of the butter. When hot, add the carrots and cook for about 1 minute. Add the cardamom and carrot juice and simmer until the carrots are tender. Remove the carrots and keep warm. Add the toasted cumin and star anise to the juice and reduce by half. Strain and return the carrot juice to the pan. Add the sherry vinegar and reduce by one quarter. Transfer to a blender, add 1/2 cup of the butter, and purée. The sauce should coat the back of a spoon. Add salt and pepper to taste.

Preheat the oven to 375°F. Salt and pepper the char. In a sauté pan over medium heat, heat the olive oil and cook the fillets, skinned side up, for 2 to 3 minutes, until brown. Turn and cook for 2 more minutes. Remove from the pan and place on a buttered baking sheet.

In a sauté pan over medium-low heat, warm both the green and white asparagus in 2 tablespoons of the butter. Add the chervil and salt and pepper to taste and toss. Remove from the pan and keep warm. Wipe out the pan and place over medium heat. Sauté the radishes and new onions in the remaining 2 tablespoons butter. Add the water and simmer until hot but firm. Keep warm.

To serve, put the char into the oven for 2 to 3 minutes, depending on the thickness, until cooked through. Portion about 3 tablespoons of the creamed leeks into the center of each of 6 warm dinner plates. Top with alternating green (3) and white (2) asparagus. Surround with the carrots, radishes, and new onions. Sauce with the carrot butter and top the asparagus with the char. Garnish with a sprinkle of chives and serve at once.

Roasted Red Snapper, Fried Zucchini with Parmesan, and Cherry Tomato Confit

his recipe demonstrates a good method for oven-roasting any thick fish fillet. The fried zucchini are not only a terrific accompaniment for this dish, they can be eaten by themselves as a snack with cocktails. The Parmesan is a compelling complement to the crispy zucchini.

The tomato confit offers a good method for oven-drying that fruit. It's a variation on oven-dried tomatoes but can be used more as a relish or side salad. These low-temperature-oven-dried tomatoes are made to be used right away, as opposed to completely drying the fruits to extract every bit of the liquid. The summer sun–ripened varieties will provide the most intensely flavored results. If cherry tomatoes are not available, small plum tomatoes or grape tomatoes will work just fine. A mixture of yellow, red, and orange tomatoes makes a colorful presentation.

CHERRY TOMATO CONFIT

2 pints cherry tomatoes (about 70 tomatoes),
 stems removed

1/2 cup olive oil

4 cloves garlic, sliced

1 teaspoon sugar

2 teaspoons kosher salt, plus more as needed

1 teaspoon cracked black pepper, plus more as needed

1 tablespoon red wine vinegar

1 teaspoon fresh thyme leaves

1/4 cup extra virgin olive oil

ROASTED RED SNAPPER

6 (6-ounce) American red snapper fillets

1/2 teaspoon kosher salt, plus more as needed

1/2 teaspoon cracked black pepper, plus more as needed

1/2 cup extra virgin olive oil

2 cloves garlic, minced

1 large shallot, minced

1/4 cup Champagne vinegar

1/2 cup dry white wine

1 cup chicken stock (page 255)

2 tablespoons freshly squeezed lemon juice

3 tablespoons chopped Italian flat-leaf parsley

1 teaspoon chopped rosemary leaves

1 tablespoon chopped tarragon leaves

Flour for dusting

2 tablespoons vegetable oil

1/4 cup butter

GARLIC CHIPS

8 cloves garlic

1 cup clarified butter or olive oil

Kosher salt

1 recipe Fried Zucchini with Parmesan (page 223)

Freshly grated Parmesan cheese, for garnish

To make the tomato confit, preheat the oven to 250°F. In a stainless steel bowl, toss the cherry tomatoes with the olive oil and the garlic, sugar, salt, and pepper. Marinate for about 20 minutes. On a cookie rack on top of a baking sheet, spread out the tomatoes in a single layer. It is all right if they touch. Place in the oven for 1½ hours, until the tomatoes are starting to shrivel but not completely dried out or brown. Remove from the oven and let cool. When cool enough to handle, remove the skins. Toss the tomatoes in a stainless steel bowl with any juices, marinade, and

CONTINUED

garlic. Stir in the red wine vinegar, thyme, and the olive oil. Add salt and pepper to taste. The tomatoes will keep, refrigerated, for up to 2 days.

To prepare the snapper, trim the fillets to about $1^{1}/_{2}$ inches thick; leave the skin on. Score each fillet with a sharp knife. Salt and pepper on both sides and refrigerate.

To make a vinaigrette, in a sauté pan over medium heat, heat 1 tablespoon of the olive oil. Add the garlic and shallots and sweat for 2 to 3 minutes. Add the vinegar and wine and bring to a boil. Decrease the heat to medium and cook for 2 minutes, until reduced to a glaze. Add the stock and reduce by three-quarters. Transfer to a blender and add the lemon juice, parsley, rosemary, and tarragon. With the blender on, slowly add in the remaining olive oil in a stream until all is emulsified. Set aside.

To bake the snapper, preheat the oven to 400°F. Remove the snapper from the refrigerator and pat dry with paper towels. Dust the skin side of the snapper with the $1/2$ teaspoon salt, $1/2$ teaspoon pepper, and flour. In a large sauté pan over medium-high heat, heat the vegetable oil and sear the snapper, skin side down, until brown and crisp. Turn over, add the butter to the pan, and place it in the oven. Roast for 5 to 6 minutes, basting every 2 minutes or so with the butter. Remove from oven and keep warm.

To make the garlic chips, slice the garlic in to $1/8$-inch-thick slices. In a sauté pan over medium-low heat, melt the butter. Add the garlic and cook until brown and crisp. Transfer to paper towels to drain and season with salt to taste.

Make the fried zucchini with Parmesan just before serving.

To serve, place 2 to 3 tablespoons vinaigrette in the center of each of 6 warm dinner plates. Top with a piece of snapper, skin side up. Divide the zucchini among the plates and sprinkle Parmesan cheese over the top. Garnish with $1/4$ cup or so of the cherry tomato confit and garlic chips.

Sea Trout with Celery Three Ways and Truffle Vinaigrette

Sea trout, also known as weakfish, are common to the Chesapeake Bay area and the Atlantic coast. It is fairly easy to come by and is inexpensive. Alternatively, fluke flounder, halibut, rockfish, or any thick, firm-fleshed whitefish will do in this recipe. Mediterranean sea bass or loup de mer *is particularly nice with this preparation.*

This is another pairing of rare and expensive ingredients with more plebian, inexpensive ones. The combination of truffles and celery works very well and the modest cost of most of the ingredients somewhat offsets the expense of the truffles. I highly recommend purchasing fresh black truffles, which are generally available at specialty stores in the winter, for this dish. If you cannot obtain them or they are out of season, frozen is the second choice; canned is third.

6 (6-ounce) portions center-cut sea trout or 12 (3-ounce) fillets

3 small heads celery

$^1/_2$ cup butter, at room temperature

2 cups chicken stock (page 255)

1 cup water

1 large celeriac, peeled and cut in large dice

1 small Idaho potato, peeled and diced

$^1/_4$ cup heavy cream

Sea salt and cracked black pepper

1 Périgord truffle

1 teaspoon sherry vinegar

1 tablespoon black truffle oil

$^1/_4$ cup black truffle juice

3 tablespoons grapeseed or other vegetable oil

3 tablespoons extra virgin olive oil

4 large radishes, sliced

1 tablespoon chopped chives

Remove any bones from the trout fillets. Refrigerate.

To prepare the celery, trim the heads and wash under cold water. Remove the large outer stalks and reserve for another use. Reserve any celery leaves. Keeping the remaining stalks attached at the bottom and trim the hearts down to 5 to 6 inches long. Finely dice the trimmings and reserve. Split the hearts in half and remove the leafy, yellow center stalks, reserving for the salad garnish.

In a braising pan large enough to hold all 6 celery heart halves, heat $^1/_4$ cup of the butter over medium heat. Add the celery hearts, cut side down, and sauté until they just start to brown. Turn and repeat on the other side. If your largest pan can't accommodate all 6 at once, you can sauté 2 or 3 hearts at a time, but once all are sautéed, braise together in the same pan Add the chicken stock and water and bring to a boil. Decrease the heat to a simmer, cover, and cook for about 30 minutes, turning every 5 minutes or so, until tender. If the liquid evaporates, add more water or stock.

Drain and reserve the liquid. Trim the celery heart bottoms, but make sure the stalks are connected. Keep warm.

To make the celeriac purée, place the celeriac and potato in a saucepan with salted water and bring to a boil. Cook for 8 to 10 minutes, until tender. Drain. Rice the celeriac and potato and mix with the heavy cream, 2 tablespoons of

CONTINUED

the butter, and salt and pepper to taste. It should be the consistency of very thick soup or runny mashed potatoes. Keep warm.

To make the truffle vinaigrette, wash the truffle and peel with a sharp paring knife, reserving the peelings. Slice the truffle in half. Using a mandoline or truffle slicer or a very sharp knife, slice 6 thin slices and dice.

Bring the celery braising liquid to a boil and reduce to 1/2 cup. Transfer to a blender, add the sherry vinegar, truffle oil, truffle juice, truffle peelings, and salt and pepper to taste, and purée. Transfer to a stainless steel bowl.

In a sauté pan over medium heat, heat 1 tablespoon of the grapeseed oil and 1 tablespoon of the extra virgin olive oil and add the minced celery stalks and trimmings. Sauté until cooked but still crunchy. Add the diced truffles and let cook for 1 or 2 minutes. Add to the vinaigrette. Whisk in the remaining extra virgin olive oil and keep warm.

To prepare the sea trout, preheat the oven to 375°F. Pat the fillets dry. In a sauté pan over medium-high heat, heat the remaining 2 tablespoons grapeseed oil and sauté the fillets, skin side up, for about 3 minutes. Turn and cook for about 2 more minutes. Brush the fillets with the remaining 2 tablespoons butter and bake for about 3 minutes, until cooked through. Remove from the heat and keep warm.

To make celery leaf-radish salad, trim the yellow center stalks reserved from the celery hearts. Chop the stalks, leaving the leaves whole. In a stainless steel bowl, combine the leaves and chopped stalks with the radishes and chives and a little of the warm truffle vinaigrette. Add salt and pepper to taste.

To serve, place about 3 tablespoons of celeriac purée in the center of each of 6 warm plates. Drizzle truffle vinaigrette around the purée. Cut each braised celery heart in half. Place one half at 12 o'clock on each plate and top with 1 or 2 sea trout fillets. Garnish with celery leaf–radish salad. Serve at once.

Halibut with Spring Vegetable Ragoût, Crabmeat Ravioli, and Lemon Butter

SERVES 6

This light seafood dish highlights the new spring vegetables and the Alaskan halibut harvest. Halibut is always one of the most popular fish we serve. The sauce, a lemon-flavored beurre fondue, is almost pure butter. The vegetables used can easily be varied with the seasons. If ramps, morels, or asparagus are preferred or available, by all means, add them to the recipe. The crab ravioli can be made in advance and refrigerated for a day, or frozen. The ravioli recipe makes twice as much as you need for this dish; the extras can be used as an appetizer by themselves with the same sauce, some fava beans, and a fresh herb garnish.

CRABMEAT RAVIOLI

1 pound pasta dough (page 266)

1 teaspoon butter

1 shallot, minced

Juice of 1/2 lemon

2 teaspoons sherry

2 tablespoons cream cheese

2 tablespoons crème fraîche

1 teaspoon kosher salt

1/2 teaspoon white pepper

8 ounces jumbo lump crabmeat, picked through for shells

1/4 cup semolina or fine cornmeal

1 tablespoon chopped chives

1 large egg

2 tablespoons water

HALIBUT

6 (5-ounce) halibut fillets, boned and skinned

Kosher salt and cracked white pepper

1/4 cup vegetable oil

4 tablespoons butter

1 small shallot, minced

1 1/2 cups beurre fondue (page 258)

1 cup fava beans, blanched and peeled

3/4 cup haricots verts, cut into 3-inch lengths and blanched

1/2 cup fresh English peas, blanched

1/2 cup snow peas, blanched and julienned

1/2 cup sugar snap peas, blanched

2 teaspoons summer savory leaves

2 teaspoons chervil leaves, plus extra sprigs for garnish

1 teaspoon coarsely chopped tarragon leaves

6 ounces jumbo lump crabmeat, picked through for shells

Juice and zest of 1 lemon, grated with a microplane zester

To make the ravioli, let the pasta dough come to room temperature. In a sauté pan over medium heat, melt the butter. When hot, add the shallot and sweat. Add the lemon juice, sherry, cream cheese, and crème fraîche and bring to a boil. Reduce by one third and add the salt and pepper. Fold in the crabmeat and chives and remove from the heat. Refrigerate for about 30 minutes, until very cold.

Make an egg wash with the egg and water. Use a pasta roller to roll out a sheet of pasta dough about 1/16-inch thick. Every 3 inches or so, place a hefty teaspoon of the crabmeat mixture on the sheet. Paint the areas around the crabmeat with the egg wash. When all are completed, cover with another thin sheet of pasta. With your hands, press the top layer of pasta around the crabmeat, being careful not to tear the pasta.

Cut out each ravioli with a 3-inch round cutter, or a square cutter if you prefer. Check that each of the ravioli is completely sealed on all sides. Sprinkle a sheet pan with the semolina. Place the ravioli on the sheet and keep refrigerated. Either use within 24 hours or freeze.

To prepare the halibut, preheat the oven to 375°F. Wash and pat the halibut fillets dry and salt and pepper them on both sides. In a sauté pan over medium heat, heat the vegetable oil and sear the halibut on one side. When they start to brown, turn, add 2 tablespoons of the butter to the pan, and sauté for 1 more minute. Place the pan in the oven and baste with the butter every 2 minutes or so for 5 to 6 minutes, until cooked. Remove from the oven and keep warm.

To prepare the ragoût, wipe out the pan and place over medium heat. Add the remaining 2 tablespoons butter and the shallot and sweat for about 2 minutes. Add 1/4 cup of the beurre fondue and the favas, haricots verts, English peas, snow peas, and snap peas and warm through. Add the savory, chervil, and tarragon and salt and pepper to taste and keep warm.

Cook the ravioli in boiling salted water. They are done when they rise to the surface. Strain and toss in a bowl with the crabmeat and 4 tablespoons of the beurre fondue. Keep warm.

To serve, add the lemon juice and zest to the remaining beurre fondue. On each of 6 warm plates, place a halibut fillet in the center and ravioli at the 3 o'clock position. Divide the vegetable medley among the plates, placing it at the 9 o'clock position. Sauce with the lemon beurre fondue. Garnish with the chervil sprigs.

HALIBUT

Halibut is a large flatfish indigenous to both the Atlantic and Pacific oceans. Alaskan halibut is the best-known—and the largest, with some specimens weighing in at over 90 pounds. The Atlantic version grows quite a bit smaller. Like its smaller cousins, flounder, turbot, and sole, the halibut is a flatfish with the eyes on the top of the head. It has gray, camouflage-like skin on the top and white skin on the bottom.

Halibut is popular even among diners who are not very fond of fish. Its flavor is sweet and mild, and, because of its size, it cuts to a wonderful, thick portion. The flesh is white and fairly lean, with a texture firmer than cod or haddock, and it is flaky but stays together when cooked. The bones are excellent for making fish stock.

Halibut works equally well using any cooking method—almost no other species can match this. Smaller halibut can be cut into steaks with the central bone intact, which makes it great for grilling, baking, or poaching.

Flounder with Artichokes, Tomatoes, Thyme, and Olives

SERVES 6

Despite the fact that artichokes are a difficult match with wines, they make a marvelous complement to whitefish, flatfish in particular. This recipe uses a purée of artichokes to make a flavorful butter sauce for the flounder. If you're splurging, try this recipe with fresh Dover sole. Turbot, halibut, haddock, or any member of the flounder family also works well. Cooked spinach makes a nice accompaniment.

18 braised baby artichokes (page 217), with the cooking liquid reserved

2 tablespoons extra virgin olive oil

2 cloves garlic, sliced

1 teaspoon thyme leaves

1/4 cup dry white wine

1 cup chicken stock (page 255)

1/2 cup butter

1/2 teaspoon kosher salt

Sea salt and cracked black pepper

1 tablespoon freshly squeezed lemon juice

6 (6-ounce) flounder fillets

1/2 cup buttermilk

1/2 cup seasoned breadcrumbs

Peanut oil for frying

3 tablespoons olive oil

12 halves tomato confit (see page 133)

18 pitted kalamata olives, for garnish

6 basil sprigs, for garnish

To make the artichoke purée, preheat the oven to 375°F. Select 12 of the nicest artichokes, cut in half, and reserve for garnish.

In a saucepan over medium heat, heat the extra virgin olive oil. Add the garlic and thyme and sweat for 2 minutes. Add the wine and chicken stock and bring to a boil. Add 1/2 cup of the artichoke cooking liquid, the remaining artichokes, and any leaves that have fallen off. Bring to a boil and when the chokes are very soft, in about 3 minutes, strain, reserving the liquid and returning it to the pan. Over high heat reduce the liquid by half and transfer the artichokes to a blender. Add one third of the cooking liquid and purée until very smooth. Strain the purée through a fine-mesh sieve and return to the blender. Add the butter, salt, and as much of the cooking liquid as needed to make a purée about the thickness of heavy cream. Remove from the blender, add salt and pepper to taste, and keep warm. This should make about 2 cups of sauce.

Salt and pepper flounder fillets and dip the top side only in the buttermilk and then in the breadcrumbs. In an oven-proof sauté pan over medium-high heat, heat the peanut oil. Place the fillets in the hot oil, breaded side down, and sauté for about 3 minutes, until brown and crispy. Turn the fillets and put the pan into the oven for about 3 minutes, until cooked. Do not crowd the pan; cook in batches if necessary.

In a sauté pan over medium heat, add 2 tablespoons of the olive oil and sauté the artichoke halves, cut side down. Cook for about 3 minutes, until brown. Turn and cook for 2 more minutes. Remove from the pan and keep warm. Add the remaining 1 tablespoon olive oil to the pan and warm the tomato confit halves in the oil.

To serve, on each of 6 warm plates, place 4 or 5 tablespoons of the artichoke sauce. Top with a breaded flounder fillet. Finish each plate with 3 artichoke halves and 2 tomato confit halves. Garnish each plate with 3 kalamata olives and a basil sprig. Serve hot. Pass the extra sauce separately.

Skate with Lentils, Bacon, Cauliflower Rissole, and Syrah

SERVES 6

Pairing seafood with lentils is a classic French flavor combination. The earthy flavor of the lentils is a nice contrast to the sweetness of the fish. Combined with two members of the cabbage family and a rich red wine–butter sauce, it makes for a wonderful dish. The lentils in this recipe can be made without the bacon for those who wish to avoid meat or pork.

This method of preparing skate starts with the skin left on and the featherbone in the middle of the wing left intact until serving. The skate is poached in a court bouillon made from a seasoned nage *(poaching liquid) and some vinegar.*

The method for cooking the cauliflower differs from classic preparations in that they are not blanched in water before cooking. The slow cooking and browning gives them a rich, buttery flavor.

LENTILS WITH BACON

2 cups dried Puy (green) lentils

1 tablespoon vegetable oil

3 bacon strips, sliced thinly

1 cup *brunoise* mirepoix (page 263)

1/4 teaspoon dried thyme

1 cup chicken stock (page 255)

1 teaspoon kosher salt

1 teaspoon freshly ground black pepper

CAULIFLOWER RISSOLE

1/4 cup butter

1 small cauliflower, trimmed and cut into 12 large florets

Kosher salt and freshly ground black pepper

SYRAH BUTTER

1 1/4 cups butter

1 shallot, minced

3/4 cup port

1 cup Syrah or other deep-red wine like Cabernet or Merlot

2 tablespoons balsamic vinegar

Kosher salt and freshly ground black pepper

1 teaspoon freshly squeezed lemon juice

SKATE

6 (1-pound) skate wings, or 3 larger wings

8 cups nage (poaching liquid)

2 lemons, halved

1 teaspoon Champagne or white wine vinegar

To make the lentils, pick through them for twigs or little pebbles. Rinse in cold water.

In a saucepan, bring 4 cups of water to a boil. Add the lentils and bring to a boil. Drain immediately and run under cold water. Spread out on a baking sheet until cooled.

In a saucepan over medium-high heat, heat the vegetable oil. Add the bacon and fry until browned and crisp. Transfer to paper towels to drain. Add the mirepoix and thyme to the saucepan and sauté until the onion is just starting to brown. Add the lentils, stock, and enough water to cover the lentils by 1 inch. Bring to a boil and skim any impurities that rise to the surface. Lower the heat and simmer for about 30 minutes, until the liquid has evaporated by one quarter. Add 2 cups of water and cook for about 15 more minutes. Add the salt and pepper and check that the lentils are tender but not mushy. If the liquid evaporates past one quarter reduced, add more water, not more stock. The lentils should have enough liquid to stir but should not be swimming. Add the cooked bacon and keep warm.

To make the cauliflower rissole, in a sauté pan over medium heat, melt the butter and add the cauliflower. Do not crowd the pan; you may need to do this in two batches. Cook until starting to brown on all sides, turning frequently. Watch the heat. Add $1/2$ cup of the stock and cook until the stock forms a glaze. The cauliflower should brown and give off cooking liquid but not burn. Add salt and pepper and remove from the pan when the cauliflower is just tender, after about 20 minutes. The cauliflower should be well cooked but not falling apart, with a little firmness at the center. Keep warm.

To make the Syrah butter, dice the butter into 1-inch cubes. In a noncorrosive saucepan, add the shallot, port, Syrah, and balsamic vinegar and bring to a boil. Cook for about 20 minutes, until reduced to a glaze. Lower the heat and whisk in the butter, one cube at a time, until all is incorporated. Add salt and pepper to taste and pass through a fine-mesh sieve. Add the lemon juice. Keep warm.

To prepare the skate, wash the wings and pat dry. In a braising pan or fish poacher, make the court bouillon by placing the nage, lemon halves, and Champagne vinegar and bring to a boil. Turn down the heat to a simmer and add the skate wings. Cook for about 15 minutes, until the feather bone in the middle of the wings comes out easily. Remove the wings from the water and peel away the skin. Keep warm. (In most bistros in France the skin would be served still on the skate. That is fine; it's just easier to eat with the skin removed.)

In a saucepan over high heat, reduce about 1 cup of the court bouillon to $1/4$ cup and add to the Syrah butter sauce.

To serve, place $1/3$ to $1/2$ cup lentils in the center of each of 6 warm dinner plates. Top with a skate fillet and place two of the cauliflower rissole at the 12 o'clock position on the plate. Surround with the Syrah butter sauce. Serve at once.

Wolf Fish Braised in Beef Juices with Parsley Root–Celeriac Purée

SERVES 6

At Kinkead's we often use meat or red wine sauces in fish preparations. This is one of the more interesting. It comes out best when you have drippings from a beef roast or fat from a prime rib.

Wolf fish is an aptly named bottom feeder whose main diet consists of clams, crabs, and other shellfish. It is dark gray, with a mouthful of jagged sharp teeth and eyes set very close together, as any predator's would be. It is one scary-looking specimen. But its flesh is white and firm and perfect for soups, stews, and poached and braised fish preparations. It is considered a trash fish and is generally very reasonably priced. You can substitute monk, striped bass, tilefish, or other firm fish.

The procedure for the parsley root–celeriac purée works for several other vegetables as well. You can substitute salsify, parsnips, or even turnips.

6 (6-ounce) wolf fish fillets

1 cup rendered fat from beef roast or 2 pounds beef fat cap from rib roast

1/2 small fennel bulb, cut into 1/4-inch dice

1 small yellow onion, cut into 1/4-inch dice

1 small carrot, peeled and cut into 1/4-inch dice

1 small leek, white part only, cut into 1/4-inch dice

1 stalk celery, peeled and cut into 1/4-inch dice

2 cloves garlic, minced

4 cups veal stock (page 256)

1 cup Syrah or other dry red wine

Juice and zest of 1 lemon

2 bay leaves

4 sprigs thyme

Kosher salt and freshly ground black pepper

All-purpose flour

1 teaspoon chopped tarragon leaves

PARSLEY ROOT–CELERIAC PURÉE

1 celeriac bulbs, peeled and cut in large dice (1 1/2 to 2 cups)

1 small Idaho potato, peeled and diced (about 1 1/4 cups)

3 parsley roots, peeled and cut up (about 1 cup)

1/4 cup butter

1/2 cup heavy cream, plus more if necessary

Kosher salt and freshly ground black pepper

Clean the wolf fish fillets and remove any pin bones. Keep chilled.

If you are using the beef fat cap, preheat the oven to 400°F and roast the fat for about 1 hour, until rendered and brown. Strain and reserve the drippings, discarding any leftover solid fat.

In a saucepan over medium heat, heat 2 tablespoons of the rendered beef fat or drippings. Add the fennel, onion, carrot, leek, and celery and sauté until they start to brown. Add the garlic and sauté for 1 minute. Drain off the fat and reserve. Add the veal stock and Syrah and raise the heat to high. Bring to a boil and add the lemon juice and zest, bay leaves, and thyme. Lower the heat and let simmer until reduced by one quarter. Skim any fat or impurities that rise to the surface and remove the bay leaves and thyme, but do not strain. Keep warm. You will have about 6 cups of stock.

To make the purée, preheat the oven to 400°F. Place the celeriac, potatoes, and parsley root in a saucepan of salted water to cover. Bring to a boil and cook until a knife

144 Kinkead's Cookbook

inserts easily into the vegetables. Drain the vegetables and pass through a ricer onto a baking sheet. Dry in the oven for 3 to 4 minutes.

In a small saucepan or microwave, bring the butter and cream to a boil. Place the dried vegetables in the bowl of an electric mixer fitted with the whisk attachment. (Leave the oven on for baking the wolf fish.) Slowly add in the hot butter-cream mixture. If too thick, add a little more cream. Add salt and pepper and pass the purée through a tamis (stainless steel drum sieve). Celeriac is fairly fibrous and needs the taming.

To prepare the wolf fish, in a braising pan over medium-high heat, heat the reserved rendered beef fat or drippings. Salt and pepper the wolf fish and sear it in the fat. Transfer the fish from the pan and pour out and discard all but 2 tablespoons of the fat. Add the flour and cook for 2 to 3 minutes, stirring, to make a roux. Add the veal stock to the braising pan and bring to a simmer, whisking from time to time. It will start to thicken. Return the wolf fish to the pan. Braise in the oven, uncovered, for 5 to 7 minutes, turning every minute or so, until the fish is tender.

Remove the fish from the pan and keep warm. Place the pan on a high heat and reduce the liquid to a sauce that easily coats a spoon. Stir in the tarragon.

To serve, place a wolf fish fillet on each of 6 warm plates. Sauce the fish with the veal sauce, making sure the vegetables are evenly divided. Garnish with the parsley root–celeriac purée.

Cod with Crab Imperial, Spoon Bread, and Mustard Sauce

*I*n the past, we at Kinkead's have been accused of presenting dishes that are really "Thanksgiving on a plate." While I take issue with most of that criticism, this dish certainly qualifies. The flavor combinations of the various elements make for a tastier dish that is far more than the sum of its parts. Because each part of the dish works so well with the others, I think the dish is much diminished without all the side dishes. Feel free to pick and choose for this or other dishes.

Aside from the use of cod (as opposed to Chesapeake rockfish) this is a dish that represents the Mid-Atlantic bounty. We have been happiest with the results using a thick, center-cut cod fillet, but striped bass or rockfish works just fine with this recipe; in fact, almost any thick, flaky whitefish will do.

CRAB IMPERIAL

1 tablespoon butter

1 tablespoon all-purpose flour

1/2 cup milk

1/4 cup cream

1 tablespoon cream sherry

1/4 teaspoon kosher salt

1/4 teaspoon white pepper

1/2 teaspoon freshly squeezed lemon juice

2 drops Tabasco Sauce

3 drops Worcestershire sauce

1/2 cup mayonnaise

4 ounces jumbo lump crabmeat

1 1/2 cups Reduction Fish Cream (page 259)

2 tablespoons coarse-grain mustard

6 (3-inch) rounds Virginia Ham and Corn Spoon Bread (page 225)

1 1/2 cups Sweet Potato–Butternut Squash Purée (page 218)

1 recipe Steamed Spinach with Garlic and Lemon (page 219)

6 (5-ounce) pieces center-cut cod fillets

2 tablespoons butter

1/2 teaspoon kosher salt

1/2 teaspoon white pepper

To prepare the crab imperial, in a saucepan over medium heat, melt the butter. Add the flour and cook, whisking, to a runny roux. Add the milk and cream and bring to a boil, whisking constantly. Add the sherry, salt, pepper, lemon juice, Tabasco, and Worcestershire and cook for 2 minutes at low heat. Let cool to room temperature. Fold in the mayonnaise and crabmeat and let cool completely but do not refrigerate.

Prepare the fish cream. Stir in the mustard until combined. Prepare the spoon bread, sweet potato–squash purée, and spinach.

To prepare the fish, preheat the oven to 375°F. Place the cod fillets on a sheet pan. Salt and pepper each piece of fish and top with 4 tablespoons of the crab imperial. Brush with the butter and bake for 8 to 10 minutes, until the fish is cooked through and the tops are starting to bubble.

To assemble, warm 6 plates and place a crab-topped cod fillet in the center of each. Spoon 4 tablespoons of the fish sauce around it. Serve with the spoon bread, sweet potato–squash purée, and spinach.

THE BOCUSE D'OR

The Bocuse d'Or, named for chef Paul Bocuse, is an international culinary competition that takes place in Lyons, France every two years. Representatives from twenty-two to twenty-five countries around the world compete for what is arguably the most prestigious individual prize in cooking. At the final competition, each participant must create and serve two dishes for twelve people: one of meat and one of seafood, each with three distinct complementary garnishes. The finals take place over two days, with half of the competitors competing on the first day and the remainder on the second. All of this takes place in an amphitheater with thousands of screaming, highly partisan fans. This is cooking as a spectator sport.

Each participant must prepare his or her original creations, making every single edible part of the dish from scratch, and present each of the two dishes in the classic French banquet style—eleven portions on a silver tray—plus a single plated version. Each chef is provided a mini kitchen equipped with all the major cooking equipment necessary; the chef must supply all knives, tools, specialty equipment, and silver trays. Five and a half hours are allowed for the chef to complete and display both trays of food. Noted chefs representing each of the competing countries then judge all the trays for originality, taste, and presentation.

Tracy O'Grady worked at Kinkead's from its opening in 1993 until her recent departure to open her own restaurant. Over a ten-year period, Tracy worked her way from garde-manger all the way to chef de cuisine. She had entered a few regional and national competitions with some success. She is self-taught, a very talented cook, and as hardworking an individual as I have ever had the pleasure of working with.

In 1999, while working as the night sous-chef at Kinkead's, Tracy decided to enter the Bocuse d'Or culinary competition. So began a two-year odyssey for Tracy that took the Kinkead's staff along for the ride. Everyone who worked at Kinkead's helped in some way to get Tracy to the Bocuse d'Or.

Chefs who regularly compete in cooking competitions of this caliber, particularly at the international level, require a great deal of financial support to compete effectively. Thus, these cooks work almost exclusively for employers who can afford to support that endeavor financially and, more important, can provide the competitor with the time off or away from the workplace to travel and practice. This means working in big hotels, country clubs, or executive dining rooms, or as executive chefs of multi-unit restaurants. Clearly, then, being sponsored by an independent restaurant puts a competitor at a significant disadvantage.

In order to compete, Tracy had to raise the funds for the silver trays, travel, equipment, and practice. This grew to about $100,000 in total. A great deal of the work required to compete competitively in international competition consists of lining up sponsors—companies or individuals who contribute money or products to help the chef compete. In fact, fundraising took up much of the time of the entire restaurant staff. From holding raffles to selling catered dinners to entertaining at the restaurant, virtually everyone pitched in.

In addition to fundraising, Tracy had to practice in a working restaurant during hours the restaurant was not serving meals (from midnight to 10:00 A.M.). She also had to work her regular shifts. While we were able to make some accommodations for her schedule, Tracy still worked a fifty-five-hour week plus practice time.

Tracy finally made it to Lyons and did a phenomenal job. The year of Tracy's competition, the meat and fish were whole baby lamb and *loup de mer* (a Mediterranean sea bass). She finished in ninth place overall (a little above average for American participants) and her fish presentation took sixth place overall. I can speak for all her coworkers when I say we were very, very proud of her.

Tracy's Bocuse d'Or Sea Bass with Clams, Garlic, and a Fennel Tart

SERVES 6

Former Kinkead's chef Tracy O'Grady served this dish at the Bocuse d'Or. If you can't find loup de mer, striped bass or black sea bass are the most comparable substitutes. Sea scallops are also an excellent substitute. At Kinkead's, more often than not we would use scallops in this dish and accompany it with Steamed Spinach with Garlic and Lemon (page 219).

5 small fennel bulbs

1 cup butter

3 thick bacon strips, sliced thinly

1/4 cup olive oil

3 cloves garlic, sliced

1/2 teaspoon thyme leaves

1 shallot, minced

1/2 small yellow garlic, sliced

1 cup Bandol rosé or other rosé wine

10 black peppercorns

2 bay leaves

1/4 teaspoon red pepper flakes

1 cup clam juice

1 cup chicken stock (page 255)

24 littleneck clams

Sea salt and freshly ground black pepper

1/2 teaspoon sugar

6 (3-inch) rounds puff pastry

1 egg yolk

6 (5-ounce) pieces loup de mer, skinned, pin bones removed

To make the fennel tart, trim the fronds from the fennel bulbs, chop, and reserve for the sauce. Trim the bottoms from 3 of the fennel heads and slice each lengthwise into equal halves.

Make fennel juice with 2 of the remaining heads and the bottom scraps by juicing the heads and the scraps in a centrifugal juicer. Reserve the liquid. (Alternatively, dice the heads and purée them in a blender with the scraps and enough water to liquefy. Pass through a fine-mesh sieve and reserve.)

In a sauté pan over high heat, poach the fennel slices in salted water and 1 tablespoon of the butter until just tender. Strain and trim the fennel slices to fit the tart pan or mold. Set aside.

In a small sauté pan over medium heat, sauté the bacon lardons until crisp. Drain the lardons and reserve the bacon fat. Wipe out the pan and add 1 teaspoon of the olive oil and 1/2 teaspoon of the bacon fat. Add the garlic slices and cook until they start to brown. Add the thyme. Remove from the heat and keep warm.

To make the sauce, in a braising pan over medium heat, heat 2 tablespoons of the olive oil. Add the shallot and onion and sauté just until they start to brown. Add the reserved chopped fennel fronds and cook for 2 minutes. Deglaze with the wine. Add the peppercorns, bay leaves, red pepper flakes, clam juice, chicken stock, and fennel juice. Reduce by one half, strain, and keep warm.

In a sauté pan over high heat, place the clams and enough of the cooking liquid to cover. Cover and steam over high

CONTINUED

heat for 2 to 5 minutes. Most should be open; discard any that are not. Remove the clams in the shells from the liquid and strain the liquid back into the rest of the cooking liquid. Cook this liquid over high heat until reduced to 1 cup.

In a blender, purée the cooking liquid and 3/4 cup of the butter with a little salt and pepper. The sauce should be the thickness of light cream. Keep warm.

Preheat the oven to 375°F. Press about 1/2 teaspoon of the butter into each of six 3-inch cast-iron pans or solid tart molds. Sprinkle with salt and the sugar and place a slice of cooked fennel in each. Over medium-high heat, cook until the fennel starts to brown. Turn each fennel slice and brown on the other side. Brush with the egg yolk and dock each puff pastry. Top with a puff pastry round and bake in the oven for 12 to 14 minutes, until the pastry is golden brown. Remove from the oven and, using a small plate or baking sheet as a base, invert the tarts so the fennel is on top. Keep warm.

Salt and pepper each fillet of fish. In a sauté pan over medium heat, heat the remaining olive oil. When hot, sauté the fillets for 2 to 3 minutes. Turn and sauté for about 2 more minutes. If the fillets are thick, they may require 3 to 4 minutes in the oven to cook through.

To serve, on each of 6 warm dinner plates, place about 4 tablespoons of the sauce. Portion out the browned bacon-garlic-thyme mixture. Place a fillet on each plate and surround with 4 clams. Place a fennel tart on each plate.

Poached Tilefish with Cauliflower Purée and Caviar

SERVES 6

ilefish, an underutilized deepwater fish common to the East Coast of the United States and to Nova Scotia, deserves to be more popular than it is. Sometimes sold under the names golden tile *or* golden bass, *its flesh is lean, white, and firm. It has a delicate, sweet, almost shellfishlike flavor, possibly due to its diet of clams and other shellfish. Slow, moist-heat preparations like poaching, steaming, and braising work best. This is an asset for those seeking low-fat or low-calorie fish dishes, as moist-heat cooking methods tend to require little or no fat.*

1/2 cauliflower, cored and cut into florets

1 small Idaho potato, peeled and diced

1/4 cup butter

2 cups heavy cream

Sea salt and cracked white pepper

4 cups fish stock (page 254)

2 large shallots, sliced

2 bay leaves

2 cups dry white wine

1 large lemon, cut into slices

12 parsley stems

10 black peppercorns

6 (6-ounce) pieces tilefish, skinned

2 teaspoons Champagne vinegar

3 ounces beluga or sevruga caviar

To make the purée, in a saucepan, bring 4 cups of salted water to a boil. Add the cauliflower and potato, lower the heat to a simmer, and cook for 5 to 7 minutes, until tender. Drain, discarding the liquid, and return the potato-cauliflower mixture to the saucepan. Add 3 tablespoons of the butter and about 3 tablespoons of the cream. With a handheld blender, process until the purée is the consistency of soupy mashed potatoes. Add salt and pepper to taste. Keep warm.

To prepare the fish, in a fish poacher or other large pan with a cover, bring the fish stock, shallots, bay leaves, wine, lemon slices, parsley stems, and peppercorns to a boil. Turn down the heat to a simmer and add the tilefish fillets. Poach for about 6 minutes, until cooked through. Remove fish from poaching liquid, sprinkle with salt, and keep warm. Strain the poaching liquid and reserve.

To make a fish cream, in a saucepan over high heat, stir the champagne vinegar until reduced to a glaze. Add 2 cups of the strained poaching liquid and reduce by three quarters. Add the remaining heavy cream and reduce to a thickness that coats a spoon easily. Add the remaining 1 tablespoon butter. Add salt and pepper to taste and keep warm.

To serve, spoon the cauliflower purée into the centers of 6 warm plates. Top each with a tilefish fillet. Surround with the fish cream. Garnish by carefully spreading a generous 1 tablespoon portion of the caviar in a layer over the entire top of the tilefish. Serve at once.

Steak Fish and Whole Fish

Grilled Swordfish Puttanesca with Braised Fennel and White Beans ⌘ 154

Grilled Mahi Mahi with Tomatillo Sauce and Jicama Slaw ⌘ 157

Grilled King Mackerel with Pistachio Savory Pesto and Escalivada ⌘ 159

Pepper-Seared Tuna with Flageolets, Grilled Portobello Mushrooms,
and Pinot Noir Sauce ⌘ 161

Tuna Milanese with Wilted Spinach, Prosciutto, and a Parsley-Caper Relish ⌘ 164

Whole Crispy Snapper with Thai Coconut Curry ⌘ 167

Grilled Swordfish Puttanesca with Braised Fennel and White Beans

Swordfish is one of the best fish to grill because it has a firm texture and stays moist when cooked at high heat. Fish that make acceptable substitutes for this preparation are tuna, cobia. mako shark, marlin, or really any firm-fleshed steak fish. The puttanesca sauce is a little time-consuming to prepare, so the recipe makes more than you need for this dish. The leftover sauce is excellent over pasta and it freezes well.

PUTTANESCA SAUCE

2 (40-ounce) cans imported whole tomatoes

4 tablespoons olive oil

1 large yellow onion, diced (about 2 cups)

5 cloves garlic, minced, plus 10 cloves, blanched, peeled, and sliced

1/2 teaspoon red pepper flakes

1 teaspoon fresh oregano leaves

2 cups white wine

2 bay leaves

3 tablespoons tomato paste

2 tablespoons capers

1 cup pitted kalamata olives

1 teaspoon kosher salt

1/2 teaspoon cracked black pepper, plus more as needed

4 tablespoons extra virgin olive oil

1 cup basil leaves, chiffonade

2 tablespoons olive oil

4 small fennel bulbs, halved

2 cups chicken stock (page 255) or water

1 tablespoon extra virgin olive oil, plus more for brushing fish

2 cloves garlic, sliced

1/4 teaspoon kosher salt, plus more as needed

1/2 teaspoon cracked black pepper, plus more as needed

4 (7-ounce) center-cut swordfish steaks (about 1 1/4 inch thick)

2 tablespoons freshly squeezed lemon juice

3 cups cooked white beans (page 266)

2 teaspoons pesto drizzle (page 262)

4 sprigs basil

To make the puttanesca sauce, drain the tomatoes and reserve the liquid. Cut the tomatoes in 1/2-inch dice and reserve.

In a large noncorrosive saucepan, heat the olive oil and sauté the onion and minced garlic. When they are translucent, add the red pepper flakes and oregano and cook for 2 more minutes. Add the diced tomatoes and cook for 4 to 5 minutes, until most of the liquid has evaporated. Add the wine, reserved tomato juice, bay leaves, and tomato paste and cook for 15 to 20 minutes, until thickened. Add the capers, olives, the blanched, garlic, and the salt and pepper and cook for 3 to 4 minutes. The volume should reduce and the flavors intensify, and it should be chunky and thick. Remove from the heat and fold in the extra virgin olive oil and the basil chiffonade.

To braise the fennel, in a large sauté pan over medium heat, heat the olive oil. When hot, sear the fennel halves, cut side down, for about 2 minutes, or until brown. Add 1 to 2 cups of the chicken stock to barely cover the fennel. Cover with an oiled piece of parchment and poach for 10 to 12 minutes, until very tender. Transfer from the heat and drain, reserving the cooking liquid. Keep the fennel halves warm.

CONTINUED

In a sauté pan over medium heat, heat the 1 tablespoon extra virgin olive oil. When hot, add the garlic slices and sauté for 1 minute. Add the fennel cooking liquid and the 1/4 teaspoon salt and reduce by half.

To prepare the swordfish, preheat a grill. Salt and pepper the swordfish on both sides and brush with extra virgin olive oil. On a grill over medium-high heat, cook the swordfish on one side for 2 to 3 minutes, rotate a quarter turn so the grill bars will make a crisscross pattern, and cook for 1 more minute. Turn and repeat on the other side.

The swordfish should be cooked through but very moist. Brush with lemon juice and more extra virgin olive oil.

To serve, warm the beans and puttanesca sauce. Place about 3/4 cup of beans in the centers of each of 4 warm dinner plates or large pasta bowls. Surround with the sauce and top with a piece of swordfish. Place 2 halves of fennel at the 11 and 1 o'clock positions. Drizzle some of the pesto over the fennel halves. Garnish with a basil sprig and serve hot.

SWORDFISH AND OVERFISHING

Swordfish was at one time the most popular big fish served in the northeastern part of the United States. Its popularity, however, has fallen off somewhat in recent years as conservationists voice concern that swordfish is being overfished to extinction. The fishermen of many countries, not just the United States, have been overfishing baby or immature swordfish, called "pups," because they are fairly plentiful and easy to catch in nets or with long lines. Larger, more mature fish are generally caught by harpoon, which is less damaging to both the fish and the ecology, but more costly. Another aspect of the problem is that swordfish pups can be portioned into sizes that provide for both an attractive plate presentation and an effective means of portion control, so these baby swordfish have become popular with restaurants serving the fish.

I agree that there should be no commercial fishing of any immature fish species. If they are caught before they can reproduce, in a short time the population will be decimated. If you use swordfish, choose steaks from large ones, 300 pounds or more, preferably harpooned rather than line caught. They will be notably more expensive, but you will be doing your part to ensure that swordfish are around for your grandchildren (and mine).

Grilled Mahi Mahi with Tomatillo Sauce and Jicama Slaw

*M*ahi mahi, or dolphin fish, is found throughout the world in warm-water climates. It is a medium firm-fleshed fish that flakes but will hold up to grilling. It has slightly darker meat than striped bass and can be used in many of the same preparations. Cobia, king mackerel, and genuine American red snapper are acceptable substitutes.

Mahi mahi are not related to the dolphin, which is a mammal. In the wild, mahi mahi are good sport fish, and when just out of the water they are one of the prettiest fish in the sea. The skin is bright turquoise and blue with streaks of yellow. It looks almost electric. Once out of the water, the bright colors fade.

This preparation takes its inspiration from the Yucatan, using chiles, cilantro, tomatillo, and lime. Suggested accompaniments are black or pinto beans and fresh hot corn tortillas or tamales. The jicama slaw recipe makes about a cup extra, which you can serve with any grilled fish or chicken dish. You can omit the butter, but note that it tempers the acidity of the lime and tomatillos, and without butter the sauce will eventually separate.

TOMATILLO SAUCE

5 tomatillos (about 8 ounces)

24 scallions

1 yellow onion, sliced thickly

1 poblano chile

6 Anaheim chiles

3 tablespoons olive oil

Kosher salt and cracked black pepper

5 cloves garlic, minced

1 teaspoon toasted cumin seeds

1/4 cup freshly squeezed lime juice

1 jalapeño, finely minced

1 cup loosely packed cilantro leaves, plus some sprigs for garnish

3 tablespoons butter

JICAMA SLAW

1/2 jicama, cut into julienne (about 1 1/2 cups)

6 radishes, julienned

3 scallions, finely chopped

2 oranges, sectioned

1/2 cup cilantro leaves, loosely packed

1/4 cup freshly squeezed lime juice

1 teaspoon red wine vinegar

1 teaspoon sugar

1 large poblano chile, roasted, peeled, and julienned (optional)

1/2 red onion, julienned

1 teaspoon vegetable oil

Kosher salt and freshly ground black pepper

GRILLED MAHI MAHI

4 (6-ounce) portions mahi mahi fillets, skin and bones removed

Kosher salt and freshly ground black pepper

2 teaspoons vegetable oil, plus more for brushing

2 Hass avocados

2 limes, cut into wedges, for garnish

To make the tomatillo sauce, preheat a charcoal or gas grill to medium-high heat. Remove and discard the husks from the tomatillos, cut them in half, and reserve. Chop 3 of the scallions and reserve. Trim the tops and bottoms of the remaining scallions. Reserve 16 of these for grilling.

CONTINUED

Toss the remaining 5 scallions and the tomatillos, onion, poblano, and Anaheim chiles in the olive oil and add salt and pepper to taste. Place all of the vegetables on the grill and cook for 2 to 3 minutes per side. Remove the vegetables and place the chiles in a plastic bag. Keep the grill warm for the fish. When cool enough to handle, peel the chiles. Dice the poblanos and reserve. Split open one side of each of the Anaheims and seed them. Place 2 Anaheims in a blender with the grilled tomatillos, scallions, and onion, and the minced garlic, cumin, and lime juice, and purée. Transfer the mixture to a noncorrosive (glass or plastic) container. This yields about 1 1/2 cups.

Without cleaning the blender, add the poblanos, the reserved chopped scallion greens, jalapeño, some salt and pepper, and the cilantro leaves and purée. This should yield about 1 1/4 cups. The sauces are puréed separately to keep a nice bright green color.

To make the jicama slaw, toss all of the ingredients together in a stainless steel bowl.

To grill the mahi mahi, season the mahi mahi fillets with salt and pepper, and then lightly brush with the vegetable oil. Grill one side for 3 to 4 minutes. Turn and cook on the other side for 2 to 3 minutes. Toss the 16 reserved scallions in the vegetable oil, place on a cooler area of the grill, and grill for 2 to 3 minutes. They should be starting to char and become limp. On another cool area of the grill, warm the 4 whole Anaheims.

Peel the avocados, cut in half, and remove the seeds. Salt and brush with oil on both sides. Cut the halves into 1/4-inch slices and fan out. Set aside.

To finish the sauce, bring the tomatillo purée to a boil. Add the cilantro purée and when it starts to simmer, whisk in the butter. Remove from the heat. Add salt and pepper to taste.

To serve, place 4 to 6 tablespoons of the sauce on each of 4 warm plates. Top each with an Anaheim chile and a mahi mahi fillet. Add to each plate 4 grilled scallions, an avocado fan, and jicama slaw. Garnish with cilantro sprigs and lime wedges.

Grilled King Mackerel with Pistachio Savory Pesto and Escalivada

King mackerel or kingfish is the largest member of the mackerel family. Although smaller mackerel are very oily and strong-tasting, kingfish tend to have a much milder, yet still full flavor. Its firm flesh is great for grilling; in fact, this dish is ideal for an outdoor summer barbecue. Any other full-flavored fish—bluefish, striped bass, tinker mackerel, or even sardines—will also work fine with this recipe.

Escalivada is a Spanish cousin to ratatouille, an eggplant and vegetable stew—the difference being that escalivada is grilled rather than sautéed.

PISTACHIO SAVORY PESTO

1/2 cup shelled pistachio meats

1/2 cup summer savory leaves

3 cloves garlic, chopped

1/2 cup extra virgin olive oil

ESCALIVADA

1/2 small eggplant, cut lengthwise into 1/2-inch slices (about 12 ounces)

1 zucchini, cut lengthwise into 1/2-inch slices

1 large white onion, cut into 1/2-inch slices

3 or 4 plum tomatoes, halved

1 red bell pepper, halved, seeded, and deribbed

1 green bell pepper, halved, seeded, and deribbed

1/4 cup olive oil

3 cloves garlic, minced

Kosher salt and freshly ground black pepper

2 teaspoons coarsely chopped oregano leaves

2 teaspoons capers

2 teaspoons red wine vinegar

2 tablespoons toasted pine nuts

KINGFISH

1/4 cup beurre fondue (page 258)

Kosher salt and freshly ground black pepper

4 fillets kingfish, 5 to 6 ounces each, skin left on

1/4 cup olive oil

3 limes, quartered

To make the pesto, place all of the ingredients in a food processor and purée to a fine paste.

To make the escalivada, heat a charcoal or wood grill to medium-low. While it is heating, salt the eggplant slices and let drain in a colander for about 30 minutes to extract some of the bitter juices. In a stainless steel bowl, toss the zucchini, onion, tomatoes, and peppers with enough olive oil to coat. Season with salt and pepper and add the eggplant.

Grill the vegetables over medium-low heat. When all are cooked, peel the pepper halves and dice all the vegetables in 1-inch chunks. Return to the bowl and add the remaining olive oil and the garlic, oregano, capers, vinegar, and pine nuts. Add salt and pepper to taste and let sit for the flavors to develop.

To prepare the kingfish, crank up the fire in the grill to medium-high. Whisk the pistachio savory pesto into the beurre fondue and keep warm. Salt and pepper the fish and brush with the olive oil. Place the fish skin side down on the grill and cook for about 2 minutes. Rotate the fish a

CONTINUED

quarter turn so the grill bars make a crisscross pattern and cook for 1 to 2 minutes more. Turn the fish over and cook for 2 to 3 minutes. Brush with olive oil and sprinkle with lime juice.

To serve, place a piece of kingfish in the middle of each of 4 warm plates. Sauce the plate with the pistachio savory pesto. Garnish with the escalivada and serve some extra pistachio savory pesto on the side.

Pepper-Seared Tuna with Flageolets, Grilled Portobello Mushrooms, and Pinot Noir Sauce

SERVES 6

This is the second-best-selling dish at Kinkead's. It's particularly popular in the fall or winter. It was inspired by a Kinkead's wine dinner that featured all red wines. Although many fish dishes go very well with red wines, I wanted a fish preparation that was designed specifically for Pinot Noir—one in which the wine not only complemented the seafood but was also an integral part of the flavor combination. The marriage of veal and fish stock for the sauce may sound odd, but it works very well, especially with the large amount of garlic in the recipe. The butter finishing of the sauce balances and mellows out the otherwise hard-edged flavors. The tuna is best served rare. Note that the mushrooms must marinate overnight before proceeding. The marinade can be used for another batch of portobellos and then discarded.

5 large portobello mushrooms

1 cup olive oil

3 cloves garlic, sliced

4 sprigs rosemary

6 sprigs thyme

2 tablespoons olive oil

1 cup finely diced mirepoix (page 263)

2 large shallots, sliced

4 cloves garlic, sliced

1 (750-ml) bottle Pinot Noir

4 tablespoons whole black peppercorns

4 cups veal stock (page 256)

2 cups fish stock (page 254)

1 tablespoon red wine vinegar

1/2 cup plus 2 tablespoons butter

40 to 48 ounces center-cut, sushi-grade tuna, trimmed of all sinew

Kosher salt and freshly ground black pepper

1/2 cup peanut or vegetable oil

3 cups cooked flageolet beans (page 266)

1 recipe Steamed Spinach with Garlic and Lemon (page 219)

To make the marinated mushrooms, separate the portobello caps from the stems. Trim and wash the mushroom stems and chop coarsely; reserve for the Pinot Noir sauce.

Toss the portobello caps, olive oil, garlic, rosemary, and thyme together and place in a container large enough to hold the caps. Marinate for at least 24 hours.

To make the sauce, in a braising pan over high heat, heat the olive oil, the chopped portobello stems, and the mirepoix and cook until the vegetables start to brown. Add the shallots and garlic and sauté for 1 more minute. Add the Pinot Noir and 1 tablespoon of the whole black peppercorns. Reduce by one half. Add the veal and fish stocks and vinegar and any reserved mushroom juices. Reduce by one half. Strain. Finish the sauce by puréeing in a blender with the 1/2 cup butter. Keep warm.

Cut the tuna into six 7-ounce portions, 1 1/4 to 1 1/2 inches thick. Keep chilled until ready to cook.

CONTINUED

Preheat a grill to medium-high heat. Salt and pepper the mushroom caps and place on the hot grill, top side down. Grill for 1 to 2 minutes, rotate a quarter turn so the grill bars will make a crisscross pattern, and grill for 1 more minute. Turn over and grill for 2 to 3 minutes. Transfer from the grill, slice each into 6 slices, and keep warm. Reserve any juices that collect for the Pinot Noir sauce.

To cook the fish, crack the remaining black peppercorns coarsely, using the bottom of a small sauté pan, and spread on a plate. Salt each tuna portion, and then press the fish down into the cracked black pepper on one side only.

In a sauté pan over high heat, heat the peanut oil and the remaining butter. When very hot, sear the tuna, pepper side down, for 1 to 2 minutes, until crisp. Turn and sear for 1 more minute. It should be very rare. For more doneness, preheat the oven to 400°F oven and cook for 1 to 2 minutes, longer for more doneness.

To serve, divide the flageolets onto 6 warm plates. On each plate place some sautéed spinach and 5 portobello slices. Slice each tuna portion diagonally and place the 2 pieces on each plate, cut side up so the rare meat shows. Place 1/4 cup of the Pinot Noir sauce around the slices.

Tuna Milanese with Wilted Spinach, Prosciutto, and a Parsley-Caper Relish

his dish takes its inspiration from the Italian classic veal milanese. Instead of a thinly pounded veal chop, we use a thin tuna steak. It is best to start with tuna steaks cut to about 3/4-inch thick, and then to gently pound them to 1/2-inch thick. Tuna does not have the textural strength of veal, so heavy pounding will tear the flesh and make it mushy. Be gentle. I recommend cooking the tuna rare to medium-rare.

For a variation try swordfish; it also gives great results. You can omit the prosciutto, but if you do, increase the salt a little. The relish recipe makes more than you need to garnish the dish, so serve the remainder on the side.

PARSLEY-CAPER RELISH

1 bunch Italian flat-leaf parsley, leaves only (about 1/2 cup loosely packed)

1 lemon, peeled, sectioned, seeded, and diced, plus 6 lemon crowns for garnish

2 tablespoons capers

1/4 cup extra virgin olive oil

1 tablespoon red wine vinegar

2 shallots, minced

2 cloves garlic, minced

Kosher salt and freshly ground black pepper

2/3 cup dried currants or raisins

1/2 cup port

6 (5- to 6-ounce) tuna steaks (about 1/2 inch thick)

3 cups dry breadcrumbs

3/4 cup freshly grated Parmesan cheese

1/2 cup olive oil

2 tablespoons chopped fresh parsley

Kosher salt and freshly ground black pepper

1/4 cup extra virgin olive oil, plus more as needed

1/2 cup clarified butter (page 257)

Buttermilk for dipping (optional)

12 button mushrooms, quartered

2 tablespoons butter

2 cloves garlic, minced

1 pound spinach (about 3 cups, loosely packed)

1/2 cup pine nuts, toasted

4 ounces prosciutto, sliced thin and cut into julienne

1 small red onion, julienned

1/2 cup red wine vinegar

2 tablespoons freshly squeezed lemon juice

Parsley sprigs, for garnish

To make the relish, coarsely chop the parsley leaves and place in a stainless steel bowl. Stir in the lemon, capers, oil, vinegar, shallots, and garlic. Let the relish sit for 5 to 10 minutes for the flavors to develop.

In a saucepan, poach the currants in the port and a little water just to cover. Cook for 3 to 4 minutes, until they are plump and most of the liquid is evaporated. Drain and discard the liquid.

To prepare the tuna, gently pound the steaks to 1/2-inch-thick paillards. In a stainless steel bowl, combine the breadcrumbs, 1/2 cup of the cheese, the olive oil, and parsley with salt and pepper to taste. In a small bowl, combine the extra virgin olive oil and the clarified butter. Salt and pepper the

CONTINUED

tuna paillards and dredge in the oil-butter mixture, then in the breadcrumbs, thoroughly coating both sides. Refrigerate for 30 minutes.

In a sauté pan over medium-high heat, heat 1 tablespoon of the oil and sauté the mushrooms until browned. Reserve.

In a sauté pan over medium-high heat, heat 2 tablespoons of the oil and when hot, add the butter. Add the breaded paillards and sauté on one side for about 2 minutes, until brown and crisp. Make sure not to crowd the sauté pan; you will probably only be able to cook 2 paillards at a time. Turn and cook the other side for 1 to 2 minutes, until brown and crisp. Keep warm.

To prepare the wilted spinach, after cooking the paillards, wipe out the pan and heat 1 tablespoon of the oil (or leftover butter-oil mixture) to the pan. Add the garlic and cook for 2 minutes. Add the spinach, pine nuts, prosciutto, and sautéed mushrooms and cook until the spinach starts to wilt. Transfer from the heat.

In a stainless steel bowl, combine the plumped currants, onion, the remaining 1/4 cup cheese, and the wilted spinach mixture. Dress with the vinegar and toss to coat.

To serve, divide the spinach mixture evenly on 6 warm dinner plates and sprinkle with lemon juice. Top each salad with a tuna paillard and top each paillard with some of the relish. Serve warm with lemon and parsley.

Whole Crispy Snapper with Thai Coconut Curry

The wok-fried whole fish dishes of China and Southeast Asia inspired this spicy dish of complex flavors. At Kinkead's, we serve the fish standing up, as if it were still swimming, an effect that can be achieved by placing the bent fish in the basket of a home fryer. You can make the dish hotter by adding more sambal or chopped Thai bird chiles. Many of the customers at Kinkead's like an additional dipping sauce for fish; if you agree, try the Vietnamese Lime Dipping Sauce (page 261).

The best fish to use for this dish is a B-liner red snapper or a black sea bass between 1 and 1½ pounds. Fish larger than that make for too big an individual portion. Have the fishmonger scale and gut it and remove the gills, but leave the head and tail on.

MARINADE

2 cups soy sauce

2 teaspoons minced fresh ginger

¼ cup rice wine or sherry

2 large egg whites

THAI COCONUT CURRY

2 tablespoons peanut or other vegetable oil

½ small red onion, finely sliced (about 1 cup)

½ stalk celery, finely sliced

1 clove garlic, minced

1 tablespoon grated fresh ginger

2 tablespoons Thai red curry paste

1 teaspoon sambal

1 tablespoon soy sauce

2 tablespoons cream sherry

1 tablespoon rice wine vinegar

1 tablespoon freshly squeezed lime juice

2 Kaffir lime leaves (optional)

1 cup chicken stock (page 255) or water

2 cups coconut milk

2 tablespoons sugar

CRISPY SNAPPER

4 (1- to 1½-pound) whole red snappers

4 to 6 cups peanut or vegetable oil for frying

4 cups cornstarch

2 potatoes, cut into 1-inch cubes

16 cauliflower florets (about ½ small head)

16 snow peas

4 scallions, finely cut diagonally

½ cup loosely packed cilantro leaves

CUCUMBER SALAD

1 cucumber, peeled, seeded, and cut into crescents

½ red onion, julienned

3 tablespoons ginger juice (page 264)

2 scallions, julienned

Kosher salt and freshly ground black pepper

To prepare the marinade, combine all of the ingredients in a stainless steel bowl and marinate for about 1 hour.

To prepare the curry, in a saucepan over medium heat, heat the peanut oil and add the onion, celery, garlic, and ginger. Sauté until the onions are translucent. Add the curry paste and sambal and sauté for another 2 to 3 minutes. Add the remaining ingredients and cook for 20 minutes. Transfer from the heat to a blender or food processor and purée. Pass through a fine-mesh sieve and reserve.

To prepare the fish, preheat the oven to 325°F. With a sharp knife, on each side of each fish make 4 to 5 deep cuts through the flesh and to the bone.

CONTINUED

In a wok, fryer, or deep cast-iron pan, heat the peanut oil to 350°F. Preheat the oven to 350°F. Place the fish in the soy marinade and let sit for a few minutes. Remove the fish from the marinade and dredge in the cornstarch to coat. Shake off any excess cornstarch and fry the fish one at a time in the hot oil for about 5 minutes per side. Keep the fish warm in the oven until all are fried.

Meanwhile, blanch the potatoes, cauliflower, and snow peas separately in boiling salted water. Refresh the snow peas in an ice-water bath. Drain the potatoes and cauliflower in a colander. Reheat the curry, add the cauliflower and potatoes, and keep warm.

To make the cucumber salad, toss the cucumber, onion, ginger juice, and scallions together in a stainless steel bowl. Add salt and pepper to taste.

To serve, warm the snow peas by sautéing in a little oil or by briefly steaming. Divide the curry sauce with the vegetables into 6 large warm pasta bowls. Top with each with one of the whole crispy snappers. Garnish with the snow peas, sliced scallions, and cilantro leaves.

Shellfish

Lobster with Bay Laurel and Sauternes Cream ∽ 170

Pan-Roasted Lobster with Ginger and String Beans ∽ 172

Salt Cod and Lobster Cakes ∽ 174

Broiled Nantucket Bay Scallops with Sherry, Braised Endive, and Bayonne Ham ∽ 175

Sea Scallops with Jerusalem Artichoke Gratin and Black Truffle Sauce ∽ 179

Soft-Shell Crabs with a Warm Crayfish, Tasso, and Artichoke Salad,
and a Corn Butter Sauce ∽ 181

Mussels with Thai Green Curry ∽ 185

Mussels with Grainy Mustard, Garlic, Rosemary, and Garlic Cream ∽ 186

Lobster with Bay Laurel and Sauternes Cream

SERVES 4

The sweetness of the Sauternes marries nicely with the natural sweetness of the lobster. Sautéed spinach is a nice accompaniment.

An alternative is to stuff the body cavities with Lobster and Macaroni Gratin (page 111) before baking. Bake for 3 to 4 minutes at 400°F, then top with the claws and proceed with the recipe as directed. Finish the gratin just before serving by topping the macaroni part only with seasoned breadcrumbs and Gruyère.

4 (1¼-pound) live lobsters

½ cup crème fraîche

Juice and grated zest of 1 lemon

Sea salt and cracked white pepper

2 cups heavy cream

12 bay laurel leaves (fresh if possible)

1 cup Sauternes

2 shallots, minced

2 cloves garlic, sliced

1 teaspoon tomato paste

2 lemons, cut into wedges, for garnish

Preheat the oven to 400°F. Flip each lobster onto its back and drive the point of a chef's knife between its eyes. Bring a large pot of salted water to a boil. Add the lobsters and cook for 2 minutes only. Transfer the lobsters from the water. Split them, remove and reserve any tomalley and roe, and reserve. Remove the raw tail meat, slice into 5 to 6 slices, and return to the shell.

Twist off the claws, return them to the water, and cook for 4 to 5 more minutes. Crack the claws and knuckles and remove and reserve the meat. Try to keep the claw meat whole. Chop the claw shells with a cleaver. Roast the claw and knuckle shells in the hot oven for 20 minutes or so. When they start to brown, transfer to a saucepan and reserve for the sauce.

Whip the crème fraîche and lemon juice until the mixture starts to thicken. Add salt and pepper to taste and keep chilled.

To make the bay laurel and Sauternes cream, in a saucepan, combine any tomalley or roe and the heavy cream, lemon zest, bay laurel leaves, Sauternes, shallots, garlic, tomato paste, and the reserved roasted shells and bring to a boil. Cook for 3 minutes, lower the heat to a simmer, and cook for about 15 minutes, until reduced by half. Pass through a china cap strainer, pressing down on the shells to extract the most flavor. Strain again through a fine-mesh chinois or cheesecloth. Let cool in the refrigerator.

When the cream mixture has cooled, fold in the whipped crème fraîche mixture and add salt and pepper to taste.

To bake, place the knuckle meat in the heads of the lobster shell halves. Spread the bay laurel and Sauternes cream over the lobsters and bake for about 5 minutes. Preheat the broiler. Top with the claws, reglaze the lobsters with more of the cream, and broil for 3 to 4 minutes, until the cream starts to brown.

Serve immediately with the lemon wedges.

LOBSTER

Though there are those who love crab and shrimp, the lobster is the king of crustaceans. Both the European (sometimes called Brittany lobster) and the American lobster species are found in cold, northern Atlantic coastal waters. The European lobster (*Homarus vulgarus*) and its slightly larger American cousin are both dark blue-green to blue-black when alive, turning red when cooked. *Homarus americanus* is the species native to the northeast Atlantic coast, from northern Canada as far south as the Carolinas. Since lobsters favor very cold water, they are most plentiful from Maine north.

Lobsters are scavengers, primarily eating decaying material on the bottom of the ocean. Lobsters are also cannibalistic and will eat other small lobsters and shrimp. They have the ability to regenerate their front claws.

Try to purchase hard-shell lobsters. Soft-shell lobsters ("shedders") are lobsters that have recently molted and have grown back a new exoskeleton. They have a soft, flexible shell and a high water content, yielding less meat per pound. There are those (especially Maine natives) who insist that the meat is sweeter. Maybe, but for me it's also mushier. They are less tough than hard-shell lobsters, especially larger ones, but to me they are less flavorful.

I have always found it a myth that larger lobsters are inherently tougher or less sweet than other lobsters (except for shedders). With a larger lobster, the ratio of edible meat to skeleton is greater. A 1-pound chicken lobster (or "chick") yields about 25 percent of the body weight in edible meat. As you move up to a 2^1/$_2$-pound lobster, the ratio is about 31 percent. The bigger the lobster, the higher the ratio of edible meat to total weight.

Lobsters are available year-round but are most available and generally the cheapest June through September. Some insist that female lobsters are more delicate in flavor and, as such, are better for eating. I have never found that sex makes any difference. However, with the female you will get the coral—the egg sac—which is edible and excellent for coloring seafood mousses, soufflés, and lobster timbales. The tomalley is the lobster's liver, which is green and edible.

The sex of the lobster can be determined in much the same way as with the blue crab. Flip the lobster over. At the end of the carapace and at the top of the tail are two small leg-like appendages. In the male these are hard, pointy, and shell-like. In the female they are larger and more like soft paddles, to hold in the roe or eggs. Another difference is that the males have smooth legs and the females have hairy legs: the small, black, hair-like spikes on the legs also help to hold in the roe.

Lobsters are named according to size and are priced by the pound. Chicks are 1 pound or less. Catching and selling lobsters under 1 pound is illegal in the United States but legal in Canada. "Quarters" are 1^1/$_4$ pounds; "halfs," 1^1/$_2$ pounds; "twos," 2 pounds; and so on. Those from 1^1/$_2$ to 3 pounds generally cost more per pound than chicks or even very large lobsters over 3^1/$_2$ pounds. If you are purchasing the lobster for its lobster meat, check the price of chicks versus, say, a 3-pound lobster. If the price is $1 or more per pound less for the chicks, buy the chicks. If the price is less than $1 per pound different, go for the big guy—the usable meat will ultimately cost less.

Lobsters begin to die the moment they leave the salt water. Putting them in tanks merely retards the process. A lobster on ice that is four days out of the water is fresher and better tasting than one that is swimming around in a tank; it may have been there for weeks.

If you are cooking only one or two lobsters, steaming is a fine way to cook them. If cooking more than two, boiling is a better way to go. Lobsters taste best when prepared simply. That is why this book has only a few whole lobster recipes. A boiled lobster, cooked properly with butter and lemon, is very hard to improve upon.

Pan-Roasted Lobster with Ginger and String Beans

SERVES 4

*T*his dish was inspired by the Chinatown stir-fry lobster dishes we would eat after getting out of work late on weekend nights. Too fired-up to go home to bed, we would head down to Chinatown for some food and a few beers (or as the establishments who served past the legal blue-law hours called it, "cold tea"). The lobster or crab would be redolent of garlic and almost spicy because of the tremendous amount of fresh ginger in the dish.

Pan-roasting lobster involves searing the crustacean and then letting it roast, covered, in the pan to extract the flavor. You can use a very heavy pan or a wok with a lid. Cutting the lobster so the meat is exposed makes the dish easier to eat.

4 (1 1/2-pound) live lobsters

6 tablespoons peanut oil or other vegetable oil

6 cloves garlic, minced

4 thumb-sized pieces ginger, peeled and finely shredded

10 scallions, chopped

1/2 cup soy sauce

2 tablespoons rice wine vinegar

4 tablespoons cream sherry

2 cups lobster stock (page 254) or chicken stock (page 255)

2 small carrots, peeled, scored with a channel knife, and thinly sliced

4 teaspoons cornstarch

2 tablespoons water

4 cups string beans, trimmed

2 teaspoons sesame oil

1 cup loosely packed cilantro leaves

Flip each lobster onto its back and drive the point of a chef's knife between its eyes. Alternatively, plunge the lobsters, head down, into boiling water for 1 minute.

Quarter the lobsters by splitting into two halves, then cutting each half into tail and body sections.

Heat a large heavy sauté pan or wok over high heat and add 4 tablespoons of the peanut oil. Add the lobster quarters and stir-fry until the shells are red. Cover the pan and cook

for 2 to 3 minutes. Add the garlic and cook for 1 minute more. Add the ginger and half of the scallions and cook for about 1 minute. Add the soy sauce, vinegar, cream sherry, and stock and bring to a boil. Transfer the lobster tails to a large bowl and keep warm. Add the carrots and cook for 2 minutes.

In a small bowl, combine the cornstarch and water. Add this "slurry" to the pan and let the sauce thicken, about 1 minute. Remove the claws, crack them open, and remove the meat. Transfer the claw meat and the mixture from the wok to the bowl with the tails and keep warm.

Wipe out the pan and return it to high heat. Add the remaining peanut oil and when hot, stir-fry the string beans. The skin on the beans will shrivel and crinkle up. Add the sesame oil and keep stirring the beans. Return the lobster and sauce to the pan and heat through.

To serve, on 4 large, warm plates arrange the lobsters so each plate has a whole lobster. Top with the string beans and carrot slices. Pour the sauce over all. Garnish with the remaining scallions and cilantro leaves.

Salt Cod and Lobster Cakes

Cod cakes are an old New England staple, served for breakfast, lunch, or dinner. They can be served as a first course or main course and were traditionally served with baked beans, brown bread, and tartar sauce. This recipe is a modification of my grandmother's cod cakes, passed down through my father. He still makes them, albeit sans the lobster. To be true to Grandma Kinkead's recipe, they should be cooked in bacon fat.

Note that the salt cod must be soaked in water for at least 8 hours ahead to soften and remove the salt.

1/2 pound salt cod

5 tablespoons bacon fat or vegetable oil

1/2 small red bell pepper, seeded, deribbed, and finely diced

1 large shallot, minced

1/2 pound fresh cod, skinned

Sea salt

1/2 pound lobster meat (from a 1- to 1 1/2-pound lobster)

1 cup all-purpose flour, plus some for breading

2 teaspoons double-acting baking powder

2 large eggs, lightly beaten

2 scallions, finely chopped

1 teaspoon chopped chives

1/4 teaspoon cracked black pepper

1 cup fine cornmeal or johnnycake meal

1 tablespoon butter

1 1/2 cups tartar sauce (page 261)

Soak the salt cod in a pan full of cold water in the refrigerator. After several hours, drain and add fresh water. Repeat two more times. When done, the water should have almost no salt taste.

In a sauté pan over medium heat, heat a little of the bacon fat or oil and sauté the bell pepper and shallot until the shallot is transparent. Transfer from the heat.

Drain the salt cod and poach in a saucepan of simmering water for about 12 minutes, or until falling apart. Add the fresh cod and cook for 2 minutes. Drain, rinse in cold water, and pick through for bones. Dry on paper towels.

Chop both cods coarsely. Chop the lobster meat. In a stainless steel bowl, place the fresh cooked cod, lobster meat, salt, the 1 cup flour, the baking powder, and the eggs and mix lightly. Add the cooked shallots and bell pepper and the scallions and chives. Mix thoroughly. Add the black pepper and add salt to taste (usually the salt in the salt cod is enough to salt the cakes).

Form the mixture into 12 or so 1-inch-thick cakes. They will be very moist. Dip the cakes in the cornmeal to coat and refrigerate for a few minutes.

To cook the cakes, in a sauté pan over medium-high heat, heat the remaining bacon fat or vegetable oil and the butter and sauté the cakes until golden brown, 2 to 3 minutes per side. Do not crowd in the pan; make in batches. Salt and pepper the cod cakes and serve immediately with the tartar sauce.

Broiled Nantucket Bay Scallops with Sherry, Braised Endive, and Bayonne Ham

SERVES 6

or several years, I was chef at Twenty-One Federal on Nantucket Island. There are many, many special things about living on that magical island, but one of the best is the accessibility to the unique Nantucket Bay scallop, which are harvested in the waters around Nantucket Sound from November 1 (October 15 if you live there) to March 31. Some years the season is over commercially in December; others, it runs until March—it all depends on the bounty of the year's catch. For that portion of the year it seems like every resident of the island is a scalloper.

At the risk of bragging, I'll state that Nantucket Bays are simply the finest scallop in the world. How am I so sure? Because even the French chefs who now work in America, and those who come to visit, all agree they are the best. God knows it kills the French to admit that anything is any good if it does not come from France.

Cooked asparagus makes a nice accompaniment to this dish.

1¹/₂ pounds Nantucket Bay scallops (other small scallops can be substituted but will not have the same natural sweetness)

1 cup cream sherry

¹/₄ cup sherry vinegar

1 shallot, minced

2 cloves garlic, sliced

1 tablespoon water

¹/₂ cup plus 2 tablespoons butter

¹/₂ teaspoon sea salt

6 heads endive, outer leaves removed

1 tablespoon sugar

1 cup heavy cream

6 slices Bayonne ham or other cured, lightly salted ham, sliced very thin

¹/₄ teaspoon cracked black pepper

¹/₂ cup shredded Gruyère

Kosher salt and freshly ground black pepper

3 Potato, Cabbage, and Leek Strudels (page 215), cut in half diagonally

3 lemons, halved

To prepare the scallops, pick through, wash and dry the Nantucket Bay scallops. Pick off the small connector hinges ("feet") and reserve. Chill the scallops until ready to cook.

To prepare a sherry-garlic butter sauce, in a noncorrosive saucepan over medium-high heat, combine the sherry, sherry vinegar, reserved "feet," and shallots and reduce by half. Strain into a second noncorrosive saucepan and discard the solids. Add the garlic and reduce almost to a glaze. Add in 1 tablespoon of water and whisk in the ¹/₂ cup of butter, a little at a time. Add ¹/₄ teaspoon of the salt and keep warm.

To braise the endives, preheat the oven to 350°F. In a braising pan over high heat, melt the remaining 2 tablespoons butter and add the whole endives. Add water to just barely

CONTINUED

cover, the remaining ¹/4 teaspoon salt, and the sugar. Lower the heat to a simmer and poach the endives, turning occasionally, until a knife is easily inserted into the center. Transfer the endives from the water and let cool.

Reduce the liquid to almost a glaze and add the heavy cream. Reduce by half.

Butter a gratin dish. Wrap each endive in a slice of the ham and place in the dish. Cover with the reduced cream and some of the cracked black pepper. Sprinkle the Gruyère on top and bake for about 30 minutes, until the top is brown and bubbling. Transfer from the oven and let rest.

Prepare and bake the potato strudels.

To broil the scallops, preheat the broiler. Divide the scallops among 6 individual gratin dishes that will just hold the scallops. Add salt and pepper to taste and ladle the sherry-garlic butter over the tops. Pass under the broiler and cook for 4 to 5 minutes, or until brown and bubbly.

To serve, place each gratin on a large plate. Place one endive and 1 strudel half on the plate and garnish with lemon.

SCALLOPS

The scallop is a bivalve of the mollusk family and one of the most sought-after of all shellfish. All scallops are best during winter months. Scallops are hermaphrodites and, depending on the species and time of life cycle, have a red, white, or black egg sac or roe and white testes. All are edible. The large white adductor muscle is what Americans commonly recognize as a scallop; in the United States, the adductor muscle is usually all that is eaten. The fishermen discard the roe and all remaining organs, generally on board the scallop boat, because scallops shells do not close completely and can spoil quickly. The roe and other organs spoil far more quickly than the adductor muscle. Occasionally, you will find scallops with roe in this country. They are almost always imported.

Scallop roe has a rich creamy texture almost like a fine seafood mousse. Diners familiar with the practice of serving the scallop with its roe in Europe may find it wasteful that we do not sell more domestic roe scallops. However, aside from being very perishable, most scallops harvested in U.S. waters tend to have a black, somewhat gritty, and visually unappealing roe. In addition, scallops that have roe (and not all do) have less flavor than those without. Even in France, the best restaurants serving scallops are opting for the superior flavor of roeless scallops in many preparations.

Scallops are sold by the pound, either fresh or frozen. They are becoming increasingly more expensive, especially genuine bay scallops. The major varieties are described below.

The largest scallop, *sea,* or *king, scallop* is caught off both Atlantic and Pacific coasts in deep water. Sea scallops vary in size from about one inch in diameter to almost three. They have a deeper flavor and denser texture than bay scallops. These are the most common and most available on the market year-round. Prime season is from January through June.

The scallop catch is often soaked in water to add weight. The scallop will act like a sponge and soak up as much as 10 percent extra weight in water. Since scallops are sold by the pound, it adds to the total sold weight and profits. The best quality are dry-pack scallops, which have not been soaked. They are always more expensive but are well worth the price. Diver scallops—sea scallops taken closer to shore by divers rather than by dredging at sea—are also generally very good because they are hand selected and almost always dry packed.

Bay scallops are smaller and more uniform in size than sea scallops and are harvested off the Atlantic coast from the Delaware to Maine. The vast majority are caught off the coast of Massachusetts. Bay scallops run in size from about 1/2 to 1 inch in diameter. The bay scallop is generally sweeter and preferable in quick sautés or marinated raw preparations like a ceviche. The most famous—and, in this chef's opinion, the very best of all scallops—is the Nantucket Bay scallop. They are so sweet you can eat them raw like candy. This scallop is best in quick-cooking preparations. Nantucket Bay scallop season is officially from November 1 to March 31, but not much is caught after the first of the year.

Calico or *southern bay scallops* are very small scallops—generally about the size of a pencil eraser or a little larger—harvested off the Carolinas and the Gulf as well as off the east coast of Central and South America. They currently sell for about $4 per pound in a supermarket. These scallops are inferior to seas and bays for a few reasons. First, they are opened by being steamed, which partially cooks them. They are small and easily overcooked. Second, calicos tend to have neither the creamy texture nor the sweet taste of the other varieties. They are not, however, bad in soups and stews and in combinations with other, more assertive shellfish.

Sea Scallops with Jerusalem Artichoke Gratin and Black Truffle Sauce

SERVES 4

*T*he prize of this dish is the truffle butter sauce. It is a decadent, unctuous, and intense mouthful of black truffle flavor. It can go with most any fish and many meats and vegetables.

Several years ago I made this sauce for the course I was serving at a charity tasting dinner with several nationally renowned chefs. After the final dessert was served, the chefs were in the kitchen nibbling on the various leftovers. I glanced over and saw two of my colleagues dipping bread into the pot with the truffle butter. One was just shaking his head, moaning, "This s—t is amazing."

Yes, the ingredients are expensive, but this dish is a special-event indulgence. You can use dry-pack sea scallops or Nantucket Bays. Get whatever kind is good and fresh. If you are using sea scallops, try to get them no more than 1 1/2 inches in diameter. If you are using Nantucket Bay scallops, you have to sear and brown the scallops quickly at high heat or they will poach in their own juices.

The gratin can also be made in individual casseroles and served as an accompaniment to any fall or winter dish.

JERUSALEM ARTICHOKE GRATIN

18 large Jerusalem artichokes (sunchokes), scrubbed

2 teaspoons freshly squeezed lemon juice

2 cloves garlic, minced

Kosher salt and freshly ground black pepper

1 cup shredded Gruyère

2 tablespoons shredded Parmesan

1/4 cup crème fraîche

1 cup heavy cream

1/2 cup butter

1/2 cup sliced button mushrooms or portobellos

1 large shallot, minced

2 cloves garlic, minced

1/4 cup Madeira

1 large black Périgord truffle, sliced

1/4 cup chicken stock (page 255) or water

Kosher salt and freshly ground black pepper

12 medium to large dry-pack sea scallops (each about 1 ounce)

2 tablespoons vegetable oil

To prepare the artichokes, peel the Jerusalem artichokes and slice 1/8 inch thick (a mandoline is best for this task). Place in water that has been acidulated with the lemon juice to cover.

To make the truffle sauce, in a sauté pan over medium-high heat, melt 1 tablespoon of the butter and sauté the mushrooms until brown. Add the shallot and garlic and sweat for 1 minute. Stir and cook until almost all the liquid is gone. Deglaze with the Madeira and add the truffle and stock. Cook until the liquid is reduced to almost a glaze. Transfer to a blender. Add the remaining butter and some salt and pepper and purée. Keep warm.

To make the gratins, preheat the oven to 375°F. Drain and dry the Jerusalem artichokes on paper towels. Butter a ceramic casserole and sprinkle in a little of the garlic. Top

CONTINUED

with a single overlapping layer of one third of the Jerusalem artichokes, some salt and pepper, and one third of the Gruyère to just cover. Repeat with the cheese for 2 more layers, using the Parmesan instead of Gruyère on the top layer. Whip the crème fraîche and heavy cream slightly and pour over the Jerusalem artichokes. Top with the remaining Gruyère. Bake for 30 to 35 minutes, until bubbling and golden.

Remove from the oven and let rest for 5 minutes. Using a circular cutter, cut out six 3-inch rounds. Alternatively, you can serve the gratin family style.

To cook the scallops, rinse and dry the and season with salt and pepper to taste. In a sauté pan over medium-high heat for dry-pack scallops, high heat for bay scallops, heat the vegetable oil. When hot, sauté each scallop for 2 to 2$^{1}/_{2}$ minutes, until quite brown on both sides Transfer from the heat and let rest for 1 to 2 minutes. If you want the scallops more cooked, bake in an oven preheated to 375°F for 1 to 2 minutes, being careful not to overcook.

To serve, place a round of the Jerusalem artichoke gratin in the center of each of 4 warm dinner plates. Surround with the truffle butter sauce and place 3 scallops on each plate at the 12, 5, and 7 o'clock positions.

Soft-Shell Crabs with a Warm Crayfish, Tasso, and Artichoke Salad, and a Corn Butter Sauce

*C*rabs molt naturally from late April to mid July, but soft-shell "farmers" use special molting tanks to extend that season to mid or late September. If you see soft-shell crabs at any other time of the year, they are not fresh, but frozen. See page 182 for more about softies. Always be careful when cooking soft-shells, as they have a tendency to explode, spraying hot fat.

12 hotel prime soft-shell crabs

1 cup milk

1/2 cup buttermilk

4 ears corn, husked

1/2 cup heavy cream

4 tablespoons butter

1/2 teaspoon sugar

Sea salt and cracked black pepper

1 celeriac

1 tablespoon plus 2 teaspoons freshly squeezed lemon juice

2 Idaho potatoes, peeled and diced (about 2 cups)

9 baby artichokes

4 ounces tasso or andouille sausage

2 tablespoons vegetable oil

1 small red onion, sliced

2 stalks celery, sliced

4 cloves garlic, minced

1/2 teaspoon chile powder

12 scallions, white parts left whole and green parts diced

18 green beans, halved and blanched

2 tablespoons red wine vinegar

3 tablespoons olive oil

1/2 pound crayfish tail meat (buy fresh or cook 36 crayfish for tails)

1/4 cup corn masa

1/2 cup all-purpose flour

2 tablespoons coarsely chopped Italian flat-leaf parsley

Clean the crabs by trimming the tails and eyes and removing the lungs and head sac. Place in a stainless steel bowl with the milk and buttermilk and refrigerate.

To make the sauce, cut the corn off of 2 of the ears and blanch in a saucepan of boiling salted water. Grate the other 2 ears with a cheese grater to extract the corn milk and grated solids. Place the corn liquid in a saucepan and bring to a boil. Transfer the corn liquid with half of the whole kernels to a blender. Add the cream, butter, sugar, and salt and pepper to taste and purée. Keep warm.

To make the salad, peel and dice the celeriac and place in 2 cups of water acidulated with the 2 teaspoons lemon juice. In separate saucepans of boiling salted water, blanch the diced potatoes and celeriac. When tender, drain and reserve. Blanch the artichokes and slice each in half.

Slice the tasso into 1/8-inch slices; if using andouille, cut into 1/3-inch slices.

In a sauté pan over high heat, heat the vegetable oil and when hot, add the blanched potatoes, celeriac, and corn kernels. Sauté, tossing frequently, until the potatoes start to brown. Add the tasso, red onion, celery, garlic, chile powder, and scallion greens and sauté for 2 more minutes. Stir in the vinegar, the 1 tablespoon lemon juice, and salt and pepper to taste. Transfer from the heat and keep warm.

In a second pan, heat half of the olive oil and sauté the artichoke halves until they are hot and starting to brown.

CONTINUED

Toss in the scallion whites, green beans, and crayfish and add salt and pepper to taste. Transfer from the heat and keep warm.

To prepare the crabs, preheat the oven to 375°F. In a stainless steel bowl, combine the corn masa and flour and season with salt and pepper. Drain the crabs and dip in the masa-flour mixture. Shake off any excess flour.

In a sauté pan over medium-high heat, heat the remaining olive oil and sauté the crabs for about 2 minutes. Turn and cook on the other side for 2 more minutes. Transfer to a baking sheet and place in the oven for about 2 more minutes, until cooked through.

To serve, toss the Italian parsley into the warm artichoke-crayfish mixture. Portion out half of the corn sauce onto 6 warm dinner plates. Place the tasso mixture in the center of each plate and surround with 2 artichoke halves and the scallion crayfish mixture. Place 2 crabs on each plate and surround with the remaining corn sauce.

SOFT-SHELL CRABS

Soft-shell crabs are blue crabs that have molted and been removed from the water before they can regrow their hard shell. For the blue crab to grow, it must molt from its hard shell and grow a new larger one. The process is fascinating to watch. After the crab molts, it has a very soft, jelly-like skin and is vulnerable to predators. It literally backs out of its old shell and scurries to find a hiding place. Soft-shells are the same size as hard-shells, but whereas bigger is better with hard-shell crabs, I like the smaller "softies." Fresh soft-shells must be purchased alive and they should have very soft shells.

Older, not as quickly removed crabs are called "paper shells"; while good, they are not quite the same delicacy. A test of how fresh the soft-shells are is to examine how fat they are. Just-out-of-the-water soft-shells are plump and filled with internal water. As they get older they lose a lot of this moisture and become flatter and drier, even when still alive. Like lobsters, the livelier, the fresher. Soft-shells can be purchased frozen, but to me, this is one of those foods that you eat fresh in season and do without the rest of the year.

Soft-shell crabs can found throughout the East Coast. Because of the colder weather in the north, most are more plentiful in the Carolinas and the Louisiana delta.

Softies must be cleaned before cooking. Scissors are the best tool for cleaning soft-shells. To clean, hold the crab, top side up, and snip off the "face"—the eyes and mouth. Next, lift up the shell on both sides and snip off the featherlike gills underneath. Finally, turn the crab over and cut off the apron or flap. This is also how you can tell the boys from the girls, as the apron is T-shaped on males and beehive-shaped on females.

Soft-shell crabs can be sautéed, deep-fried, or even grilled. One note of caution: soft-shell crabs can explode, spraying hot fat on the unsuspecting cook. Be careful not to overcook when sautéing or deep-frying.

Mussels with Thai Green Curry

*O*nce the curry base is made, the rest of this preparation is very easy. I suggest that you make extra base and freeze it for later use. Clams, shrimp, or a mixture of fish and shellfish can also be used to make this spicy soup.

This recipe requires a good number of Southeast Asian ingredients: lemongrass, Thai chiles, Thai curry paste, nuoc mam, coconut milk, and Kaffir lime leaves. All can be found in a well-stocked Thai, Vietnamese, or Asian grocery. In mainstream grocery stores in many cities, there are aisles dedicated to ethnic products. You may have good luck there. Kaffir lime is usually difficult to find, so when you locate it, buy extra; it freezes well.

Cultivated mussels are recommended for the quantity called for here, as they don't require the cleaning that wild mussels need.

120 large mussels (about 5 pounds)

2 teaspoons kosher salt, plus more as needed

2 tablespoons vegetable oil

6 scallions, white and green parts chopped separately

1 large yellow onion, diced (about 2 cups)

3 cloves garlic, chopped

1 stalk young lemongrass, center only, very finely minced

3 tablespoons Thai green chile paste

2 teaspoons nuoc mam or soy sauce

2 tablespoons peeled, grated fresh ginger

2 (10-ounce) cans coconut milk

4 Kaffir lime leaves (optional)

1/2 cup dry white wine

1/4 cup cream sherry

4 small Thai bird chiles or other fresh hot chiles, chopped

2 tablespoons freshly squeezed lime juice

1 tablespoon sugar

Cracked black pepper

1 cup cilantro leaves, for garnish

Soak the mussels in ice water with the salt for 1 hour or so. Remove the beards from the shells and discard any mussels that don't close when squeezed. Keep refrigerated.

To make the curry base, in a braising pan large enough to hold the mussels heat the vegetable oil over medium-high heat. Add the scallion whites, onion, garlic, lemongrass, and green chile paste. Sauté for 5 to 7 minutes, or until the onions are translucent. Add the nuoc mam, ginger, coconut milk, lime leaves, wine, and sherry and bring to a boil. Cook for 3 to 5 minutes. If you like, you can freeze the mixture at this point.

Add the mussels, Thai chiles, lime juice, and sugar and cover the braising pan. Cook for 3 to 4 minutes. Discard any mussels that have not opened. Add salt and pepper to taste.

To serve, fill 6 warm pasta bowls with the mussels and pour the sauce over them. Remove the lime leaves and garnish with scallion greens and lots of cilantro leaves.

Mussels with Grainy Mustard, Garlic, Rosemary, and Garlic Cream

This mussel dish is the type of easy preparation that makes a great Sunday night supper served with an interesting salad and good bread. It can be used as a first course or luncheon main course as well. The beauty of this type of bistro dish is that it is a one-pot meal—just toss everything in and bring to a boil.

Do not use dried rosemary, even in a pinch. Be sure to wash and debeard the mussels. Cultivated mussels are generally very clean, but many wild mussels have "pea crabs," which are not pleasant to pick out.

48 to 60 medium to large mussels (if cultivated, about 2 pounds)

2 teaspoons butter

4 cloves garlic, minced

1 shallot, minced

1 cup Sauvignon Blanc, Chenin Blanc, or other dry white wine

3 cups heavy cream

8 (4-inch) rosemary sprigs

1 bay leaf

2 teaspoons pommery (grainy) mustard

1/2 teaspoon sea salt

1/2 teaspoon cracked black pepper

Crusty bread (optional)

Wash the mussels, debeard, and pick through. In a noncorrosive saucepan add the butter, garlic, and shallot and sweat for 2 minutes over medium-high heat. Add the wine and cream and bring to a boil. Cook for about 3 minutes, until reduced by one quarter. Add the mussels, rosemary, bay leaf, and mustard. Cook, covered, for 3 to 4 minutes, stirring from time to time. Discard any mussels that have not opened. Stir in the salt and pepper and remove the bay leaf and rosemary.

Serve in a large warmed bowls, with the crusty bread to sop up the briny sauce.

Meat, Poultry, and Game

Dad's Chicken Braised with Mushrooms, Garlic, Sherry, and Cream

his dish is the crowning culinary achievement of my father, Robert H., Sr. I am certain that he neither invented it, nor thought he would get to see his dish being fed to the first-class passengers on US Airways flights to Europe. It was served on those flights—and as for the invention, he certainly mastered a chicken dish that was consistently delicious and left his family of ten children feeling happily fed.

The real brilliance of this dish is the classic combination of garlic, mushroom, sherry, and cream. It can be prepared as a one-pot meal and as such, it is a terrific dish for large dinner parties.

At Kinkead's, we have used variations of this recipe with guinea hen, pheasant, and poussin. We have changed the blend of mushrooms to reflect seasonal availability, using morels in spring, porcinis or cèpes in late summer, and chanterelles in the fall. When "Dad's chicken" is adorned with piles of black truffle shavings, eating it is really a life-altering experience.

It is best to get double breasts with skin and drummer attached—sometimes called a Statler breast. You will need the carcass for the stock. If you have a use for the legs, it's probably more economical to buy whole chickens and use the legs for another dish.

8 (6-ounce) chicken breasts, with skin and drummer attached

Kosher salt and freshly ground white pepper

2 cups chicken stock (page 255)

2 tablespoons vegetable oil

3 tablespoons butter

5 cloves garlic, thinly sliced, plus 5 cloves garlic, minced

1/4 cup cream sherry

1/2 ounce dried porcini, soaked in 1/2 cup hot water for 20 minutes to rehydrate

2 cups heavy cream

2 pounds button mushrooms, quartered

1/2 pound oyster, chanterelle, or other wild mushrooms

HARICOTS VERTS

1 pound haricots verts or young green beans

2 tablespoons butter

1 shallot, minced

1/4 teaspoon kosher salt

1/4 teaspoon cracked black pepper

To prepare the chicken, remove the breasts from the carcass, wash, and pat dry. Salt and pepper the breasts and refrigerate.

In a saucepan over high heat, place the bones and trimmings (not the fat) and the chicken stock and bring to a boil. Decrease the heat to simmer and cook for 30 to 45 minutes and strain, discarding the solids. Return the stock to the saucepan over high heat and reduce to 1 cup. Reserve.

In a sauté pan or braising pan over medium-high heat, heat the vegetable oil and when hot add the chicken, skin side down. Do not crowd the pan; cook in batches if necessary. When browned on all sides, remove the breasts from the pan and set aside.

CONTINUED

Add 1 tablespoon of the butter and the sliced and minced garlic to the pan, and sauté for 1 minute. Deglaze with the cream sherry. Drain the soaked porcini, saving the liquid. Strain the liquid to remove any grit. Add the liquid to the pan along with the porcini, the reduced chicken stock, and the cream. Bring to a boil and start to reduce by one third.

Preheat the oven to 400°F. In a sauté pan over medium heat, melt the remaining 2 tablespoons butter and sauté the button mushrooms on all sides until they are browned and their juices are almost completely reduced. Add them to the reducing cream sauce. Repeat with the oyster mushrooms. When all the mushrooms are incorporated, add the chicken breasts and any juices that may have accumulated.

Cover the pan, place in the oven, and cook for 8 to 10 minutes, until the chicken is cooked and bubbling.

To make the haricots verts, bring a pot of salted water to a boil. Prepare an ice-water bath. When the water is boiling, blanch the haricots verts and cook until firm but no longer crisp. Drain and plunge into the ice-water bath, drain again, and reserve.

In a sauté pan over medium-high heat, melt the butter and add the shallot. When it just starts to brown, toss in the haricots verts. Heat through and add the salt and pepper.

To serve, remove the breasts from the sauce and place 1 on each of 8 warm dinner plates. Top with a selection of the mushrooms and some of the garlic cream. Place the haricots verts on the side.

Squab with Buttery Cabbage, Quince, Turnips, and Roasted Foie Gras

The combination of cabbage and foie gras in this dish juxtaposes an expensive ingredient and an inexpensive vegetable. The rich foie gras, earthy cabbage and turnips, and the unctuous meat of the roasted squab are a terrific combination. If the whole foie gras is too dear, omit it, or substitute wild mushrooms. Squab can be replaced with duck. It will not be the same, but it will make a delicious preparation nonetheless. I prefer to cook squab medium-rare or even rare; overcooking destroys its texture and unique flavor. Fresh cooked peas make a nice accompaniment.

4 squabs

2 cups mirepoix (page 263)

1 bouquet garni (parsley, thyme, bay)

8 cups chicken stock (page 255)

2 cups Pinot Noir or Syrah

Kosher salt and cracked black pepper

Coarse sea salt

Peanut or other vegetable oil for sautéing

2 large shallots, minced, plus 2 large shallots, finely sliced

1/4 cup Armagnac or other high-quality brandy

1 Grade A foie gras (about 1 pound), chilled for 2 hours

1 small savoy cabbage, outer leaves and core removed, sliced thinly

1 cup butter

12 small white turnips, peeled and blanched

2 quince, peeled, each cut into 6 wedges

Preheat the oven to 400°F.

To prepare the squabs, remove the gizzards and reserve. Run the birds under cold water to wash. Pat dry and remove the legs and wing tips. (At this point you can either confit the legs, roast them, or use them in the stock.) Cut through the backbone of the squabs so that the breasts, rib cage, and half of the backbone are intact.

Place the wing tips and remaining bones and gizzards in a roasting pan and add the mirepoix. Roast the bones and mirepoix for about 35 minutes, until brown.

To make the sauce, transfer the bones and vegetables to a small stockpot or braising pan, adding the bouquet garni and chicken stock. Deglaze the roasting pan with the wine, scraping the bottom, and transfer to the stockpot. Bring to a boil over high heat, and then decrease the heat to a simmer and cook for about 1 hour. Strain the stock into a smaller saucepan, bring to a boil, and reduce by half.

Preheat the oven to 400°F. Salt and pepper the squab breasts. In a sauté pan over medium-high heat, heat some peanut oil and sear the squabs until brown on all sides. Add a little more oil to the same pan, add the 2 minced shallots, and sauté until they start to brown. Deglaze with half of the Armagnac and add the liquid to the reducing stock. Remove from the heat and place on a roasting pan set with a baking rack, breast side up.

Roast the squabs in the oven for 6 to 8 minutes until medium-rare (or longer for more doneness). Remove from

CONTINUED

the oven and let rest for 5 minutes in a warm (not hot) place and leave the oven on.

Season the foie gras with salt, pepper, and the remaining Armagnac. In a cast-iron pan over high heat, sear the foie gras on all sides until brown. Place the 2 sliced shallots in a roasting pan and place the seared foie gras on top of them. Place in the hot oven and roast for about 10 minutes, until just set. The internal temperature should be about 100°F. Transfer from the oven and let rest for 5 minutes. Transfer the shallots on the bottom of the pan to the squab sauce. Slice the foie gras into 4 to 8 slices.

In a large sauté pan or braising pan over high heat, place the cabbage and $1/2$ cup of the butter. Cook, stirring occasionally, until wilted and starting to brown. Add $1/4$ cup of water and cook until wilted but still with a hint of crunch. Add salt and pepper and cook until almost all the liquid is evaporated. Keep warm.

In a sauté pan over medium-high heat, melt 2 tablespoons of the butter and sauté the turnips until they start to brown. Add salt and pepper and keep warm.

In a sauté pan over medium-high heat, melt 2 tablespoons of the butter and sauté the quince slices until brown on both sides. Keep warm.

Remove the squab breasts from the carcasses and keep warm. Add the breastbones to the sauce and simmer for 5 minutes. Strain the sauce into a blender, add the remaining $1/4$ cup butter, and emulsify. Keep warm.

To serve, portion out the cabbage on the centers of 6 warm plates. Surround with the squab sauce. Place 2 turnips and 2 quince wedges on each plate. Top each portion of the cabbage with 2 squab breasts and 1 or 2 slices of foie gras. Sprinkle some coarse salt on the foie gras. Serve at once.

Muscovy Duck with Clementines, Port, and Virginia Ham

SERVES 4

*M*uscovy ducks are larger than the commonly available Peking variety. The breast is large and has a darker meat and richer flavor. They range from smaller birds (females), less than three pounds, to larger specimens, five to six pounds. The larger ducks yield two portions per breast; the smaller birds provide a generous single portion.

The duck legs in this case are made into a confit or cured meat preparation. Note that making the confit requires refrigerating for 24 hours and about 5 hours of additional cooking time.

I find the combination of clementines, port, and salty Virginia ham a particularly good marriage of flavors with the duck. The clementines are used because they are basically a seedless tangerine and are easier to use as garnish. You can use tangerines, mandarin oranges, or even regular oranges if that is what's available. This is a nice dish to prepare around the holidays, as that is when clementines are in season. Sweet Potato–Butternut Squash Purée (page 218) is a nice accompaniment.

2 (2 1/2- to 3-pound) Muscovy ducks

2 cups mirepoix (page 263)

12 cups chicken stock (page 255)

2 cups port

6 to 8 sprigs thyme

2 or 3 sprigs sage

4 large sprigs rosemary

1/4 cup butter

1/2 cup Smithfield or other Virginia ham, julienned

Kosher salt and cracked black pepper, plus more for seasoning duck breasts

1 large shallot, minced

Juice of 4 clementines or tangerines, plus zest and sections of 2 more

3 tablespoons sherry vinegar

1 recipe Steamed Spinach with Garlic and Lemon (page 219)

Bone the ducks so the legs and breasts are separate, or have the butcher do it for you. Reserve the fat, gizzards, and carcass. Chill the breasts. Make the legs into confit according to the recipe on page 265, dividing all ingredient quantities by 3.

Preheat the oven to 400°F. Chop the duck neck, gizzard, and carcass into large pieces. Place in a roasting pan with the mirepoix, and roast, turning the pieces every 10 minutes or so, until very brown.

Transfer the contents to a large stockpot and cover with the stock. Deglaze the roasting pan with 1 cup of the port and a little water and add to the stockpot. Bring to a boil over high heat and skim off any impurities that rise. Turn down to a simmer, add the thyme, sage, and rosemary, and cook for 1 to 2 hours, or until reduced by one fourth. Strain the liquid into a saucepan and discard the solids. Bring to a boil and reduce to 3 cups. Set aside.

In an ovenproof sauté pan over medium-high heat, sear the confit for about 5 minutes, until brown on all sides. They should have enough residual fat from the confit process that you will probably not need more. Place the pan in the oven and roast at 400°F for about 5 minutes, until the leg skin is very crispy. Transfer from the pan and keep warm. Deglaze the pan with a little water and add this liquid to the duck sauce.

In a small sauté pan over medium heat, melt 1 tablespoon of the butter and sauté the ham for 1 to 2 minutes. Deglaze with water. Reserve.

Salt and pepper the duck breasts. In a sauté pan large enough to hold 2 breasts, over medium-high heat, sear the breasts 2 at a time, fat side down. Reduce the heat and let cook until they are very crisp and much of the fat is rendered. Turn and cook for about 3 minutes on the other side. The breasts should be medium-rare. Remove from the heat and let rest. If more cooking is desired, place in an oven heated to 400°F for 1 or 2 minutes.

Leaving the rendered fat in the pan, add the shallot. When it is just starting to brown, deglaze with the clementine juice and sherry vinegar. Add the citrus zests and the julienned Virginia ham and reduce to about 2 tablespoons. Add the reduced duck sauce and reduce to 2 cups. Whisk in the remaining butter and add pepper to taste. The saltiness of the ham should be enough for the sauce. Warm the clementine sections in the sauce.

Prepare the spinach.

To serve, divide the spinach on the centers of 4 dinner plates. Top each with a warm crispy leg. Slice each breast into about 10 slices and fan them around the leg. Garnish with the clementine sections and top with the sauce, making sure each plate gets an equal amount of ham and zest. Serve hot. Pass the remaining sauce on the side.

Rabbit with Sweetbreads, Artichokes, and Porcini

SERVES 6

*P*rofessional chefs know that certain foods make a dish sell better, whereas others retard sales. Sweetbreads, for example, as delicious as they are, are an organ meat and are not very popular except among more sophisticated diners. You have to make a pretty sexy preparation to move sweetbreads on a restaurant menu. Artichokes and porcini are two of the gold standards for making a dish get noticed. They also go together incredibly well. Despite all this, on any given evening at Kinkead's, I can be certain that we will sell, at best, 4 to 6 portions of this dish. That's a shame, because it may be the single best dish in this entire cookbook.

ROSEMARY GARLIC RUB

1 tablespoon picked, minced rosemary leaves

2 cloves garlic, minced

4 tablespoons extra virgin olive oil

3 (2-pound) rabbits, skinned and eviscerated, leaving the saddle whole

Kosher salt and cracked black pepper

$1/2$ ounce dried porcini

$1/2$ cup water

$1/2$ cup Madeira

2 cups mirepoix (page 263)

2 teaspoons thyme leaves, stems reserved for making stock, plus extra for garnish

2 cups Verdicchio, Sauvignon Blanc, or other dry white wine

8 cups chicken stock (page 255)

2 pounds veal sweetbreads, blanched (page 264), cleaned, and trimmed

4 tablespoons all-purpose flour

4 tablespoons peanut, canola, or other vegetable oil

5 tablespoons butter, plus extra as needed

3 cloves garlic

16 ounces fresh or high-quality whole frozen porcini

4 tablespoons olive oil

1 large shallot, minced

1 tablespoon freshly squeezed lemon juice

1 recipe Braised Artichokes (page 217)

To make the rub, mash all of the ingredients into a paste.

To prepare the rabbits, cut each forequarters into small pieces. Trim the excess belly from the saddle. Cut the bottom shank of the hindquarter legs. Salt and pepper the 3 saddles and 6 hind legs. Rub with the rosemary-garlic mixture and refrigerate for several hours.

Soak the dried porcini in the water and Madeira for 20 minutes.

Preheat the oven to 400°F. Place all the rabbit trimmings in a roasting pan and roast in the oven for 10 minutes. Add the mirepoix, 1 teaspoon of the thyme leaves, and any stems, and continue roasting for about 30 minutes, turning from time to time, until all are browned.

Transfer the browned rabbit bones and mirepoix to a stockpot and deglaze the pan with the white wine, scraping the pan for debris and adding to the pot. Cover the bones with 6 cups of the stock. Drain the soaked porcini and add with the Madeira. Bring to a boil and simmer for 1 to $1^1/2$ hours. Strain, discarding the solids, and keep warm.

CONTINUED

To prepare the sweetbreads, slice them into 12 rounds ³/₄-inch thick. Salt and pepper on both sides and dredge in the flour. In a sauté pan over medium-high heat, heat 1 tablespoon of the peanut oil and sauté the rounds until crispy on both sides. Add 1 tablespoon of the butter and cook through. Transfer from the pan and keep warm.

To make the porcini, mince 1 clove of the garlic. Clean and trim the woody parts off the fresh porcini stems and slice the porcini lengthwise. In a large sauté pan over medium-high heat, heat 2 tablespoons of the olive oil and sauté the minced garlic and half of the minced shallot. When they start to brown, add the porcini slices. Be sure not to crowd them; if the pan is not large enough, cook in batches. Brown on both sides and transfer to a warm plate. Keep warm.

To roast the rabbit, preheat the oven to 375°F. In an oven-proof sauté pan over medium-high heat, heat the vegetable oil and sear the hind legs, being sure to brown them on all sides. Toss a nut of butter into the pan, place it in the oven, and roast for about 25 minutes, turning once or twice.

Sear the saddles in the same manner as the legs, but roast for only about 12 minutes, until just done in the center. Transfer all parts to a warm place and keep warm. Deglaze the pans with a little of the rabbit stock and add the liquid to the sauce.

Thinly slice the remaining 2 cloves of garlic lengthwise. In a saucepan over medium heat, melt 1 tablespoon of the butter. Add the remaining minced shallot and the sliced garlic and sweat for 1 minute. Add the remaining 1 teaspoon thyme and sweat for 1 to 2 more minutes. Add the lemon juice and rabbit stock and reduce to about 1 cup. Whisk in about 4 tablespoons butter. Keep warm.

Cut each of the 6 artichoke bottoms in half. In a sauté pan over medium-high heat, heat the remaining 2 tablespoons olive oil and sauté the artichokes, cut side down. When they start to brown, turn and heat through on all sides.

Bone the rabbit saddles and slice into four 1-inch sections. You can either enrich the sauce by cooking bones in it for an additional 20 minutes and then straining, or use them to start a new stock. Return any juices that have collected to the sauce.

To serve, on each of 6 warm plates place 1 leg, 1 whole sliced loin, 2 artichoke halves, and several slices of porcini, and surround with the sauce. Place 2 rounds of crispy sweetbreads in the center of the plate. Serve hot.

Braised Lamb Shanks with Gigantes, Thyme, and Cabernet

SERVES 6

amb shanks are a terrific braised dish for the cooler fall and winter months. This recipe calls for one large shank per person, but you may find smaller shanks that are appropriate to serve two per person; for these, the cooking time will be shorter.

For the gigantes, or giant lima beans, you can substitute any dried white bean, or you can use fresh limas or cranberry beans. Fresh beans generally cook in one quarter the time needed for dried beans. Cooked baby carrots make a nice garnish.

6 cups cooked gigantes

12 cloves garlic

1/2 cup plus 2 tablespoons vegetable oil

10 tablespoons butter

Kosher salt and cracked black pepper

6 (12- to 16-ounce) lamb shanks

2 cups mirepoix (page 263)

10 sprigs thyme

6 sprigs rosemary

1/2 teaspoon dried thyme

2 cups Cabernet Sauvignon or other full-bodied red wine

8 cups veal stock (page 256)

2 cups breadcrumbs

2 teaspoons chopped fresh parsley

1 cup aïoli (page 259)

3 salsifies, blanched in acidulated water

Prepare the gigantes and keep warm.

To make a garlic-butter purée, in a sauté pan, place the garlic and cover with the 1/2 cup of oil. Bake uncovered for about 1 hour, or until quite soft. Drain the garlic, reserving the oil, and transfer to a food processor. Add 6 tablespoons of the butter, the 2 tablespoons oil, and salt and pepper to taste. Purée and refrigerate.

Salt and pepper each shank. In a braising pan over medium heat, heat about 3 tablespoons of the reserved garlic oil. Add the shanks and sear, turning and browning, for about 20 minutes, until browned on all sides. Remove the shanks from the pan and reserve.

Preheat the oven to 350°F. In the braising pan, combine the mirepoix, 2 tablespoons of the butter, 3 sprigs of the thyme, broken up, and the dried thyme. Cook over medium-high heat for about 5 minutes, until the mixture starts to brown. Deglaze with the wine. Return the shanks to the pan and add 6 cups of the veal stock. The liquid should barely cover the shanks. Bring to a boil, cover, transfer to the oven, and cook for 1 hour. Remove the cover and cook for 1 to 1 1/2 hours, until the stock is reduced by one third. Add the remaining stock to halfway up the shanks and cook for 1 more hour, until the meat is tender but not falling off the bone. Remove the shanks from the cooking liquid and let cool. Total cooking time is 3 to 3 1/2 hours. Leave the oven on.

To finish the garlic-Cabernet sauce, strain the cooking liquid into a noncorrosive saucepan and add 6 thyme sprigs. Return to a boil and reduce by one quarter. Whisk in the remaining 2 tablespoons butter and 3 tablespoons of the garlic-butter purée. Strain and keep warm.

Season the breadcrumbs with the parsley and salt and pepper to taste. Place the shanks in a roasting pan and spread

CONTINUED

the remaining garlic-butter purée in a thin layer over the tops. Cover the purée with the seasoned breadcrumbs, pressing the crumbs into the purée. Reheat in the oven for 5 to 10 minutes, until the crumbs are browned.

Slice the salsifies on the bias. Place 1 tablespoon butter in a sauté pan over medium heat, and cook the salsify for about 3 minutes, until browned on both sides.

To serve, divide the gigantes among 6 warm dinner plates or pasta bowls. Top each with a lamb shank and surround with the garlic-Cabernet sauce. Garnish with salsify and rosemary sprigs and top with a dollop of aïoli.

Garlic-Crusted Rack of Lamb with Rosemary and Merlot

For this dish, I suggest you purchase the lamb racks from a butcher who will trim and french them for you, shortening the rib bones and scraping the rack clean of sinew. A frenched rack will weigh 2 to 2 1/2 pounds uncooked. Often when you buy frenched racks there are no extra bones or trimmings. Don't worry—the shanks will provide enough flavor. Note that the rack must be prepared by rubbing with herbs and then refrigerated for 4 hours or overnight, before you proceed.

The last two ribs on the small end of the rack always present a problem, as they often get more cooked than the rest of the rack. In any case, they are fattier and less desirable than the rest of the rack. I suggest cutting them off and saving them for the next day to cook alla milanese. Pound them thin and season with salt and pepper. Dip them in garlic oil and butter, then in breadcrumbs. Cook in clarified butter (see page 257) and serve with an arugula salad. This makes a great lunch.

If ever there were a perfect food pairing it is roasted lamb and a rich, garlicky gratin of potatoes. Creamy Potato Gratin (page 209) was made for this dish.

3 racks American lamb, frenched; trimmings reserved

Kosher salt and cracked black pepper

1/2 cup olive oil

1 bunch rosemary (6 to 8 stalks)

2 teaspoons dried thyme

24 large cloves garlic

1/2 cup vegetable oil

2 large lamb shanks

2 cups mirepoix (page 263)

2 cups Merlot

4 cups veal stock (page 256)

3 tablespoons butter

1 shallot, minced

3 tablespoons chopped fresh parsley

2 cups breadcrumbs

FAVA AND CHANTERELLE RAGOÛT

5 tablespoons butter

24 chanterelles, cleaned and sliced in half if large

1 shallot, minced

2 tablespoons olive oil

2 cloves garlic, sliced

1 cup favas, blanched and peeled

1 cup haricots verts, blanched and cut into 2-inch lengths

1/2 cup English peas, blanched

1/2 teaspoon kosher salt

1/2 teaspoon freshly ground black pepper

1 teaspoon summer savory or tarragon leaves

If the lamb has not been frenched, trim all fat from the racks and scrape the rib bones. Salt and pepper the racks and rub with 2 to 3 tablespoons of the olive oil, 3 or 4 stalks of the rosemary, and 1 teaspoon of the thyme. Refrigerate for 4 hours or overnight.

To make a garlic-butter purée, preheat the oven to 300°F. In a sauté pan, place the garlic and cover with the vegetable oil and remaining olive oil. Bake in the oven, uncovered, for about 1 hour, until quite soft. Drain the garlic, reserving the oil. In a blender or food processor, purée the garlic with a little of the reserved garlic oil, add salt and pepper to taste, and let cool.

CONTINUED

To prepare the lamb shanks, turn the oven up to 350°F. In a braising pan over medium-high heat, heat some of the garlic oil and when hot, sear the lamb shanks on all sides. Remove from the pan, add the mirepoix and the remaining dried thyme, and sauté until the mixture starts to brown. Deglaze with the Merlot and add the veal stock. Return the lamb shanks to the pan and bring to a boil. Skim off any impurities that may rise to the top. Place in the oven and cook for about 3 hours, until the meat is tender.

Remove the shanks from the cooking liquid and let cool. Add half of the remaining rosemary, return to the stove, and reduce by half. Strain, discarding the solids. When the meat is cool, dice the shank meat, discarding the bones and any tendon or gristly pieces. Return the diced shank meat to the sauce. Finish the sauce by whisking in 3 tablespoons of the butter. Keep warm.

Break the remaining rosemary into 6 nice 2-inch sprigs for garnish. Tie the rest of the rosemary with kitchen string and add to the sauce. Let it steep in the warm sauce until ready to serve.

To prepare seasoned breadcrumbs, in a sauté pan over medium heat, melt the remaining 2 tablespoons of the butter. When hot, sweat the shallots. Stir in the parsley, breadcrumbs, and 1 to 2 tablespoons of the garlic oil. Add salt and pepper to taste. Remove from the heat and let cool. The breadcrumbs should be moist but crumbly.

To roast the lamb racks, preheat the oven to 400°F. Remove the racks from the marinade and wipe dry. In a sauté pan over high heat, sear the racks on all sides. Remove from the pan and let rest for 5 minutes. Coat the top of each rack with about 3 tablespoons of the garlic purée. Divide and evenly spread the seasoned breadcrumbs over the top of the garlic purée, pressing the crumbs into the purée. Top with about 1 tablespoon of the butter. Place the racks on a baking sheet with a wire rack and roast in the oven for about 15 minutes for medium-rare or 20 minutes for more well-done. Remove from the oven and let rest for 5 minutes.

To make the ragoût, heat 2 tablespoons of the butter in a sauté pan over medium heat, and sauté the chanterelles for 2 minutes. Add half of the minced shallot and cook until the chanterelles are browned on all sides and almost all of the cooking liquid is evaporated. Set aside.

In a braising pan over medium heat, heat the olive oil and sauté the remaining shallot and the sliced garlic until the shallot is translucent. Add the chanterelles, favas, haricots verts, and peas and sauté until all are warmed through. Add the salt, pepper, savory, and the remaining tablespoons butter and stir to coat the vegetables. Keep warm.

To serve, cut each rack in half and cut each half into a 2- and a 1-rib piece. Place on 6 warm plates so the ribs interlock. Remove the rosemary branches from the sauce and discard. Sauce each portion of lamb with 4 or 5 tablespoons of the sauce. Serve with the ragoût.

Prime Sirloin au Poivre with Madeira Mushrooms

This is my wife Dianne's favorite dish. She loves a "fat juicy steak" and this is the preparation she requests most often, should I be in the mood to cook at home. While this dish has been on and off the menu many times at Kinkead's, it is a dish we have used to celebrate many Christmas Eves, anniversaries, and special occasions at the Kinkead house. It has not, however, ever been a part of Mrs. Kinkead's birthday celebration. On that day, if I know what's good for me, we had better be sipping Champagne at a competitor's fancy, expensive restaurant.

This version of pepper steak differs from some others in that cream and Madeira are added to the sauce. If you prefer tenderloin rather than sirloin, I am sure you will be pleased with the results. Use an eight-ounce filet.

The Madeira mushrooms that accompany this dish add dramatically to the flavor. Button mushrooms don't get the appreciation they deserve. Much like the maligned iceberg lettuce (now making something of a comeback), domestic button mushrooms have every bit as much flavor as almost any wild variety, with the exception of porcini (cèpes) and truffles. The trick to extracting their full flavor is to cook them properly—until they have browned and released their moisture, so their flavor intensifies.

Mrs. Kinkead prefers her steak au poivre with mashed potatoes and creamed spinach. This recipe also calls for green peppercorns; use the brined variety.

1/3 cup whole black peppercorns

4 (12-ounce) aged prime sirloin steaks (about 11/2 inch thick)

Kosher salt and freshly ground black pepper

11/2 pounds button mushrooms

3 cups veal stock (page 256)

6 tablespoons Madeira

5 tablespoons vegetable oil

4 tablespoons butter

2 cloves garlic, minced

1 tablespoon chopped fresh parsley

2 shallots, minced

1/4 cup Cognac or high-quality brandy

1/2 cup heavy cream

1 teaspoon green peppercorns, drained

Coarsely crush the peppercorns. This can be done in a coffee grinder, or you can place the peppercorns on a hard surface, like granite or a cutting board, and crush by pressing and rolling the bottom edge of a sauté pan over them. Spread out the crushed peppercorns on a dinner plate.

Trim the fat and any sinew from the steaks, reserving the fat. Salt the steaks on both sides and press one side of each steak onto the crushed pepper. Make sure the side is completely coated. Refrigerate.

Wash and trim the mushrooms, cutting off the bottom stems and reserving separately. Cut the caps into quarters.

In a saucepan, bring the veal stock to a boil. Add 4 tablespoons of the Madeira and the mushroom stems and reduce the stock to 11/2 cups. Strain through a fine-mesh

CONTINUED

sieve, pressing on the stems. Discard the stems and keep the stock warm.

In a sauté pan over medium heat, heat 1 tablespoon of the oil and 1 of the butter. When hot, add the garlic and sweat for about 1 minute. Add the mushroom quarters and sauté until they start to brown. Add the remaining 2 tablespoons of the Madeira and deglaze the pan. Reduce, cooking the mushrooms until almost all of the liquid is evaporated and they are brown on all sides. Add 1 tablespoon of the butter and some salt and pepper. Transfer from the heat and toss in the parsley. Keep warm.

In a sauté pan large enough to hold 2 steaks without crowding, bring 2 tablespoons of the oil to medium-high heat. Sear 2 steaks, pepper side down, for about 3 minutes, until browned and the pepper forms a nice crust. Turn and sear for 2 to 3 minutes, until browned on the other side for a rare to medium-rare steak. Place the steaks on an ovenproof plate and keep warm. Wipe out the pan and repeat with the other steaks. If more doneness is required, place the steaks in a preheated 400°F oven for 2 to 3 minutes.

Wipe out the pan and bring to medium-high heat. Add the remaining 2 tablespoons butter and the shallots. Sauté until they just start to brown. Deglaze with the Cognac—if you are using a gas stove, be careful, as it will flame up. Add the reduced veal stock and the cream and bring to a boil. Add the green peppercorns. Reduce the sauce to the consistency of heavy cream. Place the steaks back in the pan along with any juices that have accumulated. Add salt to taste.

To serve, place a steak in the center of each of 4 warm plates. Top with the sauce and surround with the Madeira mushrooms.

Grill-Roasted Prime Sirloin with Garlic Potato Cake and Béarnaise Sauce

SERVES 6

*T*his method of cooking is really a combination of grilling and roasting. It works well for larger cuts of meat not normally cooked completely on a grill. My friend Jeremiah Tower's term for this type of cooking is "ovening the grill." It must be stressed that although this process works on a gas grill, the real benefit comes from live-fire fuels, especially wood or mesquite charcoal. The smoke from the wood or charcoal permeates the meat to some extent and provides a lot of extra flavor.

Dry-aged prime sirloin is very expensive but is worth the treat. Figure on about fourteen ounces per person, precooked weight, or about eighty-four ounces in total for six diners. A good butcher can cut and trim this for you. Try to get the rib end, not the sirloin butt end, which has a strip of gristle through it that must be cut away. Trim some of the fat cap, but not all. With a knife, score the top fat cap with crisscross cuts about 1/2 inch deep.

Besides the béarnaise, a small watercress, peashoot, or mesclun green salad is appropriate to accompany this dish. Serve with an aged American Cabernet Sauvignon or fine red Burgundy.

1 (84-ounce) aged prime sirloin strip

2 tablespoons olive oil

2 tablespoons kosher salt

Coarsely ground black pepper

4 large Idaho potatoes

1 tablespoon butter or bacon or duck fat

4 scallions, chopped (about 1/2 cup)

1 tablespoon vegetable oil

2 cloves garlic, minced, for garnish (optional)

1 cup béarnaise sauce (page 258)

About an hour before you want to cook the sirloin, rub it with 1 tablespoon of the olive oil, 1 tablespoon of the salt, and at least 2 heaping tablespoons of cracked black pepper.

Heat the grill (preferably wood or charcoal fired) to moderately hot, leaving one side cool.

Place the sirloin on the grill, fat side down. Be alert for flare-ups. Grill for 4 to 5 minutes, rotate 90 degrees, and cook for 2 more minutes. Turn over and cook for 4 minutes. Rotate 90 degrees and move to a cooler side of the grill, cover, and let cook over the low heat for about 8 minutes. Turn over and cook slowly, covered, for about 5 minutes. Turn over and cook slowly, covered, for about 4 minutes more. Test with a meat thermometer; the sirloin should be medium-rare, or about 120°F in the center. If more doneness is desired, cook longer. Remove from the grill and keep warm for 15 minutes to rest before slicing.

To make the garlic potato cake, preheat the oven to 400°F. Place the potatoes in a pot with enough salted water to cover. Bring to a boil and cook for 5 to 7 minutes, until just tender. Drain the potatoes and, wearing an oven mitt, peel them. Discard the skins and let the potatoes cool completely. Chop coarsely.

CONTINUED

Toss the potatoes in a stainless steel bowl with 1 tablespoon of the butter, $1/2$ teaspoon of the salt and pepper, the three quarters of the chopped scallions, and the remaining 1 tablespoon of olive oil. In a cast-iron pan over medium heat, heat the remaining 1 tablespoon butter and vegetable oil. Pack the potatoes firmly in the pan. Cook, sliding a metal spatula under the cake from time to time to keep it from sticking, for about 8 minutes, until very brown on one side. Turn the cake over in the pan and cook on the other side for 1 to 2 minutes. Put the potato cake in the oven for 5 to 6 minutes. Slide out onto a serving plate and garnish with the minced garlic and remaining scallions.

To serve, slice the sirloin English style ($1/2$-inch-thick slices) and serve with wedges of the potato cake. Spoon some béarnaise sauce on top. Pass any extra béarnaise sauce on the side.

Vegetables and Side Dishes

Creamy Potato Gratin

This recipe is a variation on the French gratin dauphinois. It is a terrific partner with grilled or roast lamb, steaks, or roast beef. There is nothing light or dietetic about this potato preparation, but it sure tastes great. If you want a crispier crust, sprinkle some dried breadcrumbs and whole butter on the top about halfway through the cooking process.

4 large Idaho potatoes, peeled and placed in water to cover

2 tablespoons butter

3 cloves garlic, minced

1/4 teaspoon kosher salt

1/4 teaspoon freshly ground black pepper

2 cups shredded Gruyère

1/4 cup crème fraîche

1/4 cup shredded Parmesan cheese

1 1/2 cups heavy cream

Preheat the oven to 375°F. Slice the potatoes into 1/4-inch slices. A mandoline is best for this task. Butter a glass or ceramic baking pan and sprinkle with a little of the minced garlic. Top with an overlapping layer of potato slices and repeat with another layer. Add salt and pepper and sprinkle some Gruyère liberally over the layer. Sprinkle more minced garlic and some Parmesan over the top. Repeat for 2 more double layers of potatoes. Whisk together the crème fraîche and heavy cream. Pour it over the potatoes and top with the remaining Gruyère and Parmesan. Press down on the potatoes, making sure the cream comes over the top and to pack down the potatoes. Place the casserole on a baking sheet to catch the bubbling cream and cheese and bake for about 1 1/4 hours. If dry, add a little milk or more cream.

Gratin of Creamed Tomatoes

Vegetable gratins are always a delicious accompaniment to meat and fish main courses. They are warm, rich, and intensely flavored and the gratine top with crunchy breadcrumbs or gooey cheese is always a treat.

This dish is really an update of the classic stewed tomatoes. In this recipe, the use of oven-dried tomatoes intensifies the flavor of the gratin and make it less watery. For a variation, sprinkle a little shredded Gruyère cheese over the top of the gratin for the last 10 minutes of cooking.

1 tablespoon olive oil

2 cloves garlic, sliced thinly

1 teaspoon thyme leaves

30 oven-dried tomato halves (page 263)

3 tablespoons butter

1/4 cup heavy cream

1 cup toasted croutons, cut into 1/4-inch cubes

Kosher salt and cracked black pepper

1 teaspoon chopped chives or chervil

Preheat the oven to 350°F. Butter a 9 by 12-inch casserole or a gratin dish large enough to hold all the tomatoes in a single layer.

In a sauté pan over medium heat, heat the olive oil, add the garlic and thyme, and sweat for 1 to 2 minutes, until the garlic is softened. Add the dried tomato halves and 1 tablespoon of the butter and sweat for 2 to 3 minutes. Add the cream and bring to a boil. Add the croutons and salt and pepper to taste. Transfer the mixture to the gratin dish. Dot with the remaining butter and bake for about 40 minutes, until nicely browned. Sprinkle with chives and serve.

Jerusalem Artichoke Gratin

Jerusalem artichokes—or sunchokes, as they are popularly known, have a nutty flavor and can be served cooked through or underdone, almost like water chestnuts. They are delicious sautéed, roasted, or, as in this recipe, as a gratin.

12 to 16 large Jerusalem artichokes, scrubbed
2 teaspoons freshly squeezed lemon juice
2 tablespoons butter
2 cloves garlic, minced
1 cup shredded Gruyère
Kosher salt and freshly ground black pepper
2 tablespoon shredded Parmesan cheese
1/4 cup crème fraîche
1 cup heavy cream

Peel the Jerusalem artichokes and slice into 1/8-inch slices. A mandoline is best for this task. Place in water that has been acidulated with the lemon juice.

Preheat the oven to 375°F. Butter a ceramic casserole or individual casseroles and sprinkle on a little of the garlic. Drain and dry the Jerusalem artichoke slices in paper towels. Line the casserole with a single overlapping layer of slices. Add salt and pepper to taste, and Gruyère to just cover. Repeat for two more layers, adding the Parmesan to the top layer. Whip the crème fraîche and heavy cream slightly and pour over the casserole. Top with the remaining Gruyère. Bake for about 50 minutes, until bubbling and golden.

Champ

This potato preparation originated in Ireland. It illustrates just how ingenious those Irish cooks can be. Like many of the great peasant dishes of the world, it was invented to utilize foods that were produced locally or what was on hand. It is a nice alternative to mashed potatoes and is particularly good with roasted and braised meats. You can replace the parsnips with celeriac or turnips, or leave them out altogether if you prefer.

1/2 head white cabbage, sliced (2 cups)
3 large Idaho potatoes, peeled and cut into thirds
2 parsnips, peeled and cut into thirds
4 scallions, diced
6 tablespoons butter, plus more for garnish
Kosher salt and cracked black pepper

Bring 3 quarts of salted water to a boil. Add the cabbage and cook until tender. Drain the cabbage and chop coarsely.

In a second pot of salted water, add the potatoes and parsnips and bring to a boil. Reduce the heat to a simmer and cook for 5 to 8 minutes, until a paring knife pierces them easily. Drain and coarsely mash with a fork.

Add the cabbage, scallions, 6 tablespoons butter, and salt and pepper and mix through. Top with additional butter and serve hot.

Matthew Potatoes

This potato recipe is an adaptation of a dish we served early on in my career at Chillingsworth, a fine restaurant on Cape Cod. Pat and Nitzi Rabin have been the proprietors of this seasonal French restaurant for over thirty years. Nitzi, who is also the chef, made a version of this potato dish when I started working there in the late '70s. It was referred to variously as that "gooey potato thing" or cheesy potatoes. It never had a name that I felt fit well.

My younger brother, Matthew, was working a summer at Chillingsworth when I was sous-chef and eventually his responsibilities evolved to making these potatoes as part of his daily mise en place. *Matthew moved on with me to other restaurants and these potatoes came with him. The dish thus acquired the name Matthew Potatoes. The recipe has evolved over the years to what is offered here. They remain a decadent heart attack on a plate and are particularly delicious with roasted meat dishes.*

Incidentally, I met my wife while working at Chillingsworth. Truth be known, a lot of chefs meet their wives "fishing off the company pier."

4 large Idaho potatoes, scrubbed (about 2 pounds)

2 tablespoons butter

4 bacon strips, diced (3 to 4 ounces)

1 small yellow onion, diced (about 1 cup)

3 cloves garlic, minced

3 scallions, chopped

1 cup grated Gruyère

1/2 cup grated Monterey Jack

2 tablespoons freshly grated Parmesan cheese

1 1/2 cups heavy cream

1/2 teaspoon kosher salt, plus more for boiling potatoes

1/2 teaspoon cracked black pepper

1/2 cup dry breadcrumbs

Place the potatoes in a pot of salted water and bring to a boil. Cook until just tender. Drain and refrigerate for 2 to 3 hours until very cold. This is critical: if the potatoes are warm, the dish will be like a bad version of lumpy mashed potatoes.

When cold, peel and grate the potatoes on a grater with the largest holes. *Do not use a food processor.* Butter a baking dish and chill.

Preheat the oven to 375°F.

In a sauté pan over medium-high heat, add 1 tablespoon of the butter and the diced bacon. Sauté until crispy. Transfer the bacon from the pan of bacon drippings and drain on a paper towel. Add the onions and garlic to the pan and sauté until they just start to brown. Stir in the scallions and remove the pan from the heat.

In a stainless steel bowl, place the grated potatoes, bacon, the onion-garlic-scallion mixture from the pan (with the bacon fat), the cheeses, cream, and salt and pepper. Gently fold all the ingredients together. They should be mixed through gently; rough mixing breaks up the potatoes. The mixture should be slightly loose from the cream. If too dry, add a little more cream. Transfer the mixture to the buttered baking pan. Top with the breadcrumbs and dot with the remaining 1 tablespoon butter. Bake for 35 to 40 minutes, until brown and bubbly. Serve at once.

Potato, Cabbage, and Leek Strudel

*T*his versatile dish can be modified to fit whatever ingredients you have available. The filling can be prepared up to 2 days in advance, and the assembled, uncooked strudels freeze beautifully for at least a month. This method of preparation lends itself to many savory strudel possibilities. Some popular variations you can experiment with are bacon, onion, potato, and paprika strudel (serve with caraway sour cream); sauerkraut, onion, potato, and scallion strudel; sweet potato, ham, onion, and Anaheim chile strudel; cabbage, onion, and farmer cheese strudel; and potato, Gruyère, onion, garlic, and bacon strudel.

$^1/_2$ small head savoy cabbage, cored and sliced thinly

$^1/_4$ cup unsalted butter

Kosher salt and freshly ground black pepper

2 Idaho potatoes

1 Yukon gold potato

1 leek, white part only, minced

2 cloves garlic, minced

1 cup heavy cream

1 (1-pound) package phyllo dough

$1^1/_2$ cups clarified unsalted butter (page 257)

Bring a saucepan of salted water to a boil. Blanch the cabbage for 2 to 3 minutes. Drain and pat the cabbage dry with paper towels. In a sauté pan, heat 2 tablespoons of the butter over medium-high heat and cook the cabbage, stirring frequently. Add salt and pepper to taste. When it begins to brown, remove from the pan. Chop the cabbage coarsely and set aside.

Bring a second saucepan of salted water to a boil over high heat. Add the unpeeled potatoes and decrease heat to a simmer. Cook until a knife easily pierces the potatoes. Drain and peel. Pass the potatoes through a ricer into a stainless steel bowl and add the cabbage.

In a saucepan over medium heat, heat the remaining 2 tablespoons butter until it bubbles, then add the leeks and garlic and sweat until tender. Add the cream and reduce until most of the cream is evaporated, then add to the potato-cabbage mixture. Add salt and pepper to taste and mix thoroughly. Let cool to room temperature. This filling can be refrigerated for up to 2 days before assembling the strudel.

To complete the strudel, open the phyllo and keep the sheets covered with a damp towel while you work on each one. Paint 1 sheet with clarified butter and top with a second sheet. Brush with more butter and top with a third sheet. Cut the 3 layered phyllo sheets into thirds. Place 2 tablespoons of the potato mixture near the short edge of each section. Roll up as if wrapping a submarine sandwich, folding in the sides as you roll up the sheets to surround the filling. Brush with more butter and place on a baking sheet in the refrigerator to chill. Repeat until all of the phyllo is used up. There are usually 27 sheets in a package, so that will give you 27 strudels if none break or are discarded. The strudel can be stored in the freezer for up to 1 month before baking.

To bake, preheat the oven to 350°F. Place the desired number of strudels on an ungreased baking sheet and bake for about 12 minutes (if frozen, 15 minutes), until browned. Serve hot as a potato side dish.

Braised Artichokes

This is a good method for preparing fresh artichokes. The procedure is similar for large artichokes or small, except that with larger chokes, you are only cooking the interior heart and some of the stem, and you will need to remove all the outer leaves and the hairy interior choke, as it is not edible. With the baby choke, you only need to trim the outer hard leaves; the rest is edible.

6 large globe artichokes with long stems or 18 small artichokes with long stems
2 tablespoons vinegar
2 lemons
1 cup extra virgin olive oil
1 cup *brunoise* mirepoix (page 263)
4 cloves garlic, minced
6 thyme sprigs
4 bay leaves
1 cup dry white wine
4 cups chicken stock (page 255)
Kosher salt and freshly ground black pepper

To prepare the large artichokes, tear away all of the outer leaves and reserve in a large bowl filled with 8 cups of water acidulated with the vinegar; this keeps the leaves from browning. With a sharp paring knife, trim the stems of their outer skin. Cut the lemons in half and rub the peeled stems with 1 lemon half. Scrape out the thistly inner core and place the whole artichoke bottoms in the acidulated water.

In a shallow braising pan over medium-high heat, heat the extra virgin oil and sauté the mirepoix and garlic. When the vegetables start to brown, add the artichoke bottoms and sauté on all sides. Add the thyme, bay leaves, wine, and stock and bring to a boil. Squeeze the juice from the lemon halves into the cooking liquid and toss in the halves and salt and pepper to taste. Reduce the heat to a simmer and cook for 16 to 20 minutes, until tender. A wood skewer inserted into the artichoke should slide in and out smoothly (as in a cooked potato). Remove the artichokes from the cooking liquid and reserve some of the liquid. Set aside the artichoke bottoms in a little more of the cooking liquid.

Add the leaves to the cooking liquid and cook over high heat for 10 to 12 minutes, until tender. In a blender, purée the leaves with a little of the cooking liquid. Strain through a fine-mesh sieve, pressing on the solids to extract all the liquid. This can be used as a base for other sauces or soups. Serve warm, or store refrigerated, for up to 3 days.

To prepare baby chokes, trim away the outer tough skin on the stem with a sharp paring knife. Tear away the tough outer leaves and trim the tops. You do not need to remove the choke, as it is immature. With a paring knife, trim the hearts to neaten the presentation. As you are working, place the trimmed artichokes in a pot of acidulated water. Proceed with the braising as for larger artichokes.

Sweet Potato–Butternut Squash Purée

This side dish is a nice fall complement to ham, roast pork, venison, any bird, and even some fish dishes. You can't go wrong with this side dish at your Thanksgiving table. The trick to making this purée is to dry out the squash and sweet potatoes. For a more festive presentation of the purée, pipe it through a pastry bag with an open star tip. Be careful; the bag is very hot and can be difficult to handle. Wrap the pastry bag with a kitchen towel to protect your hands.

2 large sweet potatoes (about 1 pound)

1 small butternut squash (about 1 pound), halved lengthwise and seeded

5 tablespoons butter

1 tablespoon dark brown sugar

3 tablespoons heavy cream

Kosher salt and freshly ground black pepper

Preheat the oven to 325°F. Prick the sweet potatoes with a fork and place on a baking sheet. Place the butternut squash cut side up on the same sheet. Dot with 2 tablespoons of butter and sprinkle with the brown sugar. Bake for 50 to 60 minutes, until a knife is easily inserted into the potatoes and squash. Remove from the oven, leaving the oven on, and when cool enough to handle, peel the sweet potatoes. Scrape out the insides of the squash and reserve any liquid drippings. Pass the potatoes and squash through a ricer onto a baking sheet and bake for 4 minutes to dry out. Transfer to a saucepan over medium heat, add the remaining butter, the cream, and salt and pepper to taste, and whisk to combine. Add any reserved drippings. Serve warm.

Steamed Spinach with Garlic and Lemon

SERVES 6 (MAKES 3 CUPS)

This is one of the simplest, most satisfying ways to prepare fresh spinach. One pound of spinach equals 8 cups of loosely packed leaves or 1¹/₂ cups cooked. If you desire a more intense garlic flavor, substitute garlic oil (from making garlic confit, page 264) for the olive oil in this recipe. If trying to avoid fat, reduce the olive oil by half or omit, and omit the butter at the end.

2 pounds fresh spinach, stemmed

2 tablespoons olive oil

3 cloves garlic, sliced very thin

Kosher salt and cracked black pepper

2 tablespoons butter

3 lemons, cut into wedges

Wash the spinach but do not dry. In a sauté pan over high heat, add the olive oil and garlic and sauté for about 30 seconds, until the garlic is starting to brown. Add the wet spinach, cover, and cook for about 2 minutes, until the spinach has steamed down. Pour off any excess water and add salt, and pepper to taste, and the butter. Stir and remove from the heat. Drain well and serve hot with lemon wedges.

Spring Vegetable Ragoût

SERVES 4 (MAKES 2 CUPS)

This is a nice vegetable mixture made to complement lighter seafood dishes. Blanching the vegetables in separate pans of boiling water keeps flavors separate and doneness accurate. You can add morels, asparagus, ramps, pearl onions, or other seasonal vegetables to the blend.

1 cup haricots verts, ends trimmed and cut into 1-inch lengths

1/2 cup fava beans, shelled and unpeeled

1/2 cup fresh peas, shelled

1/2 cup shelled fresh edamame

4 tablespoons butter

1 shallot, minced

1 clove garlic, minced

6 French breakfast radishes, quartered lengthwise

6 spring onions or scallions, white part only, halved lengthwise

Kosher salt and freshly ground black pepper

4 tablespoons water

1 tablespoon summer savory or tarragon leaves, chopped

Chervil sprigs, for garnish

Bring 4 saucepans of salted water to a boil. Blanch the haricots in one, the favas in another, the peas in a third, and the edamame in the fourth. When just cooked, drain and refresh each vegetable in a separate ice-water bath. Drain the haricots, peas, and edamame. When the favas are cooled, peel off and discard the outer skins.

In a sauté pan over high heat, place 2 tablespoons of the butter and bring to a foaming boil. Add the shallot and cook until transparent. Add the garlic and cook for 1 minute. Add the radishes and cook for about 2 to 3 minutes, until warmed through. They should still be crisp. Turn down the heat and add the favas, haricots verts, peas, edamame, and new onions and cook for 2 to 3 minutes, or until warmed through. Add salt and pepper to taste.

In a small saucepan over high heat, combine the water and savory and bring to a boil. Whisk in the remaining butter and, when smooth, pour into the vegetable mixture. Toss and serve at once, garnished with chervil sprigs.

Horseradish Creamed Spinach

Creamed spinach is always a popular side dish. The addition of infused horseradish gives it an extra kick. The trick to any good creamed spinach is to dry the spinach completely after blanching. For extra zip, add an additional half-teaspoon of prepared horseradish to the creamed spinach just before serving.

2 pounds spinach, stemmed and washed thoroughly

1/4 cup butter

2 cloves garlic, minced

2 shallots, minced

2 teaspoons all-purpose flour

Pinch of nutmeg

1 cup heavy cream

1/2 cup crème fraîche

1 1/2 cups finely grated fresh or 1/2 cup processed horseradish

Kosher salt and cracked black pepper

Bring a stockpot of salted water to a boil. Add the spinach and blanch for 1 minute. Drain in a colander and immerse immediately in an ice-water bath. When chilled, drain, squeeze dry, and finish drying with a kitchen towel. When very dry, chop finely with a sharp knife, not in a food processor. Chill in the refrigerator. This can be done up to 12 hours in advance.

In a saucepan over medium heat, heat 2 tablespoons of the butter and sauté the garlic and half of the shallots for 1 minute. Add the flour and cook for 1 more minute. Add the nutmeg, heavy cream, crème fraîche, and horseradish. Bring to a boil and let thicken. Decrease the heat to medium and let simmer for 2 to 3 minutes, or until the thickness of thick soup. Strain through a fine-mesh sieve and keep warm. This makes about 1 1/4 cups of horseradish béchamel.

To serve, in a sauté pan over high heat, sweat the remaining shallots in 1 tablespoon butter. Add the chopped spinach and heat through. Add the warm horseradish béchamel and incorporate. Add the remaining 1 tablespoon butter and salt and pepper to taste. Serve immediately.

Fried Zucchini with Parmesan

ried zucchini is a terrific accompaniment to roasted or fried fish and can be a delicious snack or first course. If you are up to the challenge at home and have either a good, deep cast-iron pan or a tabletop home fryer, it is worth the effort.

4 zucchini (about 8 inches long), halved
2 cups buttermilk
2 cups all-purpose flour
$1/2$ teaspoon kosher salt, plus more for seasoning
$1/2$ teaspoon cracked black pepper
Vegetable oil for deep-frying
1 cup finely grated Parmigiano-Reggiano cheese
3 lemons, cut into wedges

Using a mandoline with the julienne cutter, cut the zucchini into $1/8$-inch julienne. Use only the green outer skin and cut only about $1/2$ inch into the interior. Do not use the seeds or soft middle; reserve those for a vegetable stock or some other use.

In a stainless steel bowl, place the zucchini julienne and the buttermilk and toss to coat completely. In a separate bowl, season the flour with the salt and pepper. Drain the zucchini. Put the seasoned flour and zucchini in a paper bag and toss the zucchini until lightly coated. Remove the zucchini and shake off the excess.

Heat 2 to 3 inches of the vegetable oil in a deep cast-iron pan or fill fryer to 350°F. Fry the zucchini in small batches, stirring to keep them from clumping together, for about 3 minutes, until golden and crisp. Using a slotted spoon, remove the zucchini from the fryer and dry on paper towels or absorbent paper plates for deep-frying (papyrus plates). Place in a stainless steel bowl and toss with the cheese and $1/2$ teaspoon salt. Serve while hot and crisp, with the lemon wedges.

Dill Crackers

These are very delicate tuile-like crackers, sometimes referred to as carta musica, *or music sheets, because their thinness is like that of old parchment paper. They can be broken up into large or small pieces; the shapes are meant to be freeform and irregular. You can make any number of variations on this theme with other herbs, cracked black pepper, fennel seeds, sesame seeds (black or white), onions, or garlic. Larger pieces break very easily, so handle them delicately.*

6 extra large egg whites
1 cup all-purpose flour
1 egg yolk
1 teaspoon sugar
1½ cups (3 sticks) butter, at room-temperature
1 teaspoon olive oil
3 tablespoons chopped fresh dill
1 teaspoon coarse sea salt

Preheat the oven to 300°F. In an electric mixer fitted with the whip attachment, whip the egg whites until frothy. Slowly add the flour, egg yolk, sugar, butter, and olive oil and mix until thoroughly incorporated. Let rest for 1 hour at room temperature. Brush a silicone rubber baking pan liner with olive oil. With a large, thin metal pastry spatula, spread one quarter to one third of the mixture about 1/32 inch thick over the entire surface. Sprinkle with a scant tablespoon of the chopped dill and a pinch of the salt to taste. Place the liner on a baking pan. Bake for 8 to 10 minutes, or until brown and crisp. Remove from the oven and let cool on a rack. Repeat this process until all of the batter is used. This will make 3 to 4 half-sheet pans. Break the large cooled crackers into several irregular 4 by 8-inch crackers. Store in a dry area, preferably in a metal tin for up to 10 days.

Virginia Ham and Corn Spoon Bread

Spoon bread, which is a cross between cornbread and a soufflé, is a true Southern tradition. No family gathering in the Southeast would be complete without a big pan of it. At Kinkead's, we add Virginia ham and Cheddar, but you can choose to add any number of savory ingredients, like sausage or bacon (pork products loom large in the Southern culinary mystique), herbs, scallions, roasted peppers, or other vegetables. Make sure that these ingredients have been cooked before adding to the batter.

Kernels from 2 ears corn
1 cup chicken stock (page 255)
$^3/_4$ cup heavy cream
$^3/_4$ cup milk
$^1/_2$ cup half-and-half
$^3/_4$ cup cornmeal
1 tablespoon sugar
2 teaspoons kosher salt
1 teaspoon freshly ground white pepper
$^1/_4$ cup butter, at room temperature
8 extra large eggs
1 teaspoon baking powder
1 cup finely diced Virginia ham
$^1/_2$ cup shredded Cheddar cheese

Preheat the oven to 350°F. Place the corn in a saucepan with enough salted water to cover and bring to a boil over high heat. Simmer for 1 to 2 minutes to cook the corn, and then strain and set aside.

In a second saucepan bring the stock, cream, milk, and half-and-half to a boil. Add the cornmeal, sugar, salt, and pepper and cook, stirring frequently with a wooden spoon. When smooth and thickened, add the butter and remove from the heat.

Separate 4 of the eggs, discarding 1 yolk and reserving the 3 yolks and 4 whites in separate bowls.

Place the 1 whole egg, the egg yolks, and baking powder in a mixing bowl. Add the corn, ham, and Cheddar and fold that mixture into the cornmeal mix. Whip the egg whites into peaks and fold into the cornmeal batter.

Spray a 8 by 8-inch pan with vegetable oil spray and pour in the batter. Bake in the oven for about 45 minutes, or until browned on top and a skewer inserted into the center comes out clean. Let rest for 3 to 5 minutes, and serve.

Maeve's Irish Soda Bread

My friend Maeve Barnes developed this recipe many years ago. Maeve has worked as the baker and pastry chef of three restaurants where I was chef over the years. This bread has been a vital part of our menus at all of them. Maeve left several years ago to start a family on Nantucket, but this bread has lived on in several more of my restaurants since then. This is the only bread we still make in-house. Of all the recipes in this book, this is the most requested by our customers.

3 cups all-purpose flour

1 cup cake flour

1 extra large egg

1 tablespoon sugar

2 teaspoons kosher salt

1/2 tablespoon baking soda

1/4 cup butter, cold, cut into 1/2-inch cubes,
plus 1 tablespoon for brushing

2 teaspoons caraway seeds

1/4 cup raisins

1/4 cup golden raisins

1 1/4 cups buttermilk

Preheat the oven to 350°F. Place the all-purpose flour, cake flour, egg, sugar, salt, and baking soda in the bowl of an electric mixer fitted with a dough hook. Add the 1/4 cup butter and mix until a coarse meal is formed. Add the caraway seeds, raisins, and buttermilk and mix until the dough comes together. Form into one round loaf, flattened slightly. With a very sharp paring knife, make a deep cross cut into the loaf. Bake for about 25 minutes, until brown. Brush with butter and bake for 5 more minutes. Remove from the oven and let cool before serving.

Desserts

❧

Rhubarb Charlotte with Strawberries and Rum

This dessert involves making a Bavarian cream—a fruit purée to which whipped cream and gelatin are added. Think of it as an elegant Jell-O, but not as rubbery. Professional pastry chefs would use sheet gelatin, which is certainly fine. Home cooks generally have easier access to powdered gelatin, so I have indicated that here.

Almost any purée of fruit can be used to make a Bavarian cream for a charlotte. You just need to remember this equation: 2 envelopes of gelatin to 2 cups purée and 1 cup whipped cream. You will also need to adjust the sugar added to the purée according to the particular fruit's natural sweetness. Peaches, purple plums, raspberries, mangoes, and apricots all make delicious Bavarian creams. Pineapple is tricky because it tends to break down the gelatin (that's why Mom never put fresh pineapple in your Jell-O).

This ladyfinger recipe makes about thirty more than you need for this charlotte; freeze the rest for another use, such as tiramisu or snacking. For a charlotte, the ladyfingers should be made a day in advance and allowed to dry out. The extra moisture of the liqueurs and Bavarian tend to make fresh ladyfingers soggy. You can also use store-bought ladyfingers.

In our presentation, we include a white chocolate ball that can be purchased at bakery supply stores.

LADYFINGERS

10 extra large eggs

1 cup plus 1/2 cup sugar

2 teaspoons pure vanilla extract

3/4 cup all-purpose flour

Confectioners' sugar for dusting

RHUBARB CHARLOTTE

Vegetable oil cooking spray

1/4 cup strawberry liqueur, cassis, or a berry-flavored brandy

1/2 cup dark rum, plus 2 tablespoons for the ladyfingers and a few drops for topping

2 pounds ripe strawberries

2 cups sugar

1 teaspoon freshly squeezed lemon juice

1/2 pound rhubarb, unpeeled, cut up

1 cup water plus 1/2 cup boiling water

1 cup plain yogurt

1/4 teaspoon salt

2 cups heavy cream

2 envelopes powdered gelatin

1/4 teaspoon pure vanilla extract

1/4 cup strawberry jam or glaze

Strawberry sorbet or ice cream, for garnish

To make the ladyfingers, preheat the oven to 375°F. Line a baking sheet with baker's parchment. Separate the eggs, discarding 2 whites. In a mixer, beat the 8 egg whites until foamy. Gradually add in 1/2 cup of the sugar until stiff peaks form. Transfer to a large stainless steel bowl and reserve.

In a mixer, beat the 10 egg yolks with the remaining 1 cup sugar and the vanilla to the golden ribbon stage. Fold the yolk mixture into the egg whites. Gradually sift in the flour.

Transfer the batter to a piping bag with a 1-inch plain tip. Pipe 3-inch fingers about 1/2 inch apart directly on the baking sheet. Dust generously with the confectioners' sugar

CONTINUED

and bake for 12 to 15 minutes, until golden brown. Let cool on the pan to room temperature before removing.

To make the charlotte, spray the interior of the selected molds with vegetable cooking oil and line with plastic wrap. Line the interior sides with the ladyfingers with the bottoms facing in. In a bowl, combine the strawberry liqueur and the 2 tablespoons rum. Brush this onto the bottoms of the ladyfingers and set aside to soak.

Hull the strawberries and slice them into wedges (quarters for medium-sized berries, sixths for larger berries). Place in a stainless steel bowl with 1 cup of the sugar and the lemon juice and toss. Let macerate for 2 to 3 hours. Stir to mix every hour or so. There should be a fair amount of strawberry juice extracted.

In a saucepan over medium heat, combine the rhubarb, 10 of the strawberry wedges, 3/4 cup of the sugar, the remaining 1/2 cup rum, and the water and cook until very mushy. Let cool. Purée in a blender with the yogurt and salt. Transfer the purée to a stainless steel bowl.

In the bowl of an electric mixer, place 1 1/2 cups of the heavy cream and whip to stiff peaks. Put the powdered gelatin in a small stainless steel bowl and add the 1/2 cup boiling water to cover and soften the gelatin. Stir to dissolve. Add about 1/2 cup of the strawberry juice from the macerated strawberries to the mixture. Stir the gelatin mixture into the rhubarb purée.

Prepare an ice-water bath in a larger stainless steel bowl and set the bottom of the bowl of gelatin-rhubarb purée in the bath. Stir until the purée just starts to thicken. Fold in the whipped cream and keep stirring the mixture until it is thicker but still pourable.

Pour the mixture into the molds three-quarters of the way up. If any is leftover, you can put it in a ramekin for a snack later. Place the filled molds in the refrigerator to chill for 2 to 3 hours or overnight. Trim the ladyfingers so they are level with the Bavarian.

Purée some of the macerated strawberries in a blender to make a purée.

To serve, whip the remaining 1 cup heavy cream with the remaining 1/4 cup sugar and the vanilla to firm peaks. Unmold the charlottes. Heat the strawberry jam with a few drops of rum and, when melted, paint the top of the charlotte. Place the whipped cream on top and surround with the macerated strawberries, a little strawberry purée, and a scoop of strawberry sorbet.

Lime Miroir with Raspberry Sauce

*T*his dessert solves the dilemma of whether to have the Key lime pie or the cheesecake. With this torte, you get a shortbread layer topped with a layer of lime cheesecake, a layer of lime Bavarian, and a tart lime glaze served with a fresh raspberry coulis. The original version was a peaches and cream cake with peaches instead of lime. It was a nice dessert but a little cloying and lacking contrast. The lime makes this torte more sweet-tart and refreshing.

This is a complex dessert to make, using many basic pastry-making techniques—sort of a mini pastry-making course in one dish. Shortbread, cheesecake, gelatin tempering, and Bavarian cream are all included. You'll need a 10-inch springform pan, a 12-inch cardboard disk, baking parchment at least 12 inches wide, a rubber spatula, stainless steel bowls, a mixer, and a propane torch (optional). While you're at it, it makes sense to double or triple the crust recipe and freeze the crusts for future cakes.

RASPBERRY SAUCE

1 pint fresh raspberries

$1/2$ cup sugar

1 tablespoon cassis or raspberry liqueur (optional)

SHORTBREAD CRUST

1 cup butter

$1/2$ cup granulated sugar

$1/4$ cup light brown sugar

$1/4$ teaspoon pure vanilla extract

$1^1/2$ cups all-purpose flour

$1/4$ teaspoon salt

CHEESECAKE LAYER

20 ounces cream cheese, at room temperature (about 5 cups)

1 cup sugar

2 tablespoons freshly squeezed lime juice

$1/4$ cup heavy cream

$1/2$ cup sour cream

$1/2$ tablespoon pure vanilla extract

4 large eggs

Vegetable oil cooking spray

LIME BAVARIAN LAYER

$2^1/2$ sheets gelatin, or 1 envelope powdered gelatin

$3/4$ cup freshly squeezed lime juice

$1/2$ cup superfine sugar

1 cup plus 2 tablespoons heavy cream

LIME GLAZE

2 sheets gelatin or $2/3$ envelope powdered gelatin

$1/2$ cup freshly squeezed lime juice

$1/2$ cup sugar

Grated zest of 1 lime

$1/2$ teaspoon pectin

1 pint fresh raspberries, for garnish

10 mint sprigs, for garnish

To make the raspberry sauce, purée the berries and sugar in a blender and strain out the seeds. Add the liqueur. Refrigerate.

To make the crust, preheat the oven to 325°F. Cream the butter, the granulated and light brown sugar, and the vanilla.

CONTINUED

Add the flour and salt and mix until everything just comes together.

Do not overmix. Line a 12-inch cardboard disk with parchment paper. Press the mixture onto the disk and bake for 15 minutes, or until brown and crisp.

To make the cheesecake layer, decrease the oven heat to 300°F and prepare a pan of water large enough to contain a 10-inch springform pan. Cream the cream cheese and sugar in the bowl of an electric mixer until fluffy. Add the lime juice, heavy cream, sour cream, and vanilla. Mix at low speed. Beat the eggs together separately and fold into the cheese mixture with a spatula until smooth.

Line the bottom of a 10-inch springform pan with parchment and spray the bottom and sides with vegetable oil cooking spray. Place in the water bath and bake for 20 minutes, or until a toothpick inserted in the center comes out clean. Cool and set aside or freeze until ready to assemble the dessert.

To make the lime Bavarian layer, bloom the gelatin leaves in cold water and when softened, drain and place in a stainless steel bowl. In a saucepan over high heat, boil the lime juice and superfine sugar until the sugar dissolves. Pour the liquid over the gelatin leaves. Mix well, until the gelatin dissolves, and let cool down. Whip the heavy cream until it forms firm peaks and fold it into the gelatin mixture. Fill a larger stainless steel bowl with ice, place the gelatin bowl on the ice, and let it chill until the Bavarian cream starts to thicken.

To make the lime glaze, bloom the gelatin leaves in cold water. In a saucepan over high heat, bring the lime juice and sugar to a boil and add the grated lime zest. Add the liquid to the gelatin, mix in the pectin, and strain. Place the glaze in a stainless steel bowl on an ice bath until it starts to thicken. Set aside.

To assemble the dessert, warm the bottom of the springform pan with a propane torch; alternatively, wrap the bottom of the pan with a towel dipped in boiling water (be careful not to burn yourself). Turn the cheesecake out onto a cardboard circle. Clean the ring; you will be reusing it. Top the cheesecake with the shortbread crust backed by the cardboard disk and turn over. Place the springform ring around the cheesecake and trim off the excess crust. Lock down the ring so there is no space between the ring and the cake. Spread the lime Bavarian layer mixture over the cheesecake layer. It should be equal in width to the cheesecake layer. Smooth out all bubbles with a propane torch or in a broiler. Place in the freezer for 30 minutes. Take out of the freezer and pour the lime glaze over the top. Refrigerate for at least 1 hour.

When ready to serve, loosen the miroir from the mold by using a propane torch to warm the outside of the ring or by warming the ring with your hands. Remove the ring and cut the miroir into wedges with a hot knife. Spoon some raspberry sauce onto the plate. Garnish with raspberries and a sprig of mint.

Banana Tart

This is a banana lover's dream. Tons of caramelized bananas in a pastry crust, all warm and gooey. Either make six 3 by 2-inch-deep tart pans or use three 6-inch cast-iron pans and cut each tart in half. Or better yet, make six whole large tarts—they'll get eaten. These tarts go well served with Saracen (page 251) or vanilla ice cream. Garnish with a little English double cream.

1¹/₂ cups butter
¹/₂ cup dark brown sugar
¹/₂ cup granulated sugar
¹/₄ cup dark rum
¹/₈ teaspoon ground cinnamon
¹/₈ teaspoon salt
3 whole vanilla beans
12 to 14 just-ripe bananas
1 tablespoon freshly squeezed lemon juice
16 ounces puff pastry
All-purpose flour for dusting

Preheat the oven to 400°F. In the bowl of an electric mixer, combine the butter, brown and white sugars, rum, cinnamon, and salt. Split the vanilla beans and scrape in the seeds from the pods. Whip with the paddle attachment until incorporated but not fluffy.

In a cast-iron pan over medium-high heat, cook the butter-sugar mixture until it caramelizes. Be careful! The caramel is like napalm; it is extremely hot and sticky and will leave a severe burn, so don't touch. Remove from the heat to cool slightly.

Peel and slice the bananas into sections about 2 inches long and sprinkle with lemon juice. Place the sections, standing up, in the tart pans. Pour on the caramelized sugar, dividing equally among the pans.

Roll out the puff pastry to about ¹/₈-inch thick. Cut rounds to just larger than the pan size and tuck in around the bananas down the insides of the tart pans. Dust with flour and brush to even out. Place in the oven and bake for 20 to 25 minutes, until the pastry is golden brown.

To serve, while still warm, invert the tart pans onto serving plates and pop out the tarts.

Almond, Fig, and Port Tart with Ginger-Mascarpone Ice Cream

As is done for most open-faced tarts, you need to "blond bake" the tart shell. The flavor of this dessert is enhanced by serving it with a glass of port or other dessert wine.

GINGER-MASCARPONE ICE CREAM

3 tablespoons grated fresh ginger

1/2 cup heavy cream

1 cup mascarpone

1 cup superfine sugar

1/2 cup buttermilk

Juice and zest of 1 lemon, grated with a microplane zester

1/2 teaspoon pure vanilla extract

TART

1 pâte brisée (page 266)

1 pint ripe fresh figs (about 22 Black Mission figs)

1/2 cup plus 1 tablespoon butter

1 cup port

Grated zest and juice of 1 lemon

1 tablespoon firmly packed light brown sugar

2 cinnamon sticks

Pinch of nutmeg

1/2 cup almond paste

1 tablespoon sugar

2 large eggs

3 tablespoons cake flour

1/4 teaspoon pure vanilla extract

1/4 cup blanched almond slivers

To make the ice cream, in a saucepan over medium heat, combine the ginger, heavy cream, mascarpone, and superfine sugar and bring to a simmer. Strain out the ginger, pressing on the solids to extract the juices. Chill the liquid. When cold, mix together with the buttermilk, lemon juice and zest, and vanilla and freeze in an ice cream maker according to the manufacturer's directions.

To make the tart, preheat the oven to 325°F. Blond bake the tart shell for 12 to 15 minutes, until very light golden.

Make 2 crisscross cuts in the tops of the figs. In a 10-inch sauté pan over medium heat, melt 1/4 cup of the butter and, when warm, place the figs, cut side up, in the butter. Cover with the port and add the lemon zest and juice, brown sugar, cinnamon sticks, and nutmeg and cover. Poach for 2 to 3 minutes, until the figs are softened but still holding their shape. Remove the figs from the liquid and cool. Reduce the remaining liquid to a syrup. Remove the cinnamon sticks.

In the bowl of an electric mixer, cream the almond paste, 1/4 cup of the butter, the sugar, eggs, flour, and vanilla until light. Add in 2 tablespoons of the fig-port syrup.

In a sauté pan, melt the remaining 1 tablespoon butter and toss the slivered almonds in it to coat. Remove from the heat. Raise the oven temperature to 350°F.

Spread the almond paste batter evenly over the bottom of the baked tart shell and top with the cooled figs. Drizzle on the remaining fig-port syrup and top with the buttered almond slivers. Bake for about 25 minutes. Rotate the tart and bake for about 10 more minutes, until golden brown. Transfer from the oven and cool.

Serve a slice of the tart with a scoop of the ginger-mascarpone ice cream.

Pineapple Tarte Tatin

Of the many upside-down tarts we make at Kinkead's, this is one of the most popular. It is a made-to-order dessert based on the classic apple Tarte Tatin. Here we replace the apples with a thick round of pineapple. What makes this version unique is that we make a sugar and rum compound butter to caramelize the fruit rather than adding the ingredients separately. It saves time and makes a more consistent tart. The recipe can be used with almost any firm fruit: apples (traditional), peaches, pears, or even bananas. Cooking time varies with the ripeness of the fruit.

English cream or pineapple, vanilla, or coconut ice cream makes a great accompaniment to this tart.

2 fresh pineapples (preferably Hawaiian)
1 1/2 cups unsalted butter
1 cup dark brown sugar
1 cup granulated sugar
1/4 cup dark rum
1/4 teaspoon ground cinnamon
1/4 teaspoon salt
3 whole vanilla beans, split
1 pound puff pastry (preferably all butter)

Peel and core the pineapples and cut each into 3 thick, (about 1 1/2 to 2 inches wide) round slices. Set aside.

In a mixer, cream the butter, brown and white sugars, rum, cinnamon, and salt.

Preheat the oven to 400°F.

On the stovetop, heat 6 individual 6-inch cast-iron pans over medium heat and portion out the creamed butter mixture into them. Top each with 1 slice of pineapple and 1/2 a vanilla bean. Cook for 3 to 5 minutes, until very caramelized. Turn each pineapple slice over and cook until brown on the other side. Turn each back to the original side but keep the vanilla bean on the bottom. The pineapple should be cooked through; cook longer if needed. Let cool in pans.

Roll out the puff pastry about 1/4 inch thick and, using a pastry cutter or knife, cut into rounds slightly larger than the diameter of the cast-iron pan. If you don't have a cutter that size, use a butter plate that is just larger than the pan as a template. Dust the rounds with flour and top each pineapple, still in its pan, with a round. Tuck the dough down around the pineapple inside of the pan. Bake in the oven for 20 to 25 minutes, until brown.

To serve, heat the pans on the stove over medium heat. When the caramel is bubbling, place a plate over the top, invert the pan, and pop out the tart. Serve hot.

Chris's Pecan and Carrot Cake Roulade

*C*hris Kujala has been Kinkead's pastry chef for four years. He is a creative, talented, quiet, and hard-working professional. One of his best qualities is that he works clean; in fact, his pastry area is always meticulously clean. A creative, even-tempered pastry chef who cleans up after himself is rare indeed.

From early on I have been a big fan of spice cakes—carrot cake in particular. This dessert is Chris's take on that American dessert standard. It goes great with Brown Sugar–Sour Cream Ice Cream (page 250) and cookies or tuiles.

CANDIED PECANS

1 egg white

1 tablespoon plus 1 teaspoon pure vanilla extract

2 teaspoons bourbon

1/4 teaspoon vanilla powder

2 cups pecan halves (3/4 pound)

1/2 cup light brown sugar

ROULADE

2 carrots, peeled and coarsely diced (about 1 1/2 cups)

1/2 teaspoon sugar

4 extra large eggs, separated

3/4 cup light brown sugar

1 cup all-purpose flour, plus more for dusting

1 cup cake flour

3/4 teaspoon baking soda

1/2 teaspoon ground cinnamon

1/4 teaspoon salt

1/4 teaspoon ground ginger

CARAMEL SAUCE

1/2 cup white sugar

1/2 cup brown sugar

1/4 cup water

Pinch of salt

1/2 cup heavy cream

2 teaspoons bourbon or brandy

2 tablespoons butter

CREAM CHEESE ICING

2 cups cream cheese

1/2 cup butter

2 tablespoons sour cream

1 teaspoon pure vanilla extract

1 cup confectioners' sugar, sifted

To make the candied pecans, preheat the oven to 300°F. In a stainless steel bowl, whip the egg white until frothy. Stir in the vanilla, bourbon, and vanilla powder. Add in the pecans and toss until well coated. Add the brown sugar and mix until all is incorporated. Spray a half sheet pan with vegetable cooking spray and spread the pecans out evenly. Bake for 20 to 30 minutes, until dry. Cool and chop half of the pecans in a food processor; they should not be too fine. Reserve the rest for garnish.

To make the roulade, turn up the oven to 400°F. Spray a half sheet pan with vegetable cooking spray and line with baking parchment. Spray again and dust with flour.

In a saucepan, boil the carrots with the sugar in water to cover for 6 to 9 minutes, until very soft. Drain and purée in a food processor.

In a stainless steel bowl, beat the egg yolks with a whisk until slightly thickened. Gradually mix in the brown sugar

CONTINUED

and whip by hand for about 5 minutes. Whip in the carrot purée. Sift together the all-purpose and cake flours with the baking soda, cinnamon, salt, and ginger. Fold into the egg yolk–brown sugar mixture.

In a separate bowl or in the bowl of an electric mixer, whip the egg whites until they form stiff peaks. Fold the whites into the batter. Spread evenly over the half sheet pan and bake for 10 to 12 minutes, until light golden brown. Let cool slightly. Place a clean dishtowel towel and cooling rack on the top, invert, and remove the pan and parchment. Roll the warm cake up lengthwise in the dishtowel to approximate the roulade. It should be fairly tight. Let cool.

To make the caramel sauce, in a saucepan over medium heat, cook the white sugar until melted and golden in color. Add the brown sugar and cook until melted. Carefully add the water, salt, cream, and bourbon and bring to a boil. Cook until thickened. Remove from the heat and fold in the butter.

To make the icing, soften the cream cheese in the bowl of an electric mixer fitted with the paddle attachment. Add the butter and sour cream and beat until smooth. Add the vanilla and sugar and mix just until smooth; do not overwork.

To assemble, unroll the carrot sheet cake and spread an even layer of the icing on one side. Roll up to make a single roulade 18 inches long by about 3 inches in diameter. Spread with a thin layer of the icing and roll it in the chopped candied pecans. Cut into angled portions and serve with ice cream and a bourbon crème anglaise, made by adding 1 to 2 tablespoons of bourbon to the basic crème anglaise (page 244). Garnish with candied pecan halves.

Angel Food Cake with Peppermint Ice Cream and Hot Fudge Sauce

If this doesn't remind you of your fifth birthday party or Christmas, nothing will. It's a fairly time-consuming recipe, but a real treat. Be sure to spray the angel food cake mold well with vegetable oil cooking spray. It will stick somewhat in any case because of the sugar and egg whites, but much less so if the pan is well seasoned.

ANGEL FOOD CAKE

1/2 cup cake flour, sifted, plus extra for dusting pans

5 extra large egg whites

1 teaspoon cream of tartar

1/8 teaspoon salt

1/2 cup sugar

1/4 teaspoon pure vanilla extract

1 teaspoon freshly squeezed lemon juice

PEPPERMINT ICE CREAM

2 cups half-and-half

1 cup sugar

2 cups spearmint or peppermint leaves or peppermint extract

6 extra large egg yolks

2 cups heavy cream

1/4 teaspoon pure vanilla extract

1/4 teaspoon peppermint extract

1 1/2 cups peppermint hard candies or peppermint sticks (with red and white stripes), plus extra for garnish

HOT FUDGE SAUCE

8 ounces bittersweet chocolate

1 cup heavy cream

1 teaspoon sugar

1 tablespoon butter

Pinch of salt

Chocolate mint sticks, for garnish

To make the cake, preheat the oven to 325°F. Spray a 10-inch cake mold or pan of six individual-sized angel food molds and dust with the cake flour.

In a stainless steel bowl, whip the egg whites with the tartar and salt. Slowly add the sugar and whip to soft peaks. Stir in the vanilla and lemon juice. Fold in the cake flour. Transfer the mixture to a pastry bag with an open tip fitted. Pipe the batter into the molds. Bake for about 20 minutes, until golden brown on top. Let cool in the molds, and then remove to a baking rack.

To make the ice cream, in a noncorrosive saucepan over medium-high heat, combine the half-and-half, sugar, and mint leaves and bring just to a simmer. Transfer from the heat and let steep for 10 minutes. Strain and return the cream to the saucepan, discarding mint leaves.

In a stainless steel bowl, temper the yolks by gradually whisking about 1 cup of the cream mixture into the yolks. Add the yolk mixture to the saucepan with the cream mixture and heat over medium heat until the mixture coats a spoon. *Do not boil.* Strain through a fine-mesh sieve and add the heavy cream and the vanilla and peppermint extracts. Freeze in an ice cream maker according to the manufacturer's directions.

CONTINUED

Chop the peppermint hard candies by pulsing in a food processor. If using a commercial ice cream maker, fold the chopped candies into the ice cream as it comes out of the ice cream maker, or if using a home ice cream maker, fold the candies in during the last minute of freezing. Return the ice cream to the freezer for 1 hour before serving.

To make the fudge sauce, in a saucepan over medium heat, bring all of the ingredients to a simmer, whisking frequently. Keep warm.

To serve, ladle some hot fudge in the center of each of 6 plates and place a slice of cake or an individual cake in the center. Ladle on some more hot fudge and top with a scoop of peppermint ice cream. Garnish with the peppermint candies and chocolate mint sticks.

Chocolate Crème Brûlée

This is technically a burnt-sugar (brûléed) chocolate pot de crème. You get the benefit of two desserts for the price of one. At Kinkead's, we serve this dessert as either a single serving or, in smaller portions, as part of a trio of flavored brûlées. The flavors change with the seasons, but this chocolate one is hands down the most popular. Customers frequently ask if they can have a trio of just the chocolate ones, so we make extras.

The 10-ounce ramekins used for shirred eggs are ideal for making this dish. Note that the cooked custards must chill for at least 2 hours or overnight.

1½ cups heavy cream

1 cup milk

6 ounces top-quality bittersweet chocolate, chopped

6 large egg yolks

½ cup superfine sugar

¼ cup brown sugar

¼ cup granulated sugar

Preheat the oven to 325°F. In a small, heavy saucepan over medium-high heat, heat the cream and milk to just simmering. Transfer from the heat, add the chocolate, and stir until melted. In a stainless steel bowl, combine the yolks and superfine sugar and beat with a wire whisk until just combined. Slowly whisk the chocolate cream into the yolks.

Set four 10-ounce ovenproof ramekins on a baking pan. Divide the custard among the ramekins. Pour enough hot water into the baking pan to come two thirds of the way up the sides of the ramekins. Bake for 35 to 40 minutes.

To test for doneness, jiggle the custard; it should be firm. Another way is to look carefully at the custard; there should be a nickel-sized circle of undercooked custard in the middle.

Transfer the ramekins from the water bath and let rest on a baking rack for 5 minutes. They will continue cooking. Cover and refrigerate for at least 2 hours or overnight.

To finish, let the custards rest for about 15 minutes at room temperature. In the bowl of a food processor, place the brown and granulated sugars and pulse several times until very fine. Sprinkle the sugar mixture thinly over the top of each custard and melt the sugar to a hard crack glaze using a propane torch or under an oven broiler. (Trust me; the propane torch does a much better job and is much faster.) If you like a harder brûlée crust, repeat the sugar melting procedure once or twice more. Serve at once.

Crème Anglaise

Crème Anglaise is extremely useful as a dessert custard sauce, as the basis for other flavored dessert sauces, and as the base for ice creams. It is a simple sauce to master. Just remember, after the eggs have been added to the cream it should never boil.

2 cups heavy cream
1 cup half-and-half
1/2 cup sugar
2 vanilla beans, split and scraped
6 large eggs yolks

In a saucepan over medium-high heat, combine the cream, half-and-half, sugar, and vanilla bean and bring to a boil. Transfer from the heat and cool slightly.

In a stainless steel bowl, whisk the yolks until blended. Warm the yolks by gradually whisking in a cup of the warm cream mixture.

Pour the yolk mixture back into the pan with the cream and cook over medium heat until the anglaise is thick enough to coat a spoon.

Strain the custard through a fine-mesh sieve into a stainless steel bowl set over an ice-water bath. Let the crème anglaise cool completely, stirring from time to time. Store keep refrigerated for up to 3 days.

Chocolate Dacquoise with Cappuccino Sauce

SERVES 8

Developed by my friend and former pastry chef, Jackie Riley, this dessert has been on the menu at Kinkead's since the opening in 1993. It is a chocolate-flavored hazelnut meringue layer, topped with chocolate mousse, a layer of chocolate ganache, and some edible gold leaf. The beehive-like confection is then served with an espresso crème anglaise. It is very rich and a chocoholic's dream.

Note that the mousse must chill for several hours or overnight. The meringue recipe makes 12 rounds; you can fill the extras with mousse to make 2 filled meringue cookies.

MOUSSE

1 1/2 cups heavy cream

4 ounces semisweet chocolate, chopped

2 1/2 ounces bittersweet chocolate, chopped

3 eggs, separated

1/4 cup sugar

Pinch of cream of tartar

MERINGUE BASE

4 large egg whites

Pinch of salt

Pinch of cream of tartar

1/2 cup sugar

1/4 cup toasted, peeled, chopped hazelnuts

1 tablespoon unsweetened cocoa powder

2 tablespoons gianduja (hazelnut-flavored chocolate)

ESPRESSO CRÈME ANGLAISE

2 cups heavy cream

1 cup light cream

1/2 cup sugar

2 whole vanilla beans, split and scraped

2 teaspoons instant coffee

1/4 cup espresso

6 large egg yolks

GANACHE

7 ounces semisweet chocolate, chopped

1 1/2 cups heavy cream

Edible gold leaf, for garnish (optional)

To make the mousse, whip the cream to soft peaks and refrigerate. Melt the chocolates together in a bain-marie over a hot-water bath. Cool down slightly. Beat the egg yolks with 1/3 of the sugar to ribbon stage. Beat the whites with the tartar. Add the remaining sugar gradually and whisk for about 2 minutes, until stiff but not dry.

Add the yolk mixture to the melted chocolate and mix rapidly. Add the whipped cream in 3 parts. Stir in one third of the whipped egg whites to loosen the mixture. Using a rubber spatula, gently fold in the remaining whites. Pour into a container and chill for 2 hours or overnight.

To make the meringues, preheat the oven to 250°F. Beat the egg whites, salt, and tartar. Add the sugar gradually and whip to medium peaks. Fold in the hazelnuts and cocoa powder. Line a baking sheet with baking parchment. Using a pastry bag fitted with a plain tip, pipe 8 to 12 circles of meringue, 3 to 3 1/2 inches across, onto the parchment (extra meringues will be used for garnish). Bake for 45 to 60 minutes, until the meringue gives when pressed gently; they should be crisp on the outside and a little chewy in the interior.

CONTINUED

Melt the gianduija, brush it onto 8 meringues, and let dry. Using a pastry bag, pipe chocolate mousse onto the meringue circles in the shape of a tapered dome; it should look like a chocolate beehive. Freeze.

To make the crème anglaise, in a saucepan, combine the heavy and light creams, the sugar, and the vanilla beans and bring to a boil. Remove from the heat and cool slightly.

Dissolve the instant coffee in the espresso. In a stainless steel bowl, whisk the yolks with the espresso mixture until blended. Temper the yolks by gradually whisking in a cup of the warm cream mixture. Pour the yolk mixture back into the pan with the cream and cook over medium heat until the anglaise is thick enough to coat a spoon. Strain the custard into a bowl set over an ice-water bath and cool completely. Store refrigerated.

To make the ganache, place the chocolate in a stainless steel bowl. Place a sauce pan over medium-high heat and bring the heavy cream to a boil. Pour it over the chocolate and stir until the chocolate is melted and blended. Let cool to room temperature.

Place the frozen dacquoise on a rack on a baking sheet. Pour about 3 tablespoons room-temperature ganache over each. Garnish with gold leaf. Chop up the leftover baked meringue in a food processor. Coat the bottom of each dacquoise with the crumbled meringue.

To serve, pour some crème anglaise on 8 plates and place a dacquoise on each. Use the leftover ganache to decorate the plate. Serve any extra crème anglaise on the side.

Lemon Curd Soufflé

This is a little different from other lemon soufflés in that when you get to the center you hit a pool of molten lemon curd. A problem with many soufflés, especially those featuring citrus, is anemic flavor; the lemon curd in the middle solves this by adding a jolt of intense lemon flavor.

By adjusting the type of fruit juice, you can make a lime, tangerine, grapefruit, or ugli fruit soufflé. In fact, passion fruit, because of its tartness, makes an excellent fruit curd and soufflé. You'll need to experiment with different amounts depending on the fruit.

Note that the lemon curd recipe makes a cup and you'll need only a half cup for the soufflé; the leftover curd will keep for 1 week refrigerated and is a delicious spread for scones or toast.

LEMON CURD

$1/4$ cup freshly squeezed lemon juice

$1/4$ cup sugar

3 egg yolks

$1/2$ cup butter

SOUFFLÉ

1 cup sugar, plus more for lining the soufflé molds

$1/4$ cup freshly squeezed lemon juice

1 tablespoon grated lemon zest

$1/2$ cup heavy cream

$1/4$ teaspoon pure vanilla extract

2 tablespoons cornstarch

$1/4$ cup water

3 eggs, separated, plus 5 egg whites

$1/4$ teaspoon cream of tartar

Pinch of salt

Blueberries, for garnish

To make the lemon curd, combine all of the ingredients in a noncorrosive saucepan. Cook over medium heat until thick and smooth. Let cool.

To make the soufflés, butter four 3-inch-diameter by $2^{1}/2$-inch-deep soufflé molds, or one 7 by 4-inch soufflé mold, and dust with a little sugar. In a noncorrosive saucepan, combine the lemon juice, zest, $2/3$ cup of the sugar, the heavy cream, and vanilla and bring to a boil. Dissolve the cornstarch in the water and add to the cream mixture. Let it thicken, whisking constantly. Whisk in the egg yolks. Remove from the heat and strain through a fine-mesh sieve into a stainless steel bowl. Set the bowl in an ice-water bath and cool completely. This is essentially pastry cream and can be made up to 2 days in advance and refrigerated.

Preheat the oven to 375°F. In a stainless steel bowl, whisk all 8 egg whites with the tartar and salt and gradually mix in the remaining $1/3$ cup sugar. Whip to soft peaks. Fold a little of the meringue into the pastry cream. Fold in more and more of the egg whites, turning the bowl as you work, until all are incorporated.

Place half of the mixture in the soufflé molds. Measure $1/2$ cup of the lemon curd and portion out into the centers. Top with the remaining soufflé mixture and scrape the tops evenly with a palette knife or spatula. Run your finger around the edge of each mold to push the mixture away from the sides. Bake for about 18 minutes, until risen about $1^{1}/2$ inches above the rims and golden brown. Serve at once, garnished with blueberries. You can serve any leftover curd on the side.

Brown Sugar–Sour Cream Ice Cream

MAKES 3 PINTS

At Kinkead's we make virtually all of our ice creams with a crème anglaise base to which flavoring is added. You can really make any flavor ice cream by mastering the concept of crème anglaise (page 244).

This ice cream is an interesting variation on vanilla and is quite good with fall fruit desserts in particular. The sour cream gives it a pleasant, tart flavor reminiscent of cheesecake.

1 cup half-and-half
2 cups heavy cream
$1/4$ cup granulated sugar
$3/4$ cup dark brown sugar
6 egg yolks
$1^1/2$ cups sour cream
$1/4$ teaspoon pure vanilla extract

In a noncorrosive saucepan over medium-high heat, combine the half-and-half, 1 cup of the heavy cream, and the granulated and brown sugars and bring just to a simmer.

In a stainless steel bowl, temper the yolks by gradually adding about $1/2$ cup of the cream mixture and whisking the yolks. Transfer the yolk mixture to the saucepan with the cream mixture and heat over medium heat until the mixture coats a spoon. *Do not boil.*

Strain through a fine-mesh sieve and add the remaining 1 cup heavy cream, the sour cream, and the vanilla. Freeze in an ice cream maker according to the manufacturer's directions.

Saracen Ice Cream

his is an adaptation of a recipe developed by Maeve Barnes, my former pastry chef at Twenty-One Federal on Nantucket. It is rum raisin ice cream taken to a more refined and elegant level. The name "Saracen" derives from the Spaniards' name for their Moorish conquerors. The flavor combination and ingredients are those that would be used in southern Spain and in the Basque regions of that country and France; the Armagnac is from southwestern France, and the currants, dates, cardamom, and spices evoke the cuisine of the North African Moors. This ice cream is particularly good served with a compote of dried figs, prunes, and apricots that have been poached in sherry. Note that the dried fruits for the ice cream must macerate overnight.

1/2 cup dried currants or raisins

1/4 cup pitted, diced dates (diced the size of the currants)

3 tablespoons water

1/4 cup Armagnac or other brandy

1 cup half-and-half

1 cup whole milk

1/2 teaspoon ground cardamom

Pinch of nutmeg

1 cup granulated sugar

6 egg yolks

2 cups heavy cream

1/4 teaspoon pure vanilla extract

In a saucepan, place the currants, dates, and water and bring to a boil. Transfer from the heat, add the Armagnac, and let macerate overnight to plump.

When the fruits are done macerating, in a noncorrosive saucepan over medium-high heat, combine the half-and-half, milk, cardamom, nutmeg, and sugar and bring just to a simmer. In a stainless steel bowl, temper the yolks by gradually adding about 1/2 cup of the cream-milk mixture while whisking the yolks. Transfer the yolk mixture to the saucepan with the cream-milk mixture and heat over medium heat until the cooked mixture coats a spoon. *Do not boil.*

Strain through a fine-mesh sieve and add any liquid remaining from the macerated currants. Add the heavy cream and vanilla. Freeze in an ice cream maker according to the manufacturer's directions. If using a commercial ice cream maker, fold the macerated currants and dates into the ice cream as it comes out of the ice cream maker. If using a home ice cream maker, fold them in during the last minute of freezing. Return the ice cream to the freezer for 1 hour before serving.

Lemon Ice Cream

I am a huge fan of anything citrus, and lemon is a flavor I particularly love in desserts. This is a tart, refreshing ice cream that can be the perfect accompaniment to a wide range of desserts. It is especially good with cakes and cakelike desserts. It also goes very well with blueberry pies, tarts, or cobblers.

4 large lemons
1 cup half-and-half
1 cup sugar
6 egg yolks
3 cups heavy cream
1/2 teaspoon pure vanilla extract

Grate all of the lemons with a microplane zester. Juice the lemons and strain out the pulp and seeds. In a non-corrosive saucepan, over medium-high heat combine half the grated zest, the half-and-half, and the sugar and bring just to a simmer. Transfer from the heat and let steep for 15 minutes.

In a stainless steel bowl, temper the yolks by gradually adding about 1 cup of the lemon cream while whisking the yolks. Pour the yolk mixture back into the saucepan and stir over high heat until thick enough to coat a spoon. *Do not boil.*

Strain through a fine-mesh sieve and add the remaining grated zest and the lemon juice. Let steep for 10 more minutes. Add the heavy cream and vanilla. Freeze in an ice cream maker according to the manufacturer's directions.

Basics

Fish Stock

This fish stock is suitable for reducing to a fish glaze or sauce. It is also good for soups and stews. For poaching, it should be diluted with half of an equal amount of water.

3 to 4 pounds bones of whitefish such as flounder, cod, or snapper

3 tablespoons olive oil

1 small yellow onion, diced (about 2 cups)

1 leek, minced (about 2 cups)

2 large shallots, diced (about 1/2 cup)

1 large carrot, peeled and diced (about 1 cup)

2 fennel fronds, chopped

2 stalks celery, diced (about 1 cup)

6 parsley stems

1 cup dry white wine

10 cups cold water

1 teaspoon whole black peppercorns

2 bay leaves

Wash the fish bones in cold water. If using carcasses with heads on, be sure to remove the gills and any blood from the carcass. Chop into manageable pieces. In a braising pan over medium-high heat, heat the olive oil. Add the onion, leek, shallots, carrot, fennel, celery, and parsley stems. Sweat until the onion and shallots are transparent. Deglaze with the white wine and cook until mostly reduced. Cover with the cold water and bring to a boil. Add the peppercorns and bay leaves. Turn down to a simmer and cook for 30 to 45 minutes, skimming the surface of impurities.

Pass through a fine-mesh strainer. Discard the solids. Strain again through a cheesecloth-lined strainer into a noncorrosive saucepan. Over medium-high heat, reduce, if necessary, to 6 cups. Store refrigerated for up to 4 days or frozen for up to 6 months.

Lobster Stock

Lobster stock is useful in making an array of soups, stews, and sauces. Although there is some expense involved, for certain preparations—in particular, lobster sauces—there is no substitute. For other preparations, like stews and shellfish soups, it's fine to use shrimp stock (page 254).

Shells of about 3 (1-pound) chicken lobsters (about 2 pounds)

1/4 cup olive oil

1 cup cream sherry

8 cups fish stock (this page), or 4 cups clam juice and 4 cups water

2 cups dry white wine

2 cups water

1 yellow onion, diced (about 1 1/2 cups)

1 small leek, minced

2 small celery stalks, diced

2 cloves garlic, unpeeled, cut in half

1 cup tomato purée

1 lemon, cut into quarters

1 teaspoon black peppercorns

Coarsely chop the lobster bodies with a cleaver or a large chef's knife. Place in a braising pan over medium-high heat. Add the olive oil and cook the lobster bodies until they are seared and browning. Transfer the lobster carcasses, one at a time, to the bowl of a food processor and pulse, until finely chopped. Deglaze the braising pan with the sherry and transfer, along with chopped lobster bodies, to a stockpot over high heat. Add the stock, wine, water, onion, leek, celery, garlic, tomato purée, lemon, and peppercorns and bring just to a boil. Decrease the heat to low and simmer for 1 to 2 hours, until the stock tastes rich enough. Pass through a strainer into a saucepan, pressing on the solids to extract the flavor. Discard the solids and bring the liquid back to a boil. Reduce by half to about 6 cups, 4 if you prefer a more reduced, stronger stock. Store refrigerated for up to 4 days or frozen for up to 6 months.

Shrimp Stock

This stock works great in shellfish soups.

1/4 cup olive oil
Shrimp shells from 3 pounds peeled shrimp or a
    combination of shrimp and crab shells
1 cup cream sherry
4 cups fish stock (page 254)
2 cups dry white wine
6 cups water
1 yellow onion, diced
1 small leek, minced
2 small celery stalks, diced
2 cloves garlic, unpeeled, cut in half
1 cup tomato purée
3 tablespoons tomato paste
1 lemon, cut into quarters
1 teaspoon black peppercorns

In a braising pan over medium-high heat, heat the olive oil and cook the shrimp shells until they are seared and browning. Deglaze with the sherry and add the remaining ingredients. Bring to a boil and cook for 2 minutes. Decrease the heat to medium and simmer for about 1 hour.

Pass through a strainer, pressing on the solids to extract the juices. Discard the solids and bring the liquid back to a boil in a saucepan. Reduce by half, to about 6 cups. Store refrigerated for up to 4 days or frozen for up to 6 months.

Chicken Stock

Chicken stock is the most versatile and most used stock in a professional kitchen. Even at Kinkead's, where seafood is our specialty, we use more chicken than fish stock. If you are going to the trouble of making stock from scratch, make a double or triple batch and freeze it in disposable 2-cup containers. It can be stored frozen for 6 months.

6 pounds raw chicken carcasses, bones, or backs and necks
1 large yellow onion, chopped (about 3 cups)
2 carrots, peeled and chopped (about 1 1/2 cups)
2 leeks, white part only, chopped (about 1 cup)
2 celery stalks (use outer stalks), chopped (about 1 1/2 cups)
1 small head garlic, cut in half crosswise through all the cloves
4 sprigs thyme
3 bay leaves
2 cups dry white wine
6 quarts water
1/2 teaspoon kosher salt

Wash the chicken bones and carcasses in cold running water.

In a large stockpot, place all of the ingredients except the salt and cover with the water. Bring to a boil over high heat. Skim the surface with a large spoon or ladle to remove any impurities that rise. After it comes to a boil, let it cook for 2 to 3 minutes. Reduce the heat to a simmer, add the salt, and cook for 3 to 4 hours. Turn off the heat and let the solids settle.

Slowly strain the stock through a cheesecloth-lined sieve. Cool and then refrigerate. Store refrigerated for up to 3 days or frozen for up to 6 months.

Veal Stock

MAKES ABOUT 12 CUPS

If you are taking the time to make veal stock at home, make a large or double batch and freeze in small plastic containers for future use. If you are making the veal stock primarily for use in sauces, reduce the stock by half before freezing. It will take up much less space in the freezer.

6 to 8 pounds veal knuckle bones, split
2 tablespoons vegetable oil
1 large yellow onion, chopped (about 2 cups)
2 carrots, peeled and chopped (about 1 heaping cup)
2 stalks celery, chopped (about 1 cup)
1/2 pound button mushrooms
1 head garlic, cut in half crosswise through all the cloves
2 cups red wine
4 tablespoons tomato paste
3 bay leaves
1 teaspoon peppercorns
Parsley, thyme, and rosemary stems

Preheat the oven to 400°F. Place the veal bones in a roasting pan and roast for 45 minutes, turning from time to time, until brown. *Do not let burn.* Meanwhile, in a braising pan over medium-high heat, heat the vegetable oil and sweat the onions, carrots, celery, mushrooms, and garlic. Add the vegetables to the roasting pan. When all are brown, transfer to a stockpot. Deglaze the roasting pan with the red wine and add the liquid to the stockpot. Add the tomato paste, bay leaves, peppercorns, and herb stems to the bones and cover with cold water to about 1 inch above the bones. Bring to a boil over high heat, skimming any impurities that rise. Decrease the heat to medium-low and simmer for 1 hour, skimming the fat and impurities as needed for the first hour or so. Top up the water if necessary to the original height. Decrease the heat to low and simmer gently for 2 to 3 hours, until the stock tastes rich enough. Strain into a large saucepan and discard the bones and vegetables. Strain again through a fine-mesh sieve into another pot.

Refrigerate and let the stock congeal. Remove any fat solids (there should be very little) from the top.

In a saucepan over high heat, bring the stock to a boil. Cook until reduced to 3 quarts. You now have a basic veal stock that will keep for a week or can be frozen.

For an even more meaty-flavored sauce, roast about 1 pound of veal trimmings or cubed stew veal for about 20 minutes, turning from time to time. The meat should be very brown. Deglaze the roasting pan with some red wine and transfer with the meat to the stockpot. Cover the roasted meat with the strained veal stock. Cook for about 1 hour, strain, and chill. This is a more expensive process, but the results are worth it. Store refrigerated for up to 4 days or frozen for up to 6 months.

Rich Brown Chicken Stock

For this chicken stock, roasted chicken bones are covered with basic chicken stock to produce a more intense chicken flavor. Rich or roasted chicken stock is generally used in sauces or as a simple jus for roast chicken rather than as a base for soups.

If being used to make a sauce, I prefer to add wine, aromatics, and other flavorings later in the process. Rich chicken stock should taste of roast chicken and not much else.

3 pounds chicken carcasses or neck and backs
1 head garlic, cut in half crosswise through all the cloves
1 small yellow onion, quartered
1 cup button mushroom stems or trimmings
1 recipe chicken stock (page 255)

Preheat the oven to 400°F. Wash and dry the chicken bones. In a roasting pan, place the chicken carcasses or bones and the garlic and onion and roast for about 30 minutes, turning frequently.

When bones are nicely browned, transfer to a stockpot. Add the mushroom stems and cover with the chicken stock. Bring to a boil over medium heat. Skim away any scum that rises. Boil for about 2 minutes. Turn down to a simmer, and let cook for 1 1/2 to 2 hours. If the liquid is not covering the bones, add a little water.

Pass through a fine-mesh sieve. Store refrigerated for up to 3 days or frozen for up to 6 months.

Clarified Butter

Clarified butter is pure butterfat, obtained by slowly cooking out the milk solids and liquids in whole butter. It has a higher flash point—the temperature at which it will burn—than whole butter, and therefore the fat can be heated to a higher temperature for cooking or sautéing. Because of the time involved, it is best to make clarified butter in larger batches; for home use I recommend a batch of 2 pounds or more.

3 1/2 pounds whole butter

Place the butter in a saucepan over medium heat. When it has melted and is starting to boil, turn the heat to very low and let the butter cook for 20 to 30 minutes, until all the liquid is evaporated and only the solids are left browning on the bottom of the pan. Using a ladle, strain off and reserve the golden butterfat and leave the solids to be discarded. Store refrigerated, in an airtight container, for up to 7 days.

Béarnaise

Béarnaise and its cousins are a sublime complement to many meats, fish, and birds.

4 tablespoons chopped tarragon leaves
2 shallots, minced
¹/₄ cup tarragon vinegar
¹/₂ cup dry white wine
¹/₂ teaspoon cracked black peppercorns
³/₄ cup clarified butter (page 257)
2 extra large egg yolks
2 tablespoons water
¹/₄ cup butter, at room temperature
¹/₂ teaspoon kosher salt
2 teaspoons chopped chervil leaves

In a noncorrosive pan over high heat, add three quarters of the tarragon and the shallots, vinegar, wine, and pepper. Bring to a boil and reduce until most of the liquid has evaporated. Let cool. In a saucepan over low heat, warm the clarified butter to about 150°F.

In a stainless steel bowl, whisk together the yolks, the water, and half of the tarragon reduction. Over medium-high heat, directly on the burner, whisk the egg yolks constantly, turning the bowl as you go, until the yolks are fluffy and just starting to cook. It is important you move the bowl constantly to avoid either scorching the eggs on the side or bottom of the bowl or scrambling the eggs.

Transfer the bowl from the burner and place on a folded kitchen towel to keep the bowl steady. Again turning the bowl constantly as you work, add the clarified butter in a stream, slowly at first, then faster once the emulsion starts to bind. When all is incorporated, whisk in the ¹/₄ cup butter, the rest of the vinegar reduction, the remaining tarragon, the salt, and the chervil. The finished béarnaise should be the same thickness the egg yolk–tarragon reduction mixture was when it came off the fire, or to "ribbon stage." Serve at once, or keep warm, not hot.

Beurre Blanc

This is the basic butter sauce of the Loire region of France. Beurre blanc can be used as the base for more complex sauces and is ideal with poached fish, especially freshwater fish.

This recipe uses heavy cream and is also slightly more acidic than some.

¹/₄ cup Champagne or white wine vinegar
¹/₂ cup dry white wine
2 shallots, minced
¹/₂ teaspoon kosher salt
¹/₄ teaspoon freshly ground white pepper
¹/₄ cup heavy cream
2 cups butter, cold, cut in small pieces

In a noncorrosive saucepan over high heat, combine the vinegar, white wine, shallots, salt, and pepper. Bring to a boil and reduce until syrupy. Add the cream and reduce until the mixture thickens. Decrease the heat to low. Whisking constantly, add the butter pieces, a few at a time, until all are incorporated. Strain through a fine-mesh sieve and keep warm until ready to use.

Beurre Fondue

This sauce is closely related to beurre blanc. Beurre fondue, also called beurre monte, *is used as a base sauce for other ingredients or it can be used to finish vegetables or fish. If beurre fondue gets too hot it will break, so keep it in a warm but not hot place. A ceramic crock works well.*

2 tablespoons water
1 cup butter, cut into ¹/₂-inch cubes
Pinch of kosher salt

In a noncorrosive saucepan over high heat, bring the water to a boil. Lower the heat to medium and whisk in the butter cubes, a few at a time, until fully incorporated. Transfer from the heat and keep warm in a bain-marie.

Reduction Fish Cream

This classic fish stock and cream reduction sauce can be used as the base for many fish and seafood sauces. This is a very rich sauce due to all the cream. Use real fish stock only, not canned clam juice or fish stock made from a base—these are either too salty or off-tasting. The better the stock, the better the sauce.

¹/4 cup Champagne vinegar

2 large shallots, minced

2 cups Sauvignon Blanc or other dry white wine

1 cup vermouth

5 cups fish stock (page 254)

3 cups heavy cream

Sea salt and freshly ground white pepper

1 teaspoon freshly squeezed lemon juice

In a noncorrosive saucepan over high heat, combine the vinegar, shallots, wine, and vermouth and reduce to almost a glaze. The volume will be reduced by more than three quarters. Add the fish stock and reduce to about 1 cup. Add the cream and reduce until the mixture coats the back of a spoon. Add salt and pepper to taste, and the lemon juice. The sauce should be the thickness of heavy cream.

Aïoli

Aïoli is a garlic and oil condiment used throughout the Mediterranean region in soups, stews, and seafood preparations. This is one of the few recipes for which we make an emulsion base with raw egg yolks. It never seems to have the right texture with cooked yolks.

2 cloves garlic

1 teaspoon coarse salt

2 extra large egg yolks, at room temperature

2 teaspoons garlic confit (page 264)

1 cup olive oil

¹/2 cup extra virgin olive oil

¹/3 cup grapeseed or other vegetable oil

1 teaspoon freshly squeezed lemon juice

¹/4 teaspoon kosher salt

¹/4 teaspoon freshly ground white pepper

Using a mortar and pestle, mash the garlic cloves to a paste with the coarse salt. In the bowl of a food processor, place this garlic paste, the egg yolks, and garlic confit. With the processor running very slowly, add the oils in a stream until all is incorporated. Add the lemon juice, salt, and pepper. If too thick, add a little water. Store refrigerated in an airtight container, for up to 5 days.

Rouille

Rouille is a spicy, rust-colored sauce often served with fish dishes. Our rouille uses aïoli as a base.

1 teaspoon vegetable oil
1 red bell pepper
1 roasted red jalapeño or other hot chile (jarred is fine)
1/2 teaspoon vinegar
2 cups aïoli (page 264)
Kosher salt and freshly ground black pepper

In a cast-iron pan over high heat, heat a little of the oil and char the red pepper and jalapeño on all sides. Place in a plastic bag and when cool enough to handle, peel, seed, and chop the peppers. Transfer to a blender and purée with the vinegar.

Transfer to a sauté pan and, over medium heat, concentrate the purée by cooking out the water for about 3 minutes. Let cool. Fold into the aïoli. Add salt and pepper to taste.

Romesco Sauce

Romesco sauce is garlic-flavored condiment from Spain. It is used much the same way as aïoli is in France, particularly as an accompaniment to seafood and fish soups and stews. The main difference in romesco is the addition of breadcrumbs and roasted red peppers to the garlic-mayonnaise base. You can adjust the heat by adding or decreasing the amount of red pepper flakes or adding jalapeños or other hot chiles to the sauce.

1/4 cup breadcrumbs
1 cup milk
1/4 cup almond slices, toasted and chopped in a food processor
1/2 teaspoon freshly squeezed lemon juice
3 cloves garlic, minced
1 piquillo pepper or other red pepper, roasted
1/2 teaspoon red pepper flakes
1/2 cup mayonnaise
Kosher salt and freshly ground black pepper

In a small bowl, soak the breadcrumbs in the milk for about 3 minutes to soften. Meanwhile, place the almonds, lemon juice, garlic, piquillo pepper, and red pepper flakes in a blender and purée. Transfer the purée to a stainless steel bowl and add the mayonnaise.

Squeeze out the breadcrumbs and discard the milk. Add the breadcrumbs to the bowl and mix thoroughly. Add salt and pepper to taste. Store refrigerated for up to 5 days.

Tartar Sauce

MAKES 3 CUPS

For many recipes used at Kinkead's, we make our mayonnaise from scratch. For preparations requiring large quantities or when the sauce is not to be served within a few hours, we use prepared mayonnaise (Hellmann's), for both food safety and convenience.

2 cups mayonnaise (good-quality store-bought is fine)
2 large eggs, hard-boiled, yolk and white grated
1 tablespoon chopped capers
8 cornichons, finely chopped
2 tablespoons finely chopped red onion
1 tablespoon chopped chives
1 tablespoon chopped tarragon
1/2 teaspoon sugar
1 tablespoon freshly squeezed lemon juice
1 teaspoon red wine vinegar
1 teaspoon tarragon vinegar
1/2 teaspoon kosher salt
1/2 teaspoon cracked black pepper
4 drops Tabasco sauce
8 drops Worcestershire sauce

Mix all the ingredients in a stainless steel bowl and refrigerate. Store refrigerated, in an airtight container, for up to 5 days.

Vietnamese Lime Dipping Sauce

MAKES 2 CUPS

This is a variation on a dipping sauce taught to us by our former pastry chef, Marguerite O'Brien.

6 limes
1 1/4 cups ginger juice (page 262)
1/4 cup sugar
1/2 cup nuoc nam
6 Thai basil leaves, chiffonade
1 clove garlic, minced
1 scallion, chopped
2 Thai chiles, finely sliced diagonally

Juice 3 of the limes and section the others. In a small saucepan, bring the ginger juice and sugar to a boil. When the sugar is dissolved, transfer from the heat and let cool to room temperature in a stainless steel bowl. Add the lime juice and sections, nuoc nam, basil, garlic, scallion, and chiles to the bowl and combine.

Basic Vinaigrette

This vinaigrette can be used on any mixed green or vegetable salad. It is particularly good with all-leaf or mesclun salads. It differs from some vinaigrettes in that the ratio of acid to oil is higher. I generally prefer dressings with more vinegar.

1/4 cup red wine vinegar
1 shallot, minced
1 clove garlic, minced
1 tablespoon Dijon mustard
1/4 cup grapeseed or vegetable oil
3/4 cup extra virgin olive oil
1/2 teaspoon kosher salt
1/2 teaspoon cracked black pepper

In a stainless steel bowl, combine the vinegar, shallot, garlic, and mustard. Combine the oils and slowly whisk in to incorporate. Add the salt and pepper.

Mustard-Chervil Vinaigrette

This vinaigrette is delicious in salads or as a dipping sauce for asparagus and other vegetables.

1/4 cup red wine vinegar
1 small shallot, minced
1 clove garlic, minced
1 tablespoon Dijon mustard
1 teaspoon honey mustard
1 teaspoon pommery mustard
4 tablespoons grapeseed or vegetable oil
1/2 cup plus 2 tablespoons extra virgin olive oil
1/2 teaspoon kosher salt
1/2 teaspoon freshly ground black pepper
2 tablespoons chopped chervil leaves
1 teaspoon chopped tarragon leaves

Place the vinegar, shallot, garlic, mustards, oils, salt, and pepper in a blender and purée. Fold in the chervil and tarragon.

Pesto Drizzle

This condiment differs from the classic Italian basil and pine nut condiment from Genoa in that it is somewhat liquid and meant to be spooned. Because of that, the olive oil content is very high. Traditionally, pesto is made with a mortar and pestle to get the full flavor of the basil, but for this more pourable version, I recommend using a food processor.

1 bunch basil leaves (about 1 cup)
1/4 cup pine nuts, toasted
1/4 cup freshly grated Parmesan cheese
1/4 teaspoon kosher salt
3/4 cup extra virgin olive oil

In a food processor, pulse the basil, pine nuts, cheese, salt, and half of the olive oil until coarsely puréed. Transfer to a stainless steel bowl and gradually add the remaining oil to the mixture. Store refrigerated, for up to 4 days.

Ginger Juice

There are two ways to make this condiment. If you have access to a centrifugal juicer, it is much easier.

1/2 cup peeled ginger
1 cup rice wine vinegar
1 teaspoon nuoc nam

In a centrifugal juicer, juice the ginger. Combine the juice with the vinegar and nuoc nam. (Alternatively, grate the ginger. Place in a blender with the vinegar and nuoc nam and purée at high speed.) Strain through a fine *chinois* or cheesecloth. Store refrigerated for up to 2 weeks.

Mirepoix

Mirepoix *is the French term for an aromatic mixture of diced vegetables used to enhance the flavor of a stock, soup, or sauce. For purposes of the recipes in this book, our recipe for mirepoix is as follows. All vegetables are to be diced in* 1/4-*inch cubes. For* brunoise, *the vegetables must be finely diced or shredded.*

1 yellow or white onion, diced (about 2 cups)
2 small carrots, peeled and diced (about 1/2 cup)
1 leek, white part only, diced (about 1/2 cup)
2 large celery stalks, diced (about 1 cup)

Combine all of the diced vegetables in a bowl.

Tomato Concassé

Concassé *is a French word meaning "chopped." Peeled, seeded, and diced tomatoes are a component of many dishes in this and many other cookbooks. Any good-quality tomato can be used; the plums generally have a higher pulp-to-seed ratio, so they are easier to handle.*

6 or 7 ripe plum tomatoes (about 1 1/2 pounds)

Bring a saucepan of water to a boil. With a paring knife, score the top and bottom of each tomato. Plunge into the boiling water for 1 minute. Remove and refresh in an ice-water bath.

When cool enough to handle, drain and peel the skin, which will be starting to curl up at the knife cuts. Slice the tomatoes in half lengthwise and squeeze out the seeds into a bowl (reserve and use for stock). Dice the tomato pulp into 1/4-inch cubes. Store refrigerated for up to 1 day.

Oven-Dried Tomatoes

When summer vine-ripened tomato varieties are not available, a possible solution is to dry tomatoes to concentrate whatever flavor is available.

These tomatoes are a very versatile condiment, most useful in the months when tomatoes are not at their best. Drying the tomato evaporates the liquid in the fruit, concentrating the flavor. Through this process, normally bland winter tomatoes become fairly edible and summer tomatoes become super-intense, delivering an out-of-this-world taste experience. Plum tomatoes are preferred because of their thicker pulp. Unlike sun-dried tomatoes, all the moisture is not extracted from oven-dried tomatoes, so they will spoil after 4 days.

24 large plum tomatoes
1/4 cup kosher salt
1/4 cup sugar
1/2 cup extra virgin olive oil
4 cloves garlic, sliced
1/2 teaspoon cracked black pepper
2 teaspoons thyme leaves

Cut the tomatoes in half lengthwise and gently squeeze out most of the seeds. Combine the salt and sugar and liberally sprinkle over the cut sides of the tomatoes. Place each, skin side down, on a baking rack and place the rack on a baking sheet. Let the tomatoes sit for about 30 minutes.

Preheat the oven to 225°F. Place the baking sheet in the oven and bake and dry for 3 to 4 hours, checking on them about every 30 minutes. Ovens differ; the longer and lower you can dry the tomatoes, the better. Stop when the tomatoes are starting to shrivel but have not entirely dried out.

Transfer from the oven and gently peel away the outer skins. Brush off any of the excess salt-sugar mix. Place in a stainless steel bowl and dress with the oil, garlic, pepper, and thyme. Layer in a flat plastic holding container or jar (they are delicate) and refrigerate. Store refrigerated for up to 4 days.

Blanching Sweetbreads

MAKES ABOUT 1¼ POUNDS TRIMMED SWEETBREADS

The term sweetbreads *is generally used to refer to the thymus gland of immature calves (veal) or lamb. They are sold in pairs. Veal sweetbreads are more likely to be found at a butcher's than at a grocery store. They are larger than lamb sweetbreads and more delicate tasting, creamy textured, and fairly bland in flavor.*

There is a good deal of controversy regarding the correct preliminary preparation of sweetbreads. One school advocates blanching in acidulated water with aromatics and white wine; another, slow oven braising with herbs and mirepoix; a third, slicing the sweetbread lobes into medallions and cooking them from the raw state.

Our standard preliminary method is something of a hybrid. The sweetbreads are soaked in cold water overnight, poached for a short time, then chilled again for a few hours or overnight under the pressure of a weighted pan to firm up the texture. The sinew and large veins are removed before proceeding with final preparation.

2 pounds sweetbreads, trimmed of fat and blood spots
8 cups ice water
2 tablespoons kosher salt
1 cup dry white wine
2 bay leaves
10 black peppercorns
2 teaspoons vinegar

Place the sweetbreads in the ice water with 1 teaspoon of the salt and soak in the refrigerator overnight. This helps extract some of the blood and whiten the sweetbreads.

In a saucepan over high heat, bring 8 cups of water, the remaining salt, the wine, bay leaves, peppercorns, and vinegar to a boil. Drain the sweetbreads, lower the heat, and poach for 2 minutes. They will be underdone in the middle. Drain and place in a roasting pan in a single layer. Top with another pan and place 1 to 2 medium cans of tomatoes in the pan to weigh it down. Refrigerate for 2 to 3 hours or overnight. Pick through the sweetbreads to remove any large veins, fat, or membranes. Store refrigerated for up to 3 days until ready to cook.

Garlic Confit

MAKES ABOUT ½ CUP OF PURÉE,
1 CUP OF WHOLE CLOVES

This recipe for slow-roasted garlic has many applications. The cloves can be used whole, puréed to add to soups and sauces or used as a coating for roasted meat or fish. Do not use elephant garlic, which is technically not real garlic but a milder member of the allium family.

3 heads garlic, cloves left whole (50 or more cloves total)
1 cup olive oil

Preheat the oven to 300°F. Place the peeled garlic in a sauté pan or Pyrex cake pan just large enough to hold it. Pour the olive oil over to just cover. Bake for 1 to 1¼ hours, until tender and just starting to brown. Drain and save the garlic-flavored oil for another use. Store the oil refrigerated for up to 1 week.

If the recipe calls for purée, put the garlic confit in a blender with ¼ cup or so of the garlic oil and blend to a fine purée. Garlic confit will keep, covered and refrigerated, for 1 week.

Duck Confit

Duck confit can be served as a main course, or in salads, soups, stews, or cassoulet. You can purchase duck legs from specialty butchers or you can confit the easier to find breasts and legs. Because of the work involved, it is best to make a large batch and refrigerate the leftovers. I do not recommend using Peking duck (the Long Island variety), as it is too mild in flavor. Pork, especially bellies, shoulders, and butts, can be prepared in the following manner as well.

Note that the duck needs to season overnight.

12 muscovy or, if you can find them, moullard duck legs
(9 to 10 pounds)
1/4 cup kosher salt
1 tablespoon sugar
3 bay leaves, crumbled
3/4 cup crushed black peppercorns
2 pounds duck fat
2 cups vegetable oil

Place a baking rack on a sheet pan. Trim the duck legs so that they have a nice fat cap but any excess is removed. Save any excess fat for rendering. Place the legs in a single layer on the baking rack.

In a stainless steel bowl, place the salt, sugar, bay leaves, and peppercorns and mix by hand to incorporate. Sprinkle 1 to 1 1/2 tablespoons of the mixture over each duck leg. The legs should be well salted but not packed in salt. You are trying to season the duck like sausage, not like salt ham. Refrigerate for 24 hours.

In a saucepan over medium-low heat, heat the duck fat trimmings, duck fat, and 1 cup of the vegetable oil and let render until the duck fat is liquid and the cracklings are starting to brown. This will take 2 to 3 hours and should yield 3 to 4 cups. Strain the liquid fat and discard any solids.

Preheat the oven to 275°F. Brush the seasoning off the duck pieces. Rinse them thoroughly and pat dry. In a braising pan just large enough to hold the duck pieces,

place the duck legs vertically, with the bone straight up. Cover with the rendered duck fat and fill with the remaining vegetable oil to not quite cover the legs. The amount will depend on the size of the pot you use.

Place in the oven and cook until the legs are tender but not fork-tender or falling apart, for 1 1/2 to 2 hours. Transfer from the oven and cool. Strain the fat, store the legs in the fat, and refrigerate.

Cooking Dried Beans

This recipe works for basically any dried bean. The cooking times might vary due to age, size, and density of the bean, but the process is the same.

Note that the beans must soak overnight. When cooking dried beans, it is important not to salt the beans too early in the cooking process—the beans will cook unevenly. The skins fall off, some are undercooked, and others get mushy.

1 pound dried flageolet, great Northern, or canelli beans (about 2 cups small beans or 1 3/4 cups large beans)
5 tablespoons olive oil
1 cup *brunoise* mirepoix (page 263)
1/2 teaspoon dried thyme
1 teaspoon kosher salt, plus more as needed
6 cups chicken stock (page 255)
3 tablespoons puréed garlic confit (page 264)
1/2 teaspoon cracked black pepper, plus more as needed

Wash the beans in 2 changes of water. Pick through for any pebbles. Place in a container with 8 cups of cold water and soak overnight. They will double in size. Drain and discard the water.

In a heavy-sided braising pan over high heat, add 8 cups of fresh cold water and the beans and bring to a boil. Drain the beans and wipe out the pot.

Over medium heat, heat 2 tablespoons of the olive oil and when hot, add the mirepoix and thyme. Sweat for about 3 minutes, then add 5 1/2 cups of the chicken stock and the blanched beans and bring to a boil. Lower the heat to a simmer and cook for 20 minutes. Skim away any impurities that rise. Add the salt and cook for about 15 minutes, until tender but not falling apart. If more liquid is needed, add water, not stock. Stir gently to keep from sticking.

When done, remove from the heat and chill. You can prepare the beans to this point and refrigerate them for up to 2 days.

To serve, in a heavy saucepan over high heat, add the remaining 3 tablespoons olive oil and one fifth of the beans. Stirring constantly, let them cook and break down. Lower the heat to simmer and add the remaining beans, 1/2 cup chicken stock, and the garlic purée, and add salt and pepper to taste. Heat through.

Pasta Dough

This dough is intended for filled pasta preparations like ravioli, agnolotti, tortellini, and the like. Although it can also be used to make extruded or fresh cut pasta, the high amount of flour and the use of whole eggs produce a thinner, more elastic dough. Cut pasta dough benefits from semolina and more yolk and less of the albumin found in egg whites.

6 large eggs
1 teaspoon kosher salt
1 tablespoon extra virgin olive oil
22 ounces all-purpose flour, by weight

In an electric mixer fitted with a dough hook, place the eggs, salt, and oil and start mixing at slow speed. Add the flour gradually and increase the mixer speed to medium. When all is incorporated, transfer from the mixer and knead by hand. The dough should be somewhat moist but not sticky. If it is too wet, add a little more flour. Let rest for about 10 minutes before rolling out.

Pâte Sablée (Basic Sweet Tart Dough)

MAKES ENOUGH FOR TWO 10-INCH TARTS

This is a basic sweet dough for making the crust for dessert (rather than savory) open tarts and tartlets. It is not recommended for American-style double-crust pies, but it will do. I prefer a flakier crust for pies, either with lots of butter or, better yet, lard.

Unlike many other recipes, for tart dough it is important to measure the flour by weight rather than volume. This is true of most baking recipes.

18 ounces all-purpose flour
1 1/4 cups plus 1 tablespoon butter, chilled
1 pinch kosher salt
1/8 teaspoon sugar
2 eggs
1/8 teaspoon freshly squeezed lemon juice

In the bowl of a food processor fitted with the metal blade, add the flour and butter and pulse to pea-sized lumps. Add the salt, sugar, eggs, and lemon juice and pulse to combine. Don't overprocess or let it clump into a ball.

Turn the dough out onto a work surface and knead a few times by hand. Divide the dough into quarters and roll out by hand into 1-inch-thick disks. Wrap with plastic wrap and refrigerate for 1 hour before using. Will keep refrigerated for up to 3 days and frozen for 1 month.

Pâte Brisée (Unsweetened Savory Tart Dough)

MAKES ENOUGH FOR TWO 10-INCH TARTS

This dough is used for savory rather than dessert tarts. Quiches, canapés, and savory vegetable tarts can all be made using this dough.

18 ounces all-purpose flour
1 1/4 cups plus 1 tablespoon butter, chilled
1/4 teaspoon kosher salt
1/4 teaspoon cider vinegar
2 extra large eggs

In the bowl of a food processor fitted with the metal blade, add the flour, butter, and salt. Pulse several times to form pea-sized lumps. Add the vinegar and eggs and pulse to form a moist, crumbly mixture. Do not overprocess.

Turn out the dough onto a work surface and knead a few times by hand. Cut in half and roll into 1-inch-thick disks. Wrap the disks in plastic wrap and refrigerate. Will keep refrigerated for up to 3 days or frozen for 1 month.

Index